The State of
BLACK
AMERICA
2006

AN OFFICIAL PUBLICATION OF THE  National Urban League   www.nul.org

120 Wall Street New York, NY 10005

The State of
BLACK
AMERICA
2006

AN OFFICIAL PUBLICATION OF THE NATIONAL URBAN LEAGUE

EDITORIAL DIRECTOR
Stephanie J. Jones

EDITOR-IN-CHIEF
George E. Curry

MANAGING EDITOR
Lisa Bland Malone

ASSOCIATE EDITORS
Rose Jefferson-Frazier
Renee R. Hanson

IMAGE PARTNERS
CUSTOM PUBLISHING

PRESIDENT AND CREATIVE DIRECTOR
John Shearer

GENERAL MANAGER
Ellen Burke

ART DIRECTOR
Louise Landry

CHARTS
Cari Colclough

COVER ILLUSTRATION
Mark Preston

CHAIRMAN
Michael J. Critelli

PRESIDENT AND CHIEF EXECUTIVE OFFICER
Marc H. Morial

SENIOR VICE PRESIDENT
DEVELOPMENT
Chandra Y. Anderson

SENIOR VICE PRESIDENT
PROGRAMS
Donald E. Bowen

SENIOR VICE PRESIDENT, ADMINISTRATION
CHIEF GOVERNANCE OFFICER &
COUNSELOR TO THE PRESIDENT
Kumiki Gibson

SENIOR VICE PRESIDENT
AFFILIATE SERVICE
Annelle Lewis

SENIOR VICE PRESIDENT
MARKETING AND COMMUNICATIONS
Michele M. Moore

SENIOR VICE PRESIDENT
FINANCE AND OPERATIONS
Paul Wycisk

NATIONAL URBAN LEAGUE POLICY INSTITUTE

EXECUTIVE DIRECTOR
Stephanie J. Jones

CHIEF OF STAFF
Lisa Bland Malone

DIRECTOR FOR LEGISLATIVE AFFAIRS
Suzanne M. Bergeron

RESIDENT SCHOLAR
Renee R. Hanson

NATIONAL URBAN LEAGUE
BOARD OF TRUSTEES
2005-2006

Officers

CHAIRMAN
Michael J. Critelli

SENIOR VICE CHAIR
Robert D. Taylor

VICE CHAIR
Alma Arrington Brown

VICE CHAIR
Martha "Bunny" M. Mitchell

SECRETARY
Alexis M. Herman

TREASURER
Willard "Woody" W. Brittain

PRESIDENT AND CEO
Marc H. Morial

The State of
BLACK
AMERICA
2006

contents

The National Urban League Opportunity Compact

by Marc H. Morial

"Support the strong, give courage to the timid, remind the indifferent, and warn the opposed."

—Whitney M. Young, Jr.

The *State of Black America 2006* report was compiled and analyzed against the backdrop of one of the most catastrophic events to ever befall our nation. Hurricanes Katrina and Rita and the tragically slow government response exposed, in the starkest and most depressing terms imaginable, the race and class gaps that our previous reports and *Equality Indexes* had highlighted. Last year's *Equality Index* documented that the status of African Americans was 0.729 of their white counterparts in the areas of economics, health, education, social justice and civic engagement. This figure was virtually unchanged from the previous two years that the National Urban League has compiled these numbers.

This year, the *Equality Index* numbers again remain virtually the same. Once again, Black Americans continue to hover at 0.73 of the status of White Americans. The fact that this number has not changed year after year is a story in itself. As we note in the *Equality Index*, the U.S. Constitution counted an African American as 3/5 of a person for purposes of taxation and state representation in Congress, an Index value of 0.60. Today, African Americans' index value stands at 0.73—0.13 improvement over the last 217 years!

This disparity between the conditions in Black America and White America is all too familiar to those impacted by these unequal economic,

9

education and social conditions. Unfortunately, the unequal status of African Americans is frequently overlooked and in many instances, outright denied. The *Equality Index* is an excellent tool that helps us quantify this disparity in clear and unambiguous ways that enable us to move beyond arguing about whether a problem exists and move straight to solving them.

Sadly, these numbers were illustrated in sharp relief last summer when America was forced to see the gaping chasm between White and Black America, the haves and the have-nots. Americans didn't like what they saw and they demanded action.

Katrina was a wake-up call for the nation to lift many from the depths of poverty. As the Urban League Movement nears the end of its first century, we celebrate the gains we have made but also see the work that still must be done.

Hurricane Katrina was this generation's Bloody Sunday. Just as millions of Americans across the country in 1965 witnessed the "iron foot of oppression" in Selma, Alabama on the Edmund Pettis bridge, last summer our nation came face-to-face with the back-of-the-hand neglect driven by poverty, race and class. In 1965, Congress responded to the outcry against racial inequality, degradation and brutality by passing the Voting Rights Act. In 2005, I was hopeful that, as the glaring inequities of poverty were stripped for all the nation to see and Americans cried out for action, our nation would once again rise to the challenge. I was hoping that after years of fits and starts, we would finally and fully close the economic, education, health, housing and justice equality gaps that leave so many of our brothers and sisters starved of opportunity and threaten the very existence of our republic.

Unfortunately, the initial flurry of concern and attention to poverty and injustice has given way to the status quo of neglect, domestic budget cuts, insensitivity and short-sighted policy priorities.

This year's report on the state of Black America moves these issues to the front burner. But more than simply describing the problems, we turn up the heat by offering concrete solutions for moving Americans from poverty to self-sufficiency to prosperity through the Opportunity

Compact, the public policy foundation of the National Urban League's five-point empowerment agenda for closing the gaps in employment, education, health and quality of life, civil rights and civic engagement.

The Opportunity Compact contains prescriptions for addressing the scourge of poverty and lays the groundwork for economic empowerment of African Americans and others in four areas: homeownership, jobs, economic development and children. The *State of Black America 2006* report opens with four essays addressing these four components. While each essay stands on its own as an independent policy analysis, together they present a cohesive and systematic approach for closing the nation's equality gaps. Outlined are prescriptions for moving from poverty to self-reliance to prosperity and wealth.

Our Opportunity Compact is more than a concept; it is a carefully-crafted action plan, a blueprint for building a nation that lifts every American, as one people, united by our commitment to a better future.

We urge our public officials, policy makers, scholars and others committed to addressing the problems of race, poverty and justice to carefully study *The State of Black America 2006* report and use it as a blueprint for finally and fully attacking the problems we all live with. Poverty, the racial divide and social injustice do not impact only those who suffer most visibly. They tear apart the fabric of our nation in ways that damage and diminish us all. Alleviating poverty and injustice is a responsibility we must never forget because liberty and justice for all is not an empty slogan, but a solemn pledge we make to our neighbors and our children.

THE NATIONAL URBAN LEAGUE EQUALITY INDEX

by Rondel Thompson and Sophia Parker of
Global Insight, Inc.

The *Equality Index* is used to compare the conditions between whites and blacks in America using multiple variables. Article I, Section 2 of the Constitution of the United States counted an African American as 3/5 of a person for purposes of taxation and state representation in Congress, an index value of 0.60. Whites have been used as the control in this index, so an index number of less than one means that blacks are doing relatively worse than whites in that category. An index value of greater than one means that blacks are doing better than whites in that category. How much progress has been made in the United States since the Constitution was adopted in 1789? The 13th Amendment, ratified in 1865, corrected the 3/5 injustice, but according to the *Equality Index*, by 2006, Black America's index value stands at 0.73, fractionally up from 0.729 in 2005. In other words, there has been a 0.13 improvement over 217 years.

The Equality Index is a compilation of five sub-indices, Health, Education, Economics, Social Justice, and Civic Engagement. Each of these subcomponents has an index value of its own. The sections following summarize how each of the individual sub-indices was constructed, the data available, and the weights used. Global Insight, Inc. (GII) attempted to use the most recent data available across these five indices to create the most current index value. Additionally, GII attempted to anticipate media criticism of our methodology and the data used primarily by employing weighting schemes to manage shortcoming in the data. Index weights are represented within the text as either a percentage of the sub-index: "Life expectancy is weighted at 15 percent," or a shorthand percentage follows the description of the data: "Live births per 1000 women was given the greatest value (0.05) in the micro-index of delivery issues." In all cases, the percentage is referring to the percent of the sub index—Health in this example—being discussed. When referring to the entire *Equality Index* itself, the text will directly mention this. "The Education sub-index comprises 25 percent of the *Equality Index*."

The weights are unchanged from last year:

Economics	30%
Health	25%
Education	25%
Social Justice	10%
Civic Engagement	10%

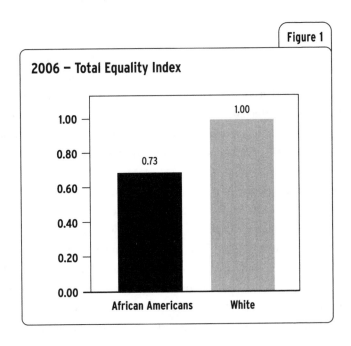

Figure 1

2006 – Total Equality Index

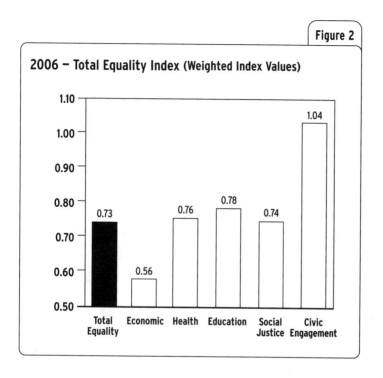

Figure 2

2006 – Total Equality Index (Weighted Index Values)

ECONOMICS—30% OF THE EQUALITY INDEX

The Economics sub-index is divided into six separate categories: Mean Income, Employment Issues, Poverty, Housing and Wealth Formation, Transportation, and Digital Divide. The weight of each category is based on relative importance and the quality of the data that was available. Of the six, Housing and Wealth Formation was given the strongest weight (34 percent), as it is the best measure of both a person's current assets and their economic potential. For example, it is easier to secure a business loan if one owns a home and can use it as collateral, thus housing can directly contribute to wealth formation. Median Income, which is assigned the second highest weight (25 percent), represents the current economic performance of the white and black employed populations. Employment Issues was given a slightly lower weight (20 percent), followed closely by Poverty (15 percent). Transportation was given the second lowest weight (5 percent). The Digital Divide was given a low weight of (1 percent). Although this is an interesting area of study, it currently has only an ancillary impact on wages and standard of living. The *Equality Index* number for Economics in 2006 was calculated at 0.56, a marginal decline over the 0.57 index number for the previous year.

This low index number means blacks are performing disproportionately worse than whites in the economic criteria. A closer look at the sub-indices that make up the Economics index will reveal the reasons for the low index number.

Housing and Wealth Formation—34% of Economics

The Housing and Wealth Formation category includes Mortgage Application Denial and Home Improvement Loans (weighted at 8 percent each), Home Ownership (1 percent) and Home Values (1 percent). The latter two were given a very small importance in the index as those values are not current snapshots, but rather based on historical material.

Home ownership, calculated at 0.64, shows yet another separation between races. Less than 50 percent of black families in America own homes. Conversely, over 70 percent of white families in America own homes. A contributing factor lies in the next series: mortgage denial was computed at 0.48. As a group, blacks experienced over twice as many mortgage denials as whites. The home improvement mortgage loans category was slightly better than mortgage denials, at 0.53. Still, blacks obtained home improvement financing at a rate that is half that of whites. Lower median income and other factors help to account for median home values, which was calculated at 0.65, translating into a $42,800 gap in black versus white home values.

There is also a huge disparity between the numbers of black and white owned businesses. The U.S. Firms by Race index, which was calculated at 0.54, illustrates the sizeable gap. The current index number of 0.54 is a large improvement over the 0.37 index number in 2005. Figure 3 shows the disparity in U.S. Firms by Race. There are nearly two times as many white-owned firms as black-owned firms in the U.S. (as compared to their relative percentages of the U.S. employment shares). The main reasons are that black firms either are not getting the seed money needed to create private wealth, and/or there is less entrepreneurial risk-taking in the black population. Both of these suppositions are supported in the *Equality Index*. Blacks are being rejected for home loans at a much higher rate than whites, and just as important, self-financing for blacks is far more difficult since the average black home is worth less than the average white home. The risk-taking argument can be supported by the higher numbers of blacks in jobs that have more security. Blacks are more likely to work in government and union jobs; both have greater job security than the average job. Of the two arguments, the index shows the greater influence is upon the first supposition, but possibly both theories are in operation.

The one caveat within this category is the elimination from the data of 50/50 ownership and other firms. There were a large number of firms that reported ownership of the firm was 50/50 black/white, and there were many firms that responded "Other," meaning the people who owned it were either of mixed ancestry, or a race not covered in the survey response.

In addition to the original components of Housing and Wealth Formation, four new categories were added: Median Net Worth[1] (8 percent), Equity in Home (8 percent), Percent of People Investing in 401k (1 percent) and Percent Investing in IRA (1 percent) further complete the wealth formation aspect of Housing and Wealth Formation. The heavier weights were given to Median Net Worth and Equity in Home as they are the strongest immediate indicators of wealth formation.

Median Income—25% of Economics

The index for Median Income is broken out into three components: Mean Male Earnings by Highest Degree Earned (8%), Mean Female Earnings by Highest Degree Earned (8%), and Median Income (8%). Mean Male Earnings produced an index value of 0.7. Not only are black males paid less than whites, but black males would have to see their mean income increase by $16,876 annually for the index to equal 1. The indicator for Mean Female Earnings of 0.83 reveals that black females are closer in earnings to their white counterparts. However, a black female would still have to earn $6,370 more each year for the index to reach 1.

Global Insight expects that over time, earnings between the two populations will converge, although they will not necessarily become equal. Data on the mean earnings by degree shows that blacks earn less than whites even when adjusted for education—this is in part due to degree choice. For example, education majors earn significantly less than business majors, a discrepancy which partly reflects the compensation for entering a less secure profession. In terms of risk versus reward, teachers and government workers are expected to earn less, as their jobs are largely immune to layoffs.

Employment Issues—20% of Economics

Employment Issues is broken out into three main categories. The Unemployment Rate portion of the index was weighted at 10%, Labor Force Participation (LFP) at ages 16-64 was weighted at 6 percent, and Unemployment Duration accounted for 4%. The Unemployment category itself is comprised of the overall unemployment rate, and also includes two categories for data on teenagers. The unemployment rate for blacks is more than twice their white counterparts, as is depicted in Figure 3. The number of unemployed black people would have to decrease by 948,500 people for the unemployment index to equal 1.

The Labor Force Participation (LFP) rate, on the other hand, showed a nominal racial difference. LFP is the number of people in a population that are either working or looking for work. The 0.98 index figure illustrates a slightly higher labor force participation rate for whites, and indicates a slightly higher number of discouraged black workers. If people feel that there is little probability of finding employment, there is a higher chance that they will drop out of the labor force. The slightly higher number of black people not in the labor force may be linked to a relatively high concentration of blacks in blue-collar positions. Historically, blue-collar jobs tend to see more attrition in times of economic hardship than white-collar jobs. In addition, the duration of a job search is higher for blue-collar jobs. It should be noted that the current LFP index number is an improvement over the 0.96 index figure from a year ago.

The LFP index number does not fully bring into perspective the difference in labor force participation, however. When this index is disaggregated by age and education level, the differences within are interesting. The LFP index for ages 16 to 19 was 0.69, but the LFP index for ages 20 to 24 showed improvement, at 0.90. The LFPs for higher age groups, simply stated as "over 25," are in addition broken out by education level. The LFP index number for Over 25 with Less than a High School Degree is 0.86.

However, the remaining LFP index values (which were all weighted at .001) all registered higher than one: High School Graduate/No College (1.09), Some College/No Degree (1.07), Associates Degree (1.03), Less than Bachelor's Degree (1.05) and College Graduate (1.06). The numbers stress importance of education. In particular, graduating from high school is a huge hurdle that can help to ensure higher labor force participation for blacks. Higher education would not only ensure higher LFP numbers but higher incomes as well.

Employment Issues also included two series that were weighted at 1.7% each. Unemployment Duration and Employment-to-Population Ratio were added to more fully describe and represent the racial employment situation.

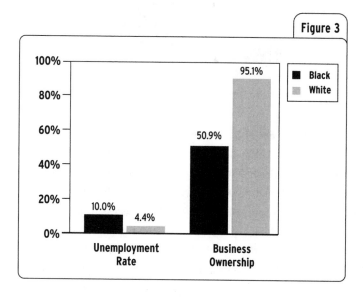

Figure 3

Poverty—15% of Economics

The Poverty category is broken out into three components: Percent of the Population Below the Poverty Line (9%), Percent Living 50 Percent Below the Poverty Line (1%) and a newly-added category, Percent Living Near the Poverty Threshold (5%). As a percentage of their population, over two times as many blacks live below the poverty line as whites. However, the overall index number for Percent Below the Poverty Level in 2006 is 0.44, a marginal improvement over the 2005 index number of 0.42.

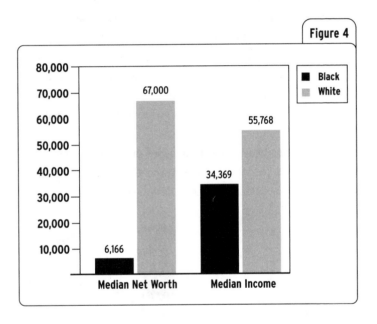

Figure 4

Transportation—5% of Economics

The newly-added Transportation category is divided into three items: Car Ownership, Driving to Work Alone, and Reliance Upon Public Transportation. These variables are important in that they speak to the ability of blacks to be mobile enough to have access to jobs that are not within their immediate vicinity. All three items produced index numbers that were below 1: Car Ownership (0.79), Driving Alone (0.84) and Reliance Upon Public Transportation (0.25). Figure 5, shows the disproportionate share of blacks that rely upon public transportation as their sole means of transport. The low index number means that nearly four times as many blacks are at the mercy of public transportation systems than whites. According to a Brookings Institution policy brief[2], many new jobs are located in suburban areas. However, public transit rarely takes urban residents to within a close proximity of those employers. The document also goes on to say that poorer families often pay more for cars due to higher finance charges. The consequences of being poor in a central urban location, which many blacks are, manifest themselves in the form of longer commutes to new jobs–longer ambulation from the suburban bus stop to the job and a relatively higher cost of purchasing a car via increased finance charges.

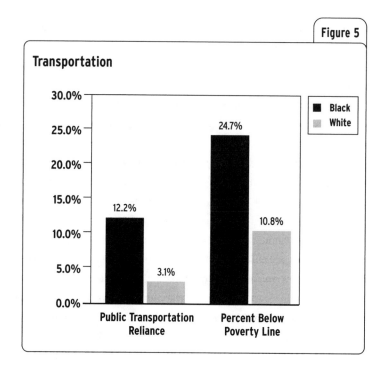

Figure 5

Transportation

Public Transportation Reliance — Black: 12.2%, White: 3.1%
Percent Below Poverty Line — Black: 24.7%, White: 10.8%

Legend: ■ Black ▨ White

Digital Divide—1% of Economics

Each of the three items within the Digital Divide category (Households with Computer at Home, Households with the Internet, and Households with Broadband) is equally weighted. While there is a pronounced disparity in Households with the Internet, the index number has improved over last year. The 2006 index number of 0.69 remains unchanged from the previous year.

HEALTH—25% OF THE EQUALITY INDEX

The Health sub-index is divided into three major categories: Death Rates and Life Expectancy, Lifetime Health Issues, and Neonatal Care and Related Issues. Of the three categories, Death Rates and Life Expectancy is the most important, so it has a weight of 45 percent within the Health Index. Lifetime Health Issues, which attempts to measure the struggles of individuals with failing or impaired health who are still to some degree functioning, was given a weight of 30 percent. Lastly, Neonatal Care and early childhood issues were given a weight of 25 percent, since this stage of development sets the table for one's entire life, but is not always directly correlated to the health problems experienced later. The overall index number for Health was calculated at 0.76, unchanged from last year's value.

Death Rates and Life Expectancy—45% of Health

The white population in the U.S. lives longer than our nation's black population, and this large disadvantage is reflected in the Health Index. Life Expectancy at Birth is weighted at 15 percent of the Health index, and the Age-Adjusted Death Rate (per 100,000) for all causes is weighted at 30 percent. In the index, we use the Death Rate for all causes to avoid "cherry picking" any sub-causes that would skew the measurement in either direction. Even with the small increase this year, however, the black population remains significantly behind the white population in the Age-Adjusted Death Rate. Diabetes, homicide, and HIV prevalence in the black community are several times greater than in the white population. Diabetes is twice as likely to occur among blacks as whites. Blacks are five times more likely to die as a victim of a homicide. The disparity in HIV deaths is even more striking—blacks are almost 10 times as likely to have HIV compared to whites. A positive note for the black community is its dramatically lower rates of chronic lower respiratory disease. In addition, the suicide rate of the nation's white population is twice that of blacks.

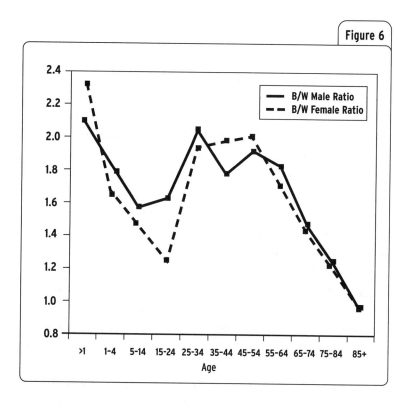

Figure 6

Figure 6 compares how many more times a black person is likely to die than a white at any given age. The category of Age-Adjusted Death rates is based on two concepts; the first, discussed previously, lists risks due to individual disease and events. Figure 6 examines the differential using the second method, an age cohort pattern. Merely quoting the life expectancy differential—blacks live on average to age 72 versus age 78 for whites —does not adequately capture the lifecycle. What the average is masking is that blacks are dying in greater percentages than whites at every stage of life due to disease, accident, behavior, or as the victim of a crime. Note that in four age cohorts: Under 1 (>1), 25-34, 35-44, and 45-54, black males and black females are more than twice as likely to die than their white counterparts. Death rates for blacks compared to whites only start to converge after age 75.

Lifetime Health—30% of Health

This subcategory is disaggregated into five sub-components. The sub-components are: Physical Condition, 10% (includes the former categories Weight Issues and AIDS); Substance Abuse, 10%; Access to Care, 5% (formerly Health Insurance); Elderly Health Care, 3%; and Mental Health, 2%. Substance Abuse and Physical Condition issues dominate the Lifetime Health subindex as they affect the largest percentages of the population. Within Physical Condition, two items of importance are Diabetes and Activity Limitation due to chronic conditions. Some of the overweight and obesity data leads to some startling conclusions. Blacks are increasingly more likely to be overweight, but even more likely than that to be obese. Obesity is weighted twice as heavily as merely overweight, since the health ramifications for being obese are far more significant, and the obesity ratio is significantly worse for blacks. What was remarkable was the intra-racial gender differences. More Hispanic and white men are overweight or obese than Hispanic and white women, whereas black women were on average more likely to be overweight or obese than black men.

Within the category of Substance Abuse, blacks fare on average better than whites. Greater usage of illegal drugs is cancelled out by less occurrence of heavy alcohol usage. Smoking is similar in both groups. The Mental Health sub-component was added this year but given a low weight, as the category only measures students. Notably, a black male student considering suicide is over five times as likely to make an attempt compared to a white male. The government reported 5.2 percent of black male students in grades 9 through 12 carry out the suicide intent and required medical attention, compared to 1.1 percent of white male students in grades 9 through 12.

The Access to Care category includes usage of prescription drugs, which is correlated with preventative health care. Additionally, data points measuring health care coverage highlight the low propensity for African Americans to have health insurance coverage. Lower rates of health insurance are highly correlated with inadequate care, impacting health throughout a person's entire life. However, poor blacks were more likely to be covered than poor whites, making the top line disparity more likely to be caused by a lower rate of employer coverage. The All People Without Insurance variable dropped considerably in the 2006 index versus 2005. The 2005 index number of 0.70 was reduced to 0.57 in 2006. While the reason for the decline is unknown, the meaning is clear. More blacks, relative to their white counterparts, are without health insurance. The implication is ominous. Take a group that suffers disproportionately from health care issues, and couple that with a higher percentage of that group not having the means to combat illness or receive preventative treatment—the outcome is a vicious cycle that holds the promise of perpetuating itself for years to come.

Neonatal & Pediatric Care, and other Early Childhood—25% of Health

Four separate components have been developed for this category: Delivery Issues, 10 percent; Children' s Health, 10 percent; Pregnancy Issues, 4 percent; and Reproduction Issues, 1 percent. Pregnancy Issues include Prenatal Care, Teenage Mothers, Mothers Health while Pregnant, Low Birth Weight of the infant, Children' s Health and Reproduction Issues.

EDUCATION—25% OF THE EQUALITY INDEX

The Education sub-index is divided into five major categories: Education Quality, Attainment, Scores, Enrollment, and Student Status. Of the five, Quality is the most important, and thus it has a weight within the index of 45 percent. Attainment, the level of education a person achieves, (20 percent) is second most important, but the dearth of both quality and degrees conferred gave it less than half the weight of Quality. Test scores are a good indication of performance, but students considered in this data had not yet achieved the final goal of graduation, so a slightly lower weighting of 15 percent was assigned for Scores. Enrollment, which takes into account the benefits of education but obscures issues such as the "warehousing" of students, was given a weight of 10 percent. Lastly, Student Status and Risk Factors (10 percent) were considered important measures of behavior, student confidence, and future accomplishments in life, but since these are closely related to attainment, a weighting of 10 percent was assigned. The overall index number for Education was calculated at 0.78 for the 2006 index, up from 0.77 in the 2005 index.

Education Quality—45% of Education

The quality of the product being received within the black community and the white community is not equal. This fact dominates how each population fares in high schools, colleges, and their jobs across America. Two broad themes emerge from these criteria: the quality, skills, and experience of the teacher, and the course curriculum of the student. The first is referred to as Teacher Quality (30 percent). This measure was consistently linked to student performance, and so was given the greatest weight. Four data series, each equally weighted at 7 percent, plus a fifth weighted at 1 percent, comprise this key determination. The first two measure the percentage of teachers lacking even a college minor in the subject they are teaching. The first series measures this factor at the middle-school level and the second at the high-school level. It does not measure what percentage of teachers achieved qualification certificates, only their prior college training in the subjects they now instruct. Middle school showed the greater black/white discrepancy—49 percent of teachers of black students did not have even a college minor in their subjects, compared to 40 percent for white students.

Two additional measures were used: teachers with less than three years experience teaching in minority schools and public school funding on education per student. Funding was measured per student in high and low poverty[3] districts based on the total amount of state and local revenues each district received for the school year. Even after applying a 40 percent adjustment for low-income students which takes into account the

26

fact that these students need more support to reach the same level as higher-income students, there still remains a funding gap. Lastly, and only given 1/7 the weight of the prior four, is a California survey that asked what percentage of teachers in minority schools are under-prepared—that is, had not completed the California preparation program and obtained a full credential before beginning to teach. This variable was proportionally weighted to the full weight of the prior four, since California educates about 15 percent of the nation' s children.

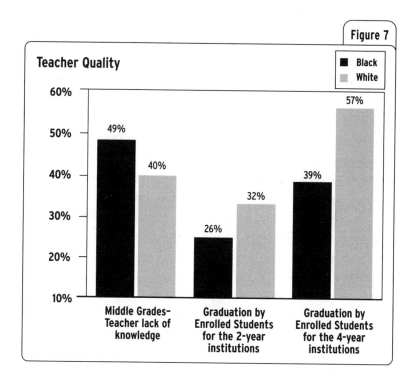

Figure 7

Teacher Quality

■ Black
▨ White

The second broad theme of this category is Course Quality (15 percent). There is some evidence that the intensity of courses taken in high school provides the most momentum for continuing education and completing college. Eight data series were included to measure the course curriculum of the student. Two series measured general strength in a student' s high school curriculum, while six others measured enrollment in Algebra II, precalculus, calculus, chemistry, English composition, and grammar. Studies have shown that one step beyond Algebra II doubles the odds that you will earn a bachelor' s degree.[4] The discrepancy between blacks and whites taking courses beyond Algebra II is still large. Whereas 65 percent and 69 percent enroll in Algebra II, respectively, only 32 percent of black students took precalculus, compared with 50 percent of whites. Calculus showed a slightly lower percentage difference (14 percent)—14 percent for blacks and 28 percent for whites. These numbers only slightly improved over last year' s index.

Attainment—20% of Education

Eight different gauges were used to measure "attained education." Each of these gauges was given an equal weight. Two of them measure graduation rates of two- and four-year schools; these data sets track students over time. Additionally, NCAA Division I schools track how many of their college freshman graduate within six years. This ratio was almost exactly equal to the data from the study of enrolled students at four-year institutions, increasing our confidence in both measures. In 2004, 26 percent of blacks graduated from two-year degree-granting schools versus 32 percent for whites. The discrepancy is higher for graduation rates at four-year degree-granting schools: 39 percent of blacks graduate compared to 57 percent for whites.

Three data sets measured the degrees earned at the associate, bachelor, and masters level. High school and college attainment for those over 25 were both also included in the index. This data suggests that even if black students immediately begin graduating from college at a greater rate than whites, it would still take many years for the ratio of college degrees in the over-25 population to equilibrate. The most improvement over 2005 in narrowing the gap between the percentage of blacks and whites who attain the same level of degrees was observed at the associates level. For bachelor's and master's degree attainment, there was only a slight improvement over last year. To determine the types of college degrees that persons over the age of 18 hold, a separate data set was used.

The data revealed that a far greater percentage of blacks chose Business, Computer, and Education than whites, while in others like Architecture, Engineering, and Law & Medicine, white concentration is greater.

Scores—15% of Education

The same measures created in 2005 to measure test scores—three micro-categories—Preschool, weighted at 10 percent of Scores; Elementary, 40 percent; and High School, 50 percent—were used for the 2006 index. One reason the Scores category was given less weight than Education Quality is that students considered in this data had not yet achieved the final goal of graduation. In addition, test scores have been shown to be less of an indication of degree completion than quality course curriculum.

The wide mix of tests creates a range of "scored education." Proficiency tests had the most data available, and included reading, math, history, geography and science scores for both 4th and 8th grade students. Both the ACT and the SAT were included, since they roughly cover different parts of the country, and their results did not significantly differ. GPA's for those taking the SAT were also included, as was writing proficiency. Finally, very young children's test scores were included, as well as the evaluated skill sets (recognizing letters, counting to 20 or higher, writing their name, and reading or pretending to read) that children had when entering preschool.

Enrollment—10% of Education

The underlying details to the already selected eleven enrollment measures were added to create a spectrum of "enrollment by age." Being enrolled in college during the more traditional age range of 18–24 was given far more importance than enrolling in college later in life. This was judged as appropriate because having a college degree at 20 rather than at 30 allows for the individual to earn higher wages for an additional 10 years. There were noticeable increases in the enrollment gap between blacks and whites for most of the age groups except ages 20–24. However, there was an improvement over last year's index in College Enrollment of Recent High School Graduates.

Student Status and Risk Factors—10% of Education

Eighteen series comprise this category, all evenly weighted. Dropping out of school is an important and widely followed statistic. Not only does it indicate students who have left the school system and thus do not "attain" the products of an education, it is also an indicator that the schools themselves are failing. The category Child in Poverty was included, since school performance is linked to conditions at home. Children with No Parents in the Labor Force was included for the same reason. Results of the next three items—Children with Disabilities, Suspended a Grade, and Repeating a Grade—illustrate the preponderance of black children to be quickly taken out of mainline classrooms.

SOCIAL JUSTICE—10% OF EQUALITY

The Social Justice index, computed at 0.74 is 6 points higher than last year's value of 0.68. The Social Justice index contains three categories: Equality Before the Law (80 percent), Governmental Equality (10 percent), and Victimization (10 percent). The index number of 0.74 indicates unequal treatment received by blacks. Figure 8 illustrates some differences among the key variables.

Equality Before the Law—80% of Social Justice

The first and most important category in the Social Justice sub-index is the equal treatment of blacks and whites before the law in our society. This is the essence of a fair and colorblind nation. Four data series captured this idea best: Stopped While Driving, Average Jail Sentence, Probation, and Prisoners as a Percent of Arrests.

Stopped While Driving (0.20) measures the percentage of drivers being pulled over for a variety of reasons. If we had simply used the total percentage, it would have produced an index of 0.85, since the average Stopped While Driving for blacks is nearly two-percentage points higher than whites—12.3 percent versus 10.4 percent. However, not all cars being stopped are equal. Speeding, Vehicle Defects, and Roadside Checks for drunk drivers do not involve subjective thinking, therefore these three items were given only the total value of the Stopped While Driving index.

Record Checks, Driver Suspected of Something, and "Other" were weighted far more heavily within Stopped While Driving. They comprise 75 percent of the index, because they are more subjective decisions. As expected, these weights caused the index value to decline—their results are less favorable to the black population. GII calculated that if using the simple total percentage figure, for the Stopped While Driving index to equalize at 1, the number of blacks stopped would have to shrink by 344,780 people.

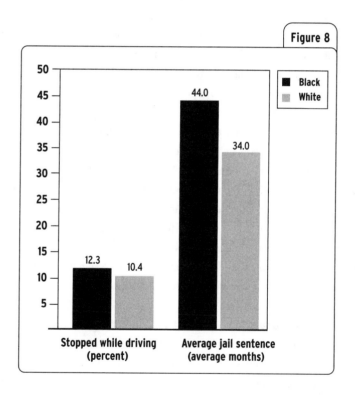

Figure 8

The index figure for Average Jail Sentence (0.20) shows that blacks are receiving, on average, a significantly longer felony sentence relative to whites. A black person's average sentence is ten months longer than a white's. This index has a value of 0.77. Obviously, this series could be open to criticism, since not all felonies are equal crimes. Depending on the mix of crimes committed, this index may be lower than .85, or even higher than 1. The Average Jail Sentence sub-categories, which show sentences for particular crimes, have been recently broken out into male and female designations. Of the sentences issued in 12 crime categories in the State Courts, sentences for black males were longer than white males in all of them. Black females found the justice system to be slightly more lenient than for black males. Of the sentences issued in 12 crime categories in State Courts, sentences for black females were longer than their white counterparts in all but four sub-categories. This brings up the question: Is the justice system not only biased against blacks, but heavily biased against black males? The data sets and scope of this document could not fully address this question.

According to Probation (0.20) figures, white male felons are more likely to get probation than black male felons. This result produced a Probation Granted index of 0.79. Again, this data series was adjusted for what kind of crime placed the person in jail, so a non-violent criminal offender was granted probation more often then a violent offender. Black females, once again, faired better than their male counterparts. The Probation Granted index was 1.14, which indicates a higher percentage of black females being granted probation compared to white females. Not included in this index, but related to the percentage of those who get probation, is how long a felon remains on probation. On average, a white felon' s probation and a black felon' s probation are the same length, 35 months.

Prisoners and Population—20% of Social Justice

The weight of the Prisoners and Population index is split evenly between its two sub-categories: In Prison as a Percent of Population (10 percent) and Prisoners as a Percent of Arrests (10 percent). The Prisoners as a Percent of Arrests index measures the transition from arrests to prisoner and the discrepancy therein. The index value of 0.32 speaks to a disproportionate amount of black arrests that result in the person becoming a prisoner. In fact, as a percentage of arrests, there are three times as many blacks that become prisoners. The operating theory is blacks are more likely to be imprisoned once arrested. Alternative theories would have to suppose that too many whites are being falsely arrested and then must be freed, or not enough blacks are being arrested based on their reported crimes.

Governmental Equality—10% of Social Justice

The Governmental Equality (0.20) index was constructed to measure government treatment of blacks in two categories. The categories are evenly weighted at 5 percent. State and Local Government Employment Median Pay, which produced a 0.85 figure, displays a discrepancy in pay between the races. Median Government pay for blacks would have to rise by $5,200 to equal whites. The next indicator relates to how many people are receiving Temporary Assistance for Needy Families (TANF) as a percent of children living below the poverty line. The index value of 0.38 illustrates that white children living in poverty are three times likely to be receiving TANF benefits than the average black child.

Victimization and Mental Anguish—10% of Social Justice

The Victimization and Mental Anguish index (0.10) has most of its weight devoted to the male and female homicide sub-indices. The Homicide indices for males and females collectively comprise 60 percent the index under this category, and the remainder is calculated with Adolescent Mortality (ages 13-19), Murder Victims (% of Population), Hate Crimes Against (% of Population), Victims of Violent Crimes (per 1,000 people), Delinquency Cases (Crimes committed by a juvenile for which they could be tried as an adult), Prisoners Under Death Sentence, Percent of Students Carrying a Weapon in School and Percent of Students who Carry a Weapon Anywhere.

Homicides Adjusted for Population, both male and female, paint a grim picture. The Homicide index number for males (0.03 weight) shows a murder rate for black males that is over six times that of white males. Under Male Homicides, black male deaths due to firearms and stabbings are near the overall index value of 0.15, while white males are more likely to die due to vehicular accidents. It is important to note that the 2006 overall Homicide index number of 0.14 is a minor but marked decline over the 0.19 index number from one year ago. The Homicide index number for females was slightly better than for males, at 0.21. The homicide rate for black females is nearly five times higher than white females. Though this seems staggering, when compared with last year, the index number for Female Homicides shows that the index increased by seven points. Lastly, the category of adolescent or teenage deaths from all causes had more black deaths than white, with an index of 0.80.

CIVIC ENGAGEMENT—10% OF EQUALITY INDEX

Civic Engagement sub-index is divided into four categories: The Democratic Progress (0.50), Volunteerism (0.30), Collective Bargaining (0.10), and Government Employment (0.10). The Civic Engagement index number was computed at 1.04, indicating that, as far as Civic Engagement goes, blacks in America are slightly more involved than whites. However, the 2006 Civic Engagement value is 0.04 points lower than the 2005 value. Figure 9 graphically demonstrates some of the differences among variables and is unchanged from the previous year's index value.

The Democratic Process—50% of Civic Engagement

This category attempts to measure the degree to which the two populations exercise their right to vote. Registering to vote and the act of voting itself are excellent proxies for how invested people are in the fabric of their nation and to what extent they feel engaged in their society. Citizens generally do not vote when they express little interest in their representatives, or when the issues being decided are not perceived to be of consequence to their daily life. Registered voters (25 percent) and actual voters (25 percent) are weighted evenly within this group. The Registered Voter index figure of 0.97 speaks to a slightly higher percentage of whites registered to vote than blacks. The number of black registered voters needs to rise by 482,000 people for the Registered Voter Index to reach 1. The Actual Voter index value of 0.93 also shows a nominal difference between blacks and whites. Interestingly, despite the tremendous effort it took to gain the right to vote, blacks participate somewhat less than whites.

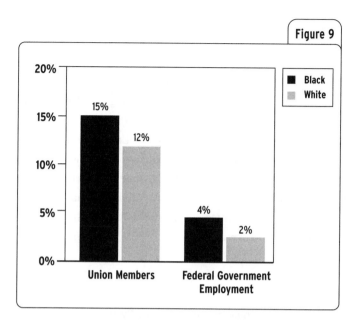

Figure 9

Community Participation—30% of Civic Engagement

Participation has six components: Volunteerism (15%), Military Volunteerism (10%) and four new series: Unpaid Volunteering of Young Adults, Attending Church, Youth Attending Church, and Youth Involved in Church Programs were all weighted equally at one half of 1%.

The 2006 Volunteerism figure of 0.68 is higher than the 2005 index figure of 0.65, but while a higher percentage of whites opt to volunteer, the index figure for Military Volunteerism is 1.13, indicating a substantially higher percentage of black volunteer in the military reserves. Part of this may be due to income supplementation, which is why military volunteerism is not pure "volunteering" and thus given a smaller weight.

Collective Bargaining—10% of Civic Engagement

The two components of this category, Unionism (% in union) and Union Represented (% in occupations that represented by Unions) are equally weighted. The Unionism index number of 1.24 reveals a significantly higher percentage of blacks in unions than whites. In addition, the Union Representation index value of 1.24 means that blacks also are more concentrated in jobs that are represented by unions. Both indices are 0.08 points lower now than in 2005.

Governmental Employment—10% of Civic Engagement

There are also two components in this category: State and Local Government Employment and Federal Government Employment. They are evenly weighted. The Federal Government Employment index tallies at 1.95, demonstrating a great difference between white and black government employment at the federal level. The State and Local Government index was calculated at 1.35. The large index numbers may speak to the security that comes along with government employment. In addition, government jobs tend to have good health benefits, which may be another attractive feature.

CONCLUSION

Overall, the Total Equality Index is virtually unchanged, registering 0.73 in both 2005 and 2006. This is not surprising, since wholesale national changes move at a glacial pace. However, changes in the sub indexes did occur; thus the comparison between the two years' index values is not straightforward. As the *Equality Index* project progresses, GII is improving the index both by updating the data as newer values become available and adding new concepts to further illustrate and better capture the totality of the black/white experience in America. In the 2005 *Equality Index*, a total of 312 data series (2005-312 in the chart below) were utilized to measure the gap between Black and White America; in the 2006 *Equality Index*, 40 new series were added for a total of 352 measuring points (2006-352).

GII kept the 2006 weights exactly as last time around for all the 5 major sub indexes and for the great majority of micro categories and even some individual series, adjusting instead the relative weights of new micro categories. For example, Education scores represent 15 percent of the total Education subindex. In 2004, seven different nationwide scores were used, each with 1/7 the weight of the 15 percent, in 2005 and 2006 a total of 14 scores were utilized each with a 1/14 weight of the 15 percent.

For purposes of comparison, GII has created charts showing the 2005 index value (2005-312) and the 2006 new index value (2006–352) below. GII also created a true apples–to–apples index comparison for the total index and the major sub-indexes (2006–312). This last index is what the 2006 value would have been had we just used the old 312 data series reflecting all the updated data available this year.

Figure 10

National Urban League/Global Insight, Inc. Equality Index

	2006-352	2005-312	2006-312	Percent Change Versus 2005	
				2006-352	2006-312
Total Equality	0.730	0.729	0.726	0.13%	-0.41%
Economic	0.561	0.568	0.566	-1.16%	-0.39%
Health	0.759	0.762	0.759	-0.47%	-0.47%
Education	0.776	0.772	0.776	0.58%	0.58%
Social Justice	0.742	0.675	0.717	9.89%	6.18%
Civic Engagement	1.037	1.081	1.009	-4.11%	-6.66%

KEY
• 2006-352 is the Equality Index calculated with additional factors in it.
• 2006-312 offers the direct comparison with the 2005 Equality Index.

In the table and accompanying charts (Figures 10, 11), the Economic sub index has the least variation, even with the addition of four new variables. This index was so highly developed the new concepts wrought very little change.

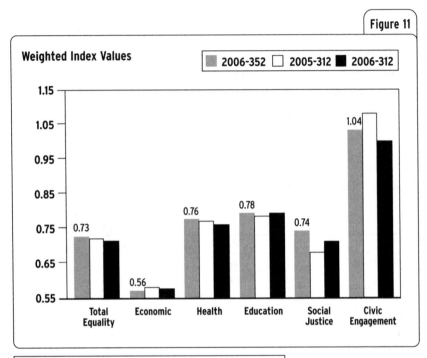

Figure 11

Weighted Index Values

■ 2006-352 □ 2005-312 ■ 2006-312

KEY
• 2006-352 is the Equality Index calculated with additional factors in it.
• 2006-312 offers the direct comparison with the 2005 Equality Index.

The Health sub index has an identical number to last year. Due to its large number of existing variables, no new variables were added this year.

Figure 12

Total Variables			
GII Equality Index	**2005**	**New**	**2006**
Total	312	40	352
Economic	35	4	39
Health	109	0	109
Education	99	0	99
Social Justice	57	36	93
Civic Engagement	12	0	12

In one of the remaining 3 subindexes, the addition of new concepts did materially impact the change from the 2005 index. Adding 36 new concepts to Social Justice had a large positive effect. While the index number for the Average Jail Sentence fell, the overall index rose, in part because of the Female Probation Granted Variable and other new female-designated variables—previously, this index did not include breakouts for gender. Including the data for black women brought the index number up because black women are treated relatively better by the system than black men.

Education added no new variables in this incarnation of the Equality index, but the Education index increased by .01. The increase comes on the strength of the Course Quality, Attainment, and Test Scores, which all posted gains this year.

Civic Engagement was the only sub-index that had a score of above 1 in 2006. However, the Civic Engagement index fell by .04 versus 2005. This is because Percent of Population Volunteering in the Military saw its index fall by 0.31 versus the 2005 value. Consequently, this caused a reduction in the overall Civic Engagement index.

NOTES

[1]Net Worth is defined as the total value of held assets minus the total value of debts. Included in net worth were interest-earning assets, checking accounts, stocks and mutual funds, real estate and motor vehicles.

[2]"High Cost or High Opportunity Cost? Transportation and Family Economic Success", the Brookings Institution, December 2005.

[3]A high poverty district was defined as those in the top 25 percent statewide in terms of the percent of students living below the federal poverty line, where the poverty rate is defined as the percentage of people age 5 to 17 living in each school district with a household income below the federal poverty line as estimated by the U.S. Census Bureau. "The Funding Gap 2005".

[4]An odds ratio indicates that every unit of change in an independent variable (in this case, each step up the math ladder) increases the odds of X happening versus the odds of X not happening by Y (the odds ratio). "The Toolbox Revisited", U.S. Department of Education, 2005.

SUMMARY FIGURES AND SPREADSHEETS

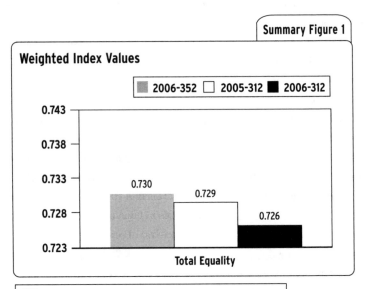

Summary Figure 1

Weighted Index Values

2006-352 ☐ 2005-312 ■ 2006-312

Total Equality

KEY
• 2006-352 is the Equality Index calculated with additional factors in it.
• 2006-312 offers the direct comparison with the 2005 Equality Index.

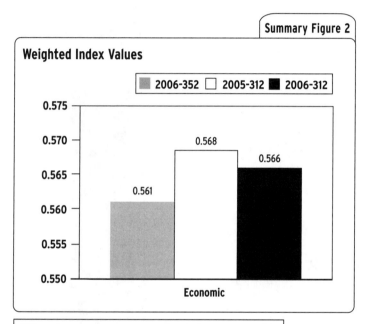

Summary Figure 2

Weighted Index Values

◾ 2006-352 ☐ 2005-312 ■ 2006-312

0.568

0.566

0.561

Economic

KEY
• 2006-352 is the Equality Index calculated with additional factors in it.
• 2006-312 offers the direct comparison with the 2005 Equality Index.

41

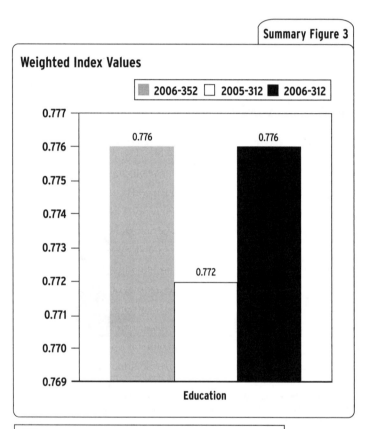

Summary Figure 3

Weighted Index Values

2006-352 ☐ 2005-312 ■ 2006-312

Education

KEY
• 2006-352 is the Equality Index calculated with additional factors in it.
• 2006-312 offers the direct comparison with the 2005 Equality Index.

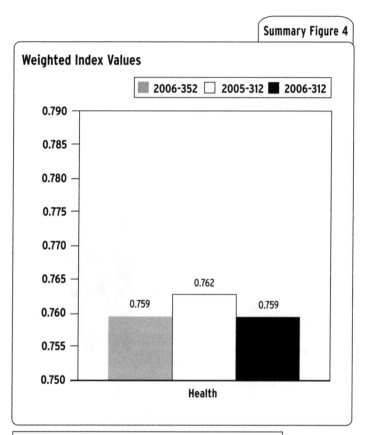

Summary Figure 4

Weighted Index Values

KEY
• 2006-352 is the Equality Index calculated with additional factors in it.
• 2006-312 offers the direct comparison with the 2005 Equality Index.

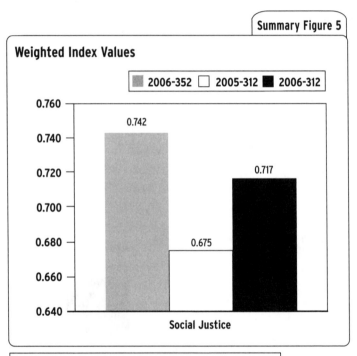

Summary Figure 5

Weighted Index Values

■ 2006-352   ☐ 2005-312   ■ 2006-312

- 0.742
- 0.717
- 0.675

Social Justice

KEY
• 2006-352 is the Equality Index calculated with additional factors in it.
• 2006-312 offers the direct comparison with the 2005 Equality Index.

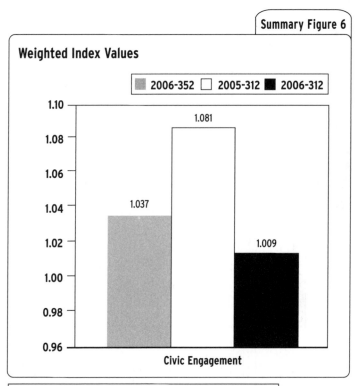

Summary Figure 6

Weighted Index Values

2006-352 ☐ 2005-312 ■ 2006-312

Civic Engagement

KEY
• 2006-352 is the Equality Index calculated with additional factors in it.
• 2006-312 offers the direct comparison with the 2005 Equality Index.

The Equality Index of Black America

Updated Series   New Series   (Index = 0.73)

	Year	Black	White	Index	DIFF ('06-'05)
ECONOMICS (30%)					
Median Income (0.25)					
Median Income (Real)	2004	34,369	55,768	62%	0.00
Mean Male Earnings by Highest Degree Earned	2001	38,478	55,354	70%	
Mean Female Earnings by Highest Degree Earned	2001	30,766	37,136	83%	
Poverty (0.15)					
Poverty Line (% Below)	2004	24.7	10.8	44%	0.01
Poverty Line (% Below 50% of Poverty Line)	2004	12.6	3.8	30%	
Population Living Near (1.00 to 1.25) Poverty Threshold (Total)	new 2004	6.2	3.2	52%	
Population Living Near Poverty Line (Under 18)	2002	27.2	16.6	61%	
Population Living Near Poverty Line (18-64)	2002	20.6	11.8	57%	
Population Living Near Poverty Line (65 and Older)	2002	33.5	27.2	81%	
Employment Issues (0.20)					
Unemployment Rate	2005	10.0	4.4	44%	0.01
Persons 16-19 Who are Unemployed	2005	0.33	0.14	43%	(0.05)
Persons 16-19 who are Idle (Not in School and not Working)	2000	0.14	0.063	45%	
Discouraged Workers (not in Workforce)	2005	35.9	33.7	94%	0.01
Labor Force Participants	2005	64.8	66.3	98%	0.02
LFPR 16 to 19	2005	32.3	46.9	69%	0.02
LFPR 20 to 24	2005	69.0	76.3	90%	0.02
LFPR over 25 - Less than High School Grad	2005	39.8	46.4	86%	0.00
LFPR over 25 - High School Graduate, no College	2005	67.9	62.5	109%	(0.00)
LFPR over 25 - Some College, no Degree	2005	74.2	69.6	107%	0.01
LFPR over 25 - Associate's Degree	2005	78.9	76.5	103%	0.02
LFPR over 25 - less than Bachelor's	2005	75.6	72.0	105%	0.01
LFPR over 25 - College Graduate	2005	82.0	77.5	106%	(0.01)

The Equality Index of Black America

| | Updated Series | New Series | (Index = 0.73) |

	Year	Black	White	Index	DIFF ('06-'05)
Unemployment Duration	2003	22.7	18.0	79%	
Employment to Pop. Ratio	2005	57.7	63.4	91%	0.00
Housing & Wealth (0.34)					
Home Ownership	2003	48.1	75.4	64%	0.00
Mortgage Application Denial	2003	24.25	11.65	48%	0.03
Home Improvement Loans	2003	54.78	29.15	53%	0.04
Home Values (Median)	2000	80,600	123,400	65%	
Median Net Worth	2000	6166	67,000	9%	
Equity in Home	2000	35000	64,200	55%	
Percent Investing in 401k	2000	19.6	32.9	60%	
Percent Investing in IRA	2000	6.5	27.5	24%	
U.S. Firms by Race (% compared to employment share)	2002	0.509	0.951	54%	0.16
Digital Divide (0.01)					
Households with Computer at Home	2001	32.6	55.7	59%	
Households using the Internet	2003	45.2	65.1	69%	
Households with Broadband Access	2003	13.9	25.7	54%	
Transportation (0.05)					
Car Ownership	new 2000	70.2	89.2	79%	
Drive Alone	new 2000	65.9	78.8	84%	
Reliance on Public Transportation	new 2000	12.2	3.1	25%	
Economic Weighted Index				56%	
HEALTH INDEX (25%)					
Death Rebates & Life Expectancy (0.45)					
Life Expectancy at Birth	2002	72.3	77.7	93%	
Male	2002	68.8	75.1	92%	
Female	2002	75.6	80.3	94%	

The Equality Index of Black America

	Updated Series		New Series	(Index = 0.73)

	Year	Black	White	Index	DIFF ('06-'05)
Life Expectancy at 65 (additional expected years)					
Male at 65	2002	16.6	18.2	91%	
Female at 65	2002	14.6	16.6	88%	
	2002	18	19.5	92%	
Age-Adjusted Death Rates (per 100,000) - all causes	2002	1,083.3	837.5	77%	
Age-Adjusted Death Rates (per 100,000) - Heart Disease	2002	308.4	239.2	78%	
Ischemic Heart Disease	2002	203.0	171.0	84%	
Age-Adjusted Death Rates (per 100,000) - Stroke (Cerebrovascular)	2002	76.3	54.6	72%	
Age-Adjusted Death Rates (per 100,000) - Cancer	2002	238.8	195.6	82%	
Trachea, Bronchus, and Lung	2002	61.9	57.5	93%	
Colon, Rectum, and Anus	2002	26.8	19.5	73%	
Prostate	2002	62.0	25.8	42%	
Breast	2002	34.0	25.6	75%	
Age-Adjusted Death Rates (per 100,000) - Chronic Lower Respiratory	2002	31.2	46.9	150%	
Influenza and Pneumonia	2002	24.0	22.6	94%	
Chronic Liver Disease and Cirrhosis	2002	8.5	9.0	106%	
Age-Adjusted Death Rates (per 100,000) - Diabetes	2002	49.5	22.2	45%	
Age-Adjusted Death Rates (per 100,000) - HIV	2002	22.5	2.1	9%	
Unintentional Injuries	2002	36.9	38.0	103%	
Motor Vehicle-Related Injuries	2002	15.0	16.0	107%	
Age-Adjusted Death Rates (per 100,000) - Suicide	2002	5.3	12.9	243%	
Age-Adjusted Death Rates (per 100,000) - Suicide Males	2002	9.8	21.4	218%	
Age-Adjusted Death Rates (per 100,000) - Suicide Males ages 15-24	2002	11.3	19.3	171%	
Age-Adjusted Death Rates (per 100,000) - Suicide Females	2002	1.6	5.1	319%	
Age-Adjusted Death Rates (per 100,000) - Suicide Females ages 15-24	2002	1.7	3.4	200%	
Age-Adjusted Death Rates (per 100,000) - Homicide	2002	21.0	2.8	13%	
Age-Adjusted Death Rates (per 100,000) - Homicide Male	2002	36.4	3.7	10%	

The Equality Index of Black America

Updated Series   New Series   (Index = 0.73)

Description	Year	Black	White	Index	DIFF ('06-'05)
Age-Adjusted Death Rates (per 100,000)- Homicide Males ages 15-24	2002	83.1	5.5	7%	
Age-Adjusted Death Rates (per 100,000)- Homicide Female	2002	6.9	1.9	28%	
Age-Adjusted Death Rates (per 100,000)- Homicide Females ages 15-24	2002	10.3	2.2	21%	
Age-Adjusted Death Rates (per 100,000) by age cohort: >1 Male	2002	1,351.5	643.5	48%	
Age-Adjusted Death Rates (per 100,000) by age cohort: 1-4 Male	2002	54.4	30.3	56%	
Age-Adjusted Death Rates (per 100,000) by age cohort: 5-14 Male	2002	28.9	18.3	63%	
Age-Adjusted Death Rates (per 100,000) by age cohort: 15-24 Male	2002	172.6	106.7	62%	
Age-Adjusted Death Rates (per 100,000) by age cohort: 25-34 Male	2002	264.5	130.9	49%	
Age-Adjusted Death Rates (per 100,000) by age cohort: 35-44 Male	2002	434.7	244.9	56%	
Age-Adjusted Death Rates (per 100,000) by age cohort: 45-54 Male	2002	983.0	509.9	52%	
Age-Adjusted Death Rates (per 100,000) by age cohort: 55-64 Male	2002	2,039.2	1,126.5	55%	
Age-Adjusted Death Rates (per 100,000) by age cohort: 65-74 Male	2002	4,024.5	2,824.1	70%	
Age-Adjusted Death Rates (per 100,000) by age cohort: 75-84 Male	2002	8,169.6	6,801.7	83%	
Age-Adjusted Death Rates (per 100,000) by age cohort: 85+ Male	2002	15,635.5	16,641.9	106%	
Age-Adjusted Death Rates (per 100,000) by age cohort: >1 Female	2002	1,172.0	504.8	43%	
Age-Adjusted Death Rates (per 100,000) by age cohort: 1-4 Female	2002	39.5	23.8	60%	
Age-Adjusted Death Rates (per 100,000) by age cohort: 5-14 Female	2002	19.9	13.6	68%	
Age-Adjusted Death Rates (per 100,000) by age cohort: 15-24 Female	2002	54.4	43.8	81%	
Age-Adjusted Death Rates (per 100,000) by age cohort: 25-34 Female	2002	116.4	60.3	52%	
Age-Adjusted Death Rates (per 100,000) by age cohort: 35-44 Female	2002	272.3	138.3	51%	
Age-Adjusted Death Rates (per 100,000) by age cohort: 45-54 Female	2002	579.4	292.1	50%	
Age-Adjusted Death Rates (per 100,000) by age cohort: 55-64 Female	2002	1,184.2	710.5	60%	
Age-Adjusted Death Rates (per 100,000) by age cohort: 65-74 Female	2002	2,545.0	1,846.0	73%	
Age-Adjusted Death Rates (per 100,000) by age cohort: 75-84 Female	2002	5,584.4	4,787.9	86%	
Age-Adjusted Death Rates (per 100,000) by age cohort: 85+ Female	2002	13,734.2	14,504.3	106%	

The Equality Index of Black America

| | Updated Series | New Series | (Index = 0.73) |

	Year	Black	White	Index	DIFF ('06-'05)
Lifetime Health (0.30)					
Physical Condition (0.10)					
Overweight and Obese: 18+ years (% of population)	2002	68.9	57.5	83%	
Men 20 years and Over (% of population)	2002	62.6	69.4	111%	
Women 20 years and Over (% of population)	2002	77.1	57.2	74%	
Obese (% of population)	2002	34.8	22.2	64%	
Men 20 years and over (% of population)	2002	27.8	28.0	101%	
Women 20 years and over (% of population)	2002	48.8	30.7	63%	
Diabetes: Physician Diagnosed in ages 20+ (% of population)	2000	11.7	4.8	41%	
Activity Limitation due to Chronic Condition: All ages (% of population)	2000	15.0	12.4	83%	
AIDS cases per 100,000 males ages 13+	2003	109.2	13.6	12%	
AIDS cases per 100,000 females ages 13+	2003	49.0	2.2	4%	
Substance Abuse (0.10)					
Any Illicit Drug Ages 12+ (% of population)	2003	8.7	8.3	95%	
Binge Alcohol (5 drinks in 1 day, 1x a month) ages 12+ (% of population)	2003	19.0	23.6	124%	
Heavy Alcohol use Ages 12+ (% of population)	2003	4.5	7.7	171%	
Tobacco: both Cigarette & Cigar ages 12+ (% of population)	2003	30.0	31.6	105%	
Mental Health (0.02)					
Students who Consider Suicide: Male	2002	10.3	12.0	117%	
Students who Carry out Intent and Require Medical Attention: Male	2002	5.2	1.1	21%	
Percent of Students that act on Suicidal feeling: Male	2002	50.5	9.2	18%	
Students who Consider Suicide: Female	2002	21.2	14.7	69%	
Students who Carry out Intent and Require Medical Attention: Female	2002	2.4	2.2	92%	
Percent of Students that act on Suicidal Feeling: Female	2002	11.3	15.0	132%	
Access to Care (0.05)					
One Prescription Drug in Past Month (% of population)	2000	40.1	47.4	85%	

The Equality Index of Black America

Updated Series | New Series | (Index = 0.73)

	Year	Black	White	Index	DIFF ('06-'05)
Private Insurance Payment for Health Care: under 65 years old (% of population)	2000	40.5	55.1	74%	
Private Insurance: 65 years & over (% of population)	2002	36.5	66.4	55%	
All People Without Health Insurance	2004	0.197	0.113	57%	(0.13)
All People under 65 Without Health Insurance	2002	19.2	12.6	66%	
All People in poverty Without Health Insurance	2002	0.264	0.314	119%	
Population under 65 Covered by Medicaid	2002	21.5	8	37%	
Elderly Heath Care (0.03)					
Population over 65 Covered by Medicaid	2002	19.4	5	26%	
Medicare Expenditures per Beneficiary	2000	12328	10,475	85%	
Disabled Medicare Beneficiary (percent)	2000	23.3	11.5	49%	
Living with Spouse: Medicare Beneficiaries	2000	30	51	59%	
Living with Children & Others: Medicare Beneficiaries		32.3	13.8	43%	
Reproduction and Pediatric Care (Mothers Health, Births & Early Childhood) (0.25)					
Pregnancy Issues (0.04)					
Prenatal Care begins in 1st Trimester	2002	75.2	88.6	85%	
Prenatal Care begins in 3rd Trimester	2002	6.2	2.2	35%	
Percent of Births to Mothers 19 and under	2002	18	7.8	43%	
Percent of Live Births to Unmarried Mothers	2002	68.4	23	34%	
Mothers with less than 12 years of Education (Percent of Live Births)	2002	24.3	11.7	48%	
Mothers who Smoked Cigarettes during Pregnancy (Percent)	2002	8.8	15	170%	
Low Birth Weight (Percent of Live Births)	2002	13.39	6.91	52%	
Reproduction Issues (0.01)					
Abortions (Per 100 live births)	2001	49.1	16.5	34%	
Women using Contraception (Percent in Population)	1995	62.1	66.1	94%	
Men - Contraception: Permanent (Sterilization - Percent of Population)	1995	1.7	13.6	13%	
Delivery Issues (0.10)					

The Equality Index of Black America

	Updated Series	New Series	(Index = 0.73)

	Year	Black	White	Index	DIFF ('06-'05)
Live Births per 1000 Women	2002	66.6	39.4	59%	
All Infant Deaths: Neonatal and Post (per 1000 Live Births)	2002	13.9	5.8	42%	
- Neonatal Deaths (per 1000 Live Births)	2002	9.3	3.9	42%	
- PostNeonatal Deaths (per 1000 Live Births)	2002	4.6	1.9	41%	
Maternal Mortality (per 100,000 Live Births)	2002	22.9	4.4	19%	
Children's Health (0.1)					
Babies Breastfed (percent)	1994	27.4	61.2	45%	
No Child health Care Visit in past 12 Months (% of Children up to 6 Years Old)	2002	5.9	6.4	92%	
Vaccinations of Children below poverty: Combined Vacc. Series 4:3:1:3 (percent of Children 19-35 Months)	2003	70	79	89%	
Uninsured Children	2004	0.13	0.076	58%	(0.21)
Children Covered by Medicaid	2002	0.412	0.201	49%	
Overweight and Obese, Boys 6-11 years old (% of population)	2002	17.0	14.0	82%	
Overweight and Obese, Girls 6-11 years old (% of population)	2002	22.8	13.1	57%	
AIDS Cases per 100,000 All Children Under 13	2003	3.0	0.2	7%	
Health Weighted Index				**76%**	
EDUCATION (25%)					
Quality (0.45)					
Teacher Quality (0.30)					
Middle Grades - Teacher Lacking at least a College Minor in Subject Taught	2000	49%	40%	85%	
HS - Teacher Lacking at least a College Minor in Subject Taught	2000	28%	21%	91%	
Per Student Funding in Low and High Poverty Districts (dollars)	2002	6,383	7,731	83%	
Teachers with <3 Years Experience (High vs. Low Minority schools)	2000	0.21	0.1	48%	
Distribution of Under Prepared Teachers (California only) Small vs. High Minority*	2002	0.15	0.03	20%	
*had not completed a preparation program and obtained a full credential before beginning to teach					
Course Quality (0.15)					
All College Entrants what percent have strong HS Curriculum (Algebra II plus other courses)	1999	0.45	0.73	62%	

The Equality Index of Black America

| | Updated Series | | New Series | |

	Year	Black	White	Index	DIFF ('06-'05)
Of all College Graduates what percent had a strong HS Curriculum (Algebra II plus other courses)					
HS Students: Enrolled in Chemistry	1999	0.75	0.86	87%	0.11
HS Students: Enrolled in Algebra II	2000	0.6	0.63	95%	0.10
Students Taking: Precalculus	2000	0.65	0.69	94%	0.01
Students Taking: Calculus	2005	0.32	0.5	64%	0.02
Students Taking: English Composition	2005	0.14	0.28	50%	(0.01)
Students Taking: Grammar	2005	0.5	0.67	75%	0.01
	2005	0.59	0.7	84%	
Attainment (0.20)					
Graduation by Enrolled Students For the 2-year Institutions:	2004	26%	32%	82%	0.03
Graduation by Enrolled Students For the 4-year Institutions:	2004	39%	57%	67%	0.00
NCAA Div. I College Freshmen Graduating within 6 Years	2005	43%	63%	68%	
Degrees Earned (Assoc)	2003	1.8%	2.4%	72%	0.05
Degrees Earned (Bach)	2003	1.8%	3.4%	53%	0.01
Degrees Earned (Master)	2003	0.5%	0.8%	56%	0.02
HS Educational Attainment (25 and over)	2004	81%	86%	94%	0.00
College Educational Attainment (25 and over)	2004	18%	28%	64%	0.02
Degree Holders (% of Persons over 18)					
Agriculture	1996	0.7	1.2	58%	
Architechture	1996	1	2.8	36%	
Business	1996	23	19.7	117%	
Communications	1996	2.1	2.3	91%	
Computer	1996	3.4	2.1	162%	
Education	1996	20.9	17	123%	
Engineering	1996	2.8	7.2	39%	
Literature	1996	1.7	2.8	61%	
Foreign Language	1996	0.4	0.7	57%	

The Equality Index of Black America

Updated Series   New Series   (Index = 0.73)

	Year	Black	White	Index	DIFF ('06-'05)
Health Sciences	1996	4.1	3.8	108%	
Law	1996	1.8	3	60%	
Liberal Arts	1996	5.3	4.9	108%	
Math	1996	3	1.8	167%	
Medicine	1996	0.3	2.3	13%	
Natural Science	1996	3.1	4.7	66%	
Nursing & Public Health	1996	0.9	1.1	82%	
Philosophy	1996	1.1	1.6	69%	
Pre-professional	1996	0.8	0.3	267%	
Psychology	1996	4.2	3.3	127%	
Social Sciences	1996	6.6	4.4	150%	
Other	1996	13	13	100%	
Scores (0.15)					
Preschool 10% of Total Scores (0.015)					
Children's School Readiness Skills: ages 3-5 (percent with 3 or 4 skills*)	2001	35	43	81%	
*Skills: Recognizes all letters, Counts to 20 or higher, Writes name, Reads or pretends to read					
Elementary 40% of Total Scores (0.06)					
- Proficiency Test Scores for Selected Subjects (NAEP) Elementary Ages					
Geography Scores for 8th Graders (public & private)	2001	234	273	86%	
History Scores for 8th Graders (public & private)	2001	243	271	90%	
Math 13 yr old (8th Grade)	2004	262	288	91%	0.03
Math 9 yr old (4th Grade)	2004	224	247	91%	0.02
Reading 13 yr old (8th Grade)	2004	244	266	92%	0.02
Reading 9 yr old (4th Grade)	2004	200	226	88%	0.02
Science 9 yr old	1999	199	240	83%	
Science Scores for 8th Graders (public schools)	new 2000	121	160	76%	

The Equality Index of Black America

			Updated Series	New Series	(Index = 0.73)
	Year	Black	White	Index	DIFF ('06-'05)
Writing Proficiency at or above Basic 4th Grade	new 2002	79	91	87%	
Writing Proficiency at or above Basic 8th Grade	new 2002	75	91	82%	
High School 50% of Total Scores (0.075)					
- High School Scores					
Writing Proficiency at or above Basic 12th Grade	new 2002	59	80	74%	
Science 17 yr old	1999	254	306	83%	
High School GPA's for those taking the SAT	2005	2.99	3.37	89%	0.01
SAT	2005	864	1068	81%	(0.00)
ACT	2005	17	21.9	78%	(0.01)
Enrollment (0.10)					
School Enrollment: ages 3-34 (% of population)	2003	59.2	55.4	107%	
Preprimary School Enrollment	2003	62.7	65.8	95%	(0.09)
3 and 4 years old	2003	55.6%	55.3%	101%	(0.06)
5 and 6 years old	2003	94.4%	94.7%	100%	
7 to 13 years old	2003	98.3%	98.3%	100%	
14 and 15 years old	2003	97.9%	97.3%	101%	
16 and 17 years old	2003	94.3%	95.0%	99%	
18 and 19 years old	2003	61.9%	64.4%	96%	
20 and 21 years old	2003	41.3%	48.2%	86%	
22 to 24 years old	2003	27.4%	26.7%	103%	
25 to 29 years old	2003	12.2%	11.0%	111%	
30 to 34 years old	2003	8.6%	6.2%	139%	
35 and over	2003	2.8%	1.8%	156%	
College Enrollment by Age Cohort (15 and over)	2003	7.6%	7.0%	110%	(0.09)
15 to 17 years old	2003	1.4%	1.2%	117%	(1.19)
18 to 19 years old	2003	30.1%	47.7%	63%	(0.08)

The Equality Index of Black America

■ Updated Series ■ New Series (Index = 0.73)

	Year	Black	White	Index	DIFF ('06-'05)
20 to 21 years old	2003	34.1%	47.3%	72%	0.02
22 to 24 years old	2003	23.5%	28.8%	82%	(0.00)
25 to 29 years old	2003	10.7%	11.8%	91%	(0.09)
30 to 34 years old	2003	7.9%	6.6%	119%	(0.22)
35 years old and over	2003	2.4%	1.7%	142%	(0.15)
College Enrollment of Recent High School Graduates	2003	66.20	57.50	115%	0.33
Adult Education Participation	2001	43.00	47.00	91%	
Student Status & Risk Factors (0.10)					
High School Dropouts: Status Dropouts - not completed HS and not enrolled, regardless of when dropped	2003	14%	12%	82%	(0.02)
Children in Poverty	2000	0.331	0.093	28%	
Children in Extreme Poverty (50% below Poverty Line)	2002	0.15	0.04	23%	
Children with No Parent in the Labor Force	2000	0.203	0.055	27%	
School Age Children (5-15) with a Disability	2000	0.07	0.057	81%	
Elementary & Secondary Students: Suspended	1999	0.15	0.35	43%	
Elementary & Secondary Students: Repeated Grade	1999	0.09	0.18	50%	
Center Based, Child Care of Preschool Children	2001	63.1	59.1	94%	0.12
Parental Only, Child Care of Preschool Children	2001	15.1	25.3	60%	0.01
Teacher Stability: Remained in Public School	2001	84.3	85.0	99%	0.03
Teacher Stability: Remained in Private School	2001	83.2	79.0	105%	0.15
Zero Days Missed in School Year (percent)	2002	16.5	13.1	126%	(0.87)
3+ Days Late to School (percent of Students Reporting)	2002	46.1	33.6	73%	(0.11)
Never Cut Classes (percent of Students)	2002	84.8	88.2	96%	(0.05)
Home Literacy Activities (Age 3 to 5)					
Read to 3 or more times a Week	2001	77	89	87%	
Told a Story at least once a Month	2001	51	81	63%	
Taught Words or Numbers three or more times a Week	2001	78	75	104%	

The Equality Index of Black America

	Updated Series	New Series	(Index = 0.73)

	Year	Black	White	Index	DIFF ('06-'05)
Visited a Library at least once in last Month	2001	31	39	79%	
Education Weighted Index				**78%**	
SOCIAL JUSTICE (10%)					
Equality Before the Law (0.80)					
Stopped While Driving					
Speeding	1999	12.3	10.4	85%	
Vehicle Defect	1999	43.4	53.7	124%	
Roadside Check for Drinking Drivers	1999	13.4	10.4	78%	
Record Check	1999	1.4	2.5	179%	
Driver Suspected of Something	1999	11	9.1	83%	
Other	1999	2.4	2.3	96%	
	1999	28.4	22	77%	
Average Jail Sentence (in Average Months)	2002	44	34	77%	(0.07)
Average Sentence for Murder - Male	new 2002	240	213	89%	
Average Sentence for Sexual Assault - Male	new 2002	95	85	89%	
Average Sentence for Robbery - Male	new 2002	92	78	85%	
Average Sentence for Aggravated Assault - Male	new 2002	48	36	75%	
Average Sentence for Other Violent - Male	new 2002	40	36	90%	
Average Sentence for Burglary - Male	new 2002	44	37	84%	
Average Sentence for Larceny - Male	new 2002	23	22	96%	
Average Sentence for Fraud - Male	new 2002	30	25	83%	
Average Sentence for Drug Possession - Male	new 2002	23	20	87%	
Average Sentence for Drug trafficking - Male	new 2002	45	38	84%	
Average Sentence for Weapon Offenses - Male	new 2002	30	27	90%	
Average Sentence for Other Offenses - Male	new 2002	23	22	96%	
Average Sentence for Murder - Female	new 2002	247	121	49%	
Average Sentence for Sexual Assault - Female	new 2002	34	43	126%	

The Equality Index of Black America

		Updated Series	New Series	(Index = 0.73)

	Year	Black	White	Index	DIFF ('06-'05)
Average Sentence for Robbery - Female	new 2002	57	54	95%	
Average Sentence for Aggravated Assault - Female	new 2002	29	25	86%	
Average Sentence for Other Violent - Female	new 2002	25	39	156%	
Average Sentence for Burglary - Female	new 2002	20	20	100%	
Average Sentence for Larceny - Female	new 2002	16	16	100%	
Average Sentence for Fraud - Female	new 2002	23	20	87%	
Average Sentence for Drug Possession - Female	new 2002	15	14	93%	
Average Sentence for Drug trafficking - Female	new 2002	33	30	91%	
Average Sentence for Weapon Offenses - Female	new 2002	23	17	74%	
Average Sentence for Other Offenses - Female	new 2002	19	14	74%	
Probation Granted for Felons (% granted) - Male	new 2002	27	34	79%	
Probation Granted for Murder	new 2002	4	6	67%	
Probation Granted for Robbery	new 2002	11	14	79%	
Probation Granted for Burglary	new 2002	23	27	85%	
Probation Granted for Fraud	new 2002	37	42	88%	
Probation Granted for Drug Offenses	new 2002	31	42	74%	
Probation Granted for Felons (% granted) - Female	new 2002	47	45	104%	
Probation Granted for Murder	new 2002	5	17	29%	
Probation Granted for Robbery	new 2002	24	31	77%	
Probation Granted for Burglary	new 2002	24	32	75%	
Probation Granted for Fraud	new 2002	57	50	114%	
Probation Granted for Drug Offenses	new 2002	45	49	92%	
In Prison as a % of Population	2003	41	34	83%	
Prisoners as a % of Arrests	2001	24.61	7.78	32%	
Government Equality (0.10)					
State and Local Government Employment Median Pay	1999	29.6	34.8	85%	

The Equality Index of Black America

Updated Series ▪ New Series ▪ (Index = 0.73)

	Year	Black	White	Index	DIFF ('06-'05)
TANF compared to Children's Poverty (eligible and receiving TANF)	2001	1.21	3.19	38%	
TANF - % of Families Covered (On TANF Share of Population)	2001	0.27	0.04	14%	
Victimization & Mental Anguish (0.10)					
Homicides (Adj. for Population) - Male	2002	0.048	0.007	14%	
Homicide rate per 100,000: Firearm (aged 15-34)	2001	785.4	86.0	11%	
Homicide rate per 100,000: Stabbings (aged 15-34)	2001	50.8	14.3	28%	
Homicide rate per 100,000: Vehicular (aged 15-34)	2001	10.7	21.7	202%	
Homicide (Adj. for Population) - Female	2002	0.0037	0.0008	21%	
Adolescent Mortality ages 13-19 (All Injury Deaths and Rates per 100,000)	2001	48.6	39.01	80%	
Murder Victims (% of Pop.)	2003	0.02	0.00	20%	0.00
Hate Crimes Against (Incidents % of Pop.)	2003	0.01	0.00	6%	0.01
Victims of Violent Crimes	2003	29.10	21.50	74%	(0.08)
Delinquency Cases (Cases com. By Juvie that Adult could be pros.)	2003	92.50	46.00	50%	0.00
Prisoners under Death Sentence	2003	0.00	0.00	24%	0.00
% Students Carrying Weapons in School (9-12 Grade)	2003	7.00	6.00	86%	(0.11)
% Students Carrying Weapons Anywhere (9-12 Grade)	2003	17.00	17.00	100%	(0.18)
Firearm-Related Death (All Ages, Males)	2002	37.80	16.30	43%	
Ages 1-14	2002	1.80	0.70	39%	
Ages 15-24	2002	87.10	15.60	18%	
Ages 25-44	2002	60.60	18.40	30%	
Ages 35-44	2002	85.60	17.40	20%	
Ages 45-64	2002	36.90	19.30	52%	
Age 65 and Older	2002	18.60	19.40	104%	
Firearm-Related Death (All Ages, Females)	2002	14.20	29.80	210%	
Ages 15-24	2002	4.20	2.80	67%	
	2002	8.10	2.50	31%	

The Equality Index of Black America

■ Updated Series ■ New Series (Index = 0.73)

	Year	Black	White	Index	DIFF ('06-'05)
Ages 25-44	2002	6.70	4.10	61%	
Ages 45-64	2002	3.00	3.80	127%	
Age 65 and Older	2002	1.20	2.30	192%	
Social Justice Weighted Index				**74%**	
CIVIC ENGAGEMENT (10%)					
Democratic Process (0.5)					
Registered Voters	2004	64.4	67.9	95%	(0.02)
Actually Voted	2004	56.3	60.3	93%	(0.01)
Community Participation (0.3)					
Percent of Population Volunteering for Military Reserves	2004	0.5%	0.4%	113%	(0.31)
Volunteerism	2004	20.8	30.5	68%	0.03
Unpaid Volunteering of Young Adults	2000	40.9	32.2	127%	
Attend Church (% Considering self Religious)	2001	49	37	132%	
Church Attendance among Youth (Weekly %)	1996	41	38	108%	
Youth Group Participation (2 Years or more)	1996	59	57	104%	
Collective Bargaining (0.1)					
Unionism (members)	2004	15.1	12.2	124%	(0.08)
Union Rep.	2004	16.7	13.5	124%	(0.08)
Governmental Employment (0.1)					
Federal Government Employment	2003	4.1%	2.1%	195%	
State and Local Government Employment	2003	15.7%	11.6%	135%	
Civic Engagement Weighted Index				**104%**	

Black Homeownership:
A Dream No Longer Deferred?

by Lance Freeman

Homeownership has long been synonymous with the American Dream. It has come to symbolize stability, the achievement of middle-class status and having "made it" in American society. Numerous studies show that the majority of Americans prefer homeownership to renting. For example, one report found that 86 percent of Americans believed that ownership was preferable to renting. This same study found that 74 percent of Americans thought that people should purchase their home as soon as they could (Fannie Mae 1994; Rohe, Van Zandt and McCarthy 2000). For Black Americans, however, the quest for homeownership has often been a dream deferred. Various discriminatory policies and practices converged to make homeownership an unlikely proposition for blacks through most of the 20th century. Homeownership is both an important indicator of the progress blacks have achieved and an important mechanism for upward mobility and reducing racial inequality.

Black Homeownership Trends Across the 20th Century

Throughout the 20th century, black homeownership rates have lagged significantly behind whites as shown in Figure 1. For the most part, the black homeownership rate has been between 35 and 50 percentage points lower than the rate for whites. The rates have moved, however, in a remarkably parallel fashion. The century can be divided roughly in three eras in terms of trends in homeownership. During the first 40 years, black homeownership rates were about half that of whites, and no progress was made in closing the gap. In fact, the black homeownership rate declined between 1920 and 1940, reflecting the turbulence of the Great Depression. Add to that the relatively low incomes of most blacks and the rampant housing discrimination faced by them during this time, the low homeownership rates are not surprising.

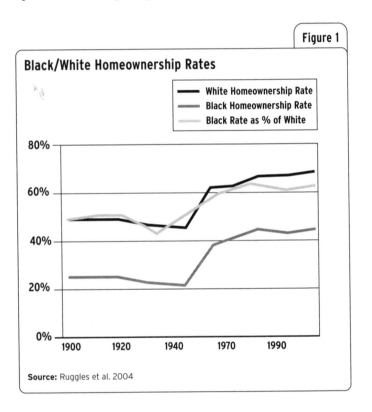

Figure 1

Black/White Homeownership Rates

Source: Ruggles et al. 2004

During the next era, between 1940 and 1980, homeownership boomed among all Americans, including African Americans. The homeownership rate for blacks doubled during this period and closely tracked the rise in homeownership rates among whites. The seeds for this explosion were planted in the 1930s when the federal government implemented several reforms that made homeownership more accessible. The Great Depression devastated the real estate industry while millions of Americans lost their homes through foreclosure. A desire to help the housing industry recover and relieve the anxiety of many homeowners prompted the federal government to take action.

Prior to the 1930s, acquiring a home typically required a sizable down payment and a mortgage with a large "balloon" payment at the end of the loan, typically five to 10 years. This was particularly disadvantageous to blacks, many of whom couldn't afford the down payment or balloon payment at the end of the mortgage's term. Among the key interventions by the federal government was the introduction of the self-amortizing, long-term mortgage. The extended term and the elimination of the balloon payment made mortgage payments lower, uniform over the life of the loan, more accessible and therefore made homeownership more achievable. The federal government also insured many mortgages through the Federal Housing Authority (FHA), thereby reducing the risks for banks to underwrite mortgages. After World War II, the federal government further increased access to homeownership through the Veteran's Administration (VA) whereby the costs of mortgages for millions of former G.I.s were subsidized by the federal government. This made homeownership even more accessible for millions of Americans.

For blacks, the federal innovations that made homeownership more accessible, however, must have seemed like a party to which they were not invited. Indeed, the federal government abetted banks' discriminatory practices by refusing to insure either loans made in older inner-city neighborhoods, where blacks were concentrated, or loans made to African Americans seeking to buy in white neighborhoods. Banks regularly excluded blacks when underwriting mortgages. Financial institutions that did lend to blacks typically charged them higher rates. Many blacks, frozen out of the formal mortgage market, had to rely on individuals for financing where interest rates were usually higher (Weaver 1948).

Despite these obstacles, after the 1930s, black homeownership rates began a steady rise that lasted over the next four decades. Prodding from civil rights advocates prompted the FHA and VA to underwrite at least some home mortgages for blacks. Despite under serving blacks, the gargantuan size of the FHA/VA meant that perhaps as many as 300,000 homes purchased by blacks and as much as 40 percent of all the new housing occupied by African Americans in the 1950s were subsidized by the FHA/VA (Wiese 2004, 140). In addition, by enabling millions of whites to purchase homes in newer suburban neighborhoods, their former homes created a new market for blacks. The homes made available by whites fleeing to the suburbs, combined with rising black incomes across the middle of the 20th century, contributed to the increasing homeownership rates among blacks that were illustrated in Figure 1.

The Civil Rights Era witnessed the culmination of the black protest movement to achieve equality in American society, which led to the implementation of a variety of policies, intended to dismantle discriminatory housing barriers. A number of these policies were targeted at housing discrimination. These included: the Fair Housing Act of 1968, the Equal Credit Opportunity Act of 1974, the Home Mortgage Disclosure Act of 1975 (HMDA) and the Community Reinvestment Act of 1977 (CRA). Despite these significant policy initiatives, the gap in homeownership rates between whites and blacks barely changed during the 1970s and 1980s (Wachter and Megbolugbe 1992). In fact, during the 1980s, blacks actually lost ground, with the gap between them and whites increasing slightly.

The persistently low levels of black homeownership, along with the impact of two landmark studies in Atlanta (Dedman 1989) and Boston (Munnell et al. 1992) suggesting that blacks continued to face discriminatory barriers in accessing credit to purchase homes, set the stage for a third and final push. It inaugurated a new policy regime in the mortgage lending market (Wyly et al. 2001). For example, during the 1990s, the federal government required Fannie Mae and Freddie Mac to more aggressively purchase mortgages taken out by low-income and minority borrowers. This should have made banks more eager to lend to blacks, knowing that it would now be easier to sell these loans to Fannie Mae or Freddie Mac. The U.S. Department of Housing and Urban Development (HUD) also lowered FHA insurance premiums and increased FHA loan limits (U.S. Department of Housing and Urban Development, 2001b). Because FHA has traditionally been an important vehicle for blacks that lacked access to conventional credit, these initiatives could have significantly increased their access to homeownership.

The Home Mortgage Disclosure Act (HMDA) was also modified during the 1990s so that banks were required to keep track not only of census tracts where they made loans, but the individual characteristics of borrowers and applicants. Moreover, the number of institutions that were covered under HMDA's provisions was expanded and regulators began publishing the Community Reinvestment Act (CRA) rating of every bank. These reforms made it easier for community activists to prod financial institutions to lend in low-income and minority communities and led to an increase in community lending agreements during the 1990s (Schwartz 1998). In 1995, the CRA was further modified with the aim of holding financial institutions accountable based on their actual performance rather than intentions or efforts to meet fair lending guidelines. The focus on actual performance would presumably have led to outcomes more favorable to blacks.

The impacts of the policy reforms are suggested in Figure 2. Between 1994 and 2004, the black homeownership rate rose from 42.3 percent to 49.1 percent, the highest rate in history. Moreover, the black homeownership rate grew faster than the white homeownership rate and by 2004, the black homeownership rate as a percentage of the white homeownership rate was at an all-time high. At least some of the improvement in homeownership rates experienced by blacks can be attributed, in part, to these policy reforms (Freeman and Hamilton 2004; Freeman 2005). Despite these impressive gains, however, the black homeownership rate in the first decade of the 21st century was only beginning to approach the white homeownership rate of 1900.

What does It Mean for Wealth Accumulation?

The importance of trends in black homeownership is more than just academic. Homeownership has many financial benefits, including increased security and as a means of accumulating wealth. Homeownership can contribute to financial stability because most homes are purchased with long-term fixed rate mortgages. Homeowners will therefore be insulated from housing inflation. Because housing prices have been rising over time, this can amount to a substantial savings over the course of a 30-year mortgage (Rohe, McCarthy, Van Zandt 2000).

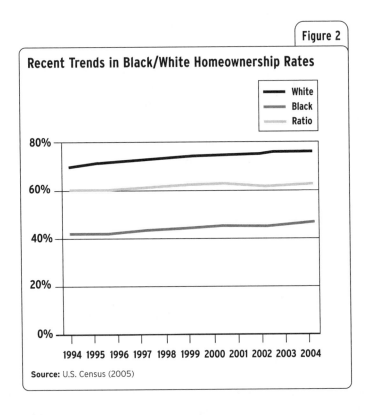

Figure 2

Recent Trends in Black/White Homeownership Rates

- White
- Black
- Ratio

Source: U.S. Census (2005)

Homeownership can also be an important engine of wealth accumulation. As a household pays off its mortgage, the difference between what is owed and the value of the house, their equity, is a form of "forced" savings. In addition, because the value of housing has trended upwards over time, homeowners realize increases in their wealth through the appreciation of their homes. Finally, a person's home is typically the largest item in their asset portfolio (Rohe, McCarthy, Van Zandt 2000). For most Americans it is the way that they accumulate substantial wealth.

Recently, social scientists have begun to focus on the importance of wealth as a determinant of life chances. Although many proponents of racial inequality focus on income disparities, racial disparities in wealth are much larger. More importantly, it might be more important in determining socioeconomic outcomes (Conley 1999; Oliver and Shapiro 1995).

While black income as a percentage of white income has hovered in the range of 55–70 percent in the past few decades, black wealth as a percentage of white wealth has typically been found to be less than 20 percent (Conley 1999; Oliver and Shapiro 1995).

In the minds of many, the large and persistent gap in homeownership between whites and blacks is a likely culprit in explaining wealth gaps. Because more whites are homeowners and homeownership is the engine that fuels the accumulation of wealth, one would expect wealth levels among blacks to be lower than those found for whites. Indeed, Figure 3 below shows a large wealth disparity between whites and blacks at the close of the last century. Achieving parity in homeownership rates between blacks and whites is clearly an important first step towards closing the gaps in wealth illustrated in Figure 3.

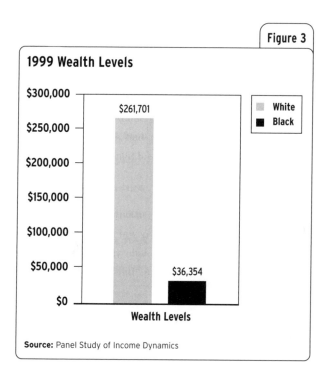

Figure 3

1999 Wealth Levels

White $261,701

Black $36,354

Wealth Levels

Source: Panel Study of Income Dynamics

The gap in wealth depicted in Figure 3, however, is driven by more than just gaps in homeownership rates. Figure 4 below shows wealth levels for whites and blacks broken down by tenure status. Black homeowners do have substantially more wealth than black renters. But black homeowners' wealth is still only 20 percent of white homeowners' wealth. While this is an improvement from the gap shown in Figure 3, where blacks' wealth was only 13 percent of whites', it still represents a sizable disparity.

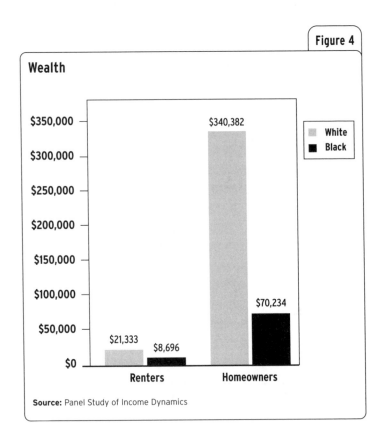

Figure 4

Wealth

Source: Panel Study of Income Dynamics

Although black homeowners have lower levels of wealth than their white counterparts, home equity is a much more important component of their total asset portfolio. Financial experts estimate that a person's home should account for 10 percent of their asset portfolio. Most Americans have much larger proportions of their wealth tied in their homes. As Figure 5 below shows, black homeowners have 70 percent of their wealth tied up in their homes. From an investment perspective, this is very risky. Should housing prices stagnate, many blacks will see the vast majority of their wealth stagnate as well. While increasing blacks' access to home-ownership is an important step in closing gaps in wealth, other aspects of blacks' asset portfolios should not be ignored.

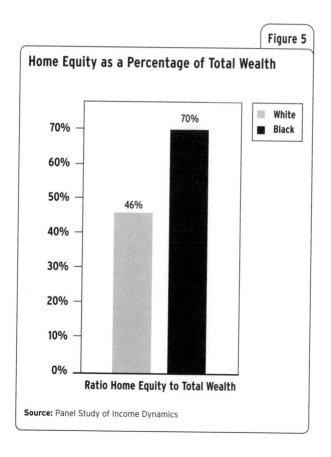

Figure 5

Home Equity as a Percentage of Total Wealth

White
Black

70%
46%

Ratio Home Equity to Total Wealth

Source: Panel Study of Income Dynamics

Achieving the American Dream

Black Americans have had to overcome numerous obstacles to achieve the American dream. Yet, at the dawn of the 21st century, black homeownership rates stand at an all-time high. If blacks are to achieve full equality in America, however, there is still much to be done. Black homeownership rates are still approximately 25 percentage points below those of whites. If progress on the homeownership front is to continue, the policy reforms previously described must be continued and not weakened. The CRA, which encourages banks to invest in low-income and minority neighborhoods, is a critical mechanism for providing mortgages to would-be homeowners. Efforts to roll back CRA requirements by limiting the number of banks subject to CRA regulations are likely to undermine progress blacks have made in achieving on the homeownership front.

But, as Figure 4 made abundantly clear, simply increasing black homeownership will not by itself close the wealth gap. Blacks have much less equity in their homes yet housing is still the major component of black wealth—perhaps dangerously so. Blacks have less home equity than their counterparts, largely because black homeowners are poorer than whites and consequently live in less costly homes.

But there are other culprits behind the lower levels of housing equity. Perhaps foremost is the high level of residential segregation between blacks and whites in most cities that has created a dual housing market whereby demand for homes in black neighborhoods is limited to black home seekers. With much of the potential market looking for housing elsewhere, homes in black neighborhoods tend to have lower values and appreciate more slowly (Harris 1999). Residential segregation also means that many middle-class and home-owning blacks live in neighborhoods that are overwhelmingly black, where poverty rates are higher and amenities and services lower than that found for middle-class home owning whites (Massey, Condran and Denton 1987). This, too, will lead to lower property values in black neighborhoods and consequently less home equity and wealth among homeowners.

Black homeowners' lower wealth relative to their white counterparts is also because of the higher interest rates blacks pay to finance the purchase of their homes. More than half a century ago, Robert Weaver documented the higher financing rates black homeowners paid to acquire their homes (Weaver 1948). This pattern persists today. My own calculations of the American Housing Survey show, that on average, black homeowners had mortgages with interest rates that were six-tenths of a percentage point higher than their white counterparts. Over the course of a 30-year, $200,000 mortgage, the difference in interest payments totals $28,000, a sizable amount of equity lost to interest payments.

The higher interest rates paid by blacks may reflect, in part, accurate assessments of the higher risk posed by some black borrowers. The explosion of sub-prime lending in recent years has made credit more available to households that might have formerly been rejected. But there is also evidence that shows that some sub-prime borrowers could qualify for prime rate loans. For example, Lax, Manti, Raca and Zorn (2004) have shown that some sub-prime borrowers have credit profiles that would seem to qualify them for prime rate loans. A lack of financial sophistication and prior bad experiences applying for credit, however, made some potential prime rate borrowers settle for readily accessible sub-prime loans. Blacks who tend to have lower levels of education and less experience with financial instruments are especially vulnerable to marketing by sub-prime lenders.

It is beyond the scope of this paper to address in depth the myriad challenges that residential segregation and/or sub-prime lending pose for black homeownership. Suffice it to say that fair housing and fair lending policy can make a difference. In particular, auditing is a tried and true method for detecting discrimination. When coupled with real enforcement of anti-bias laws, this can have a significant impact on curbing discrimination. Audits pair individuals with similar circumstances to see if race leads to disparate treatment. A broad-based program of testing in home buying and mortgage seeking could substantially reduce discriminatory barriers faced by blacks in their quest to become homeowners. It is clear that if we want the American dream to mean the same thing for blacks that it does for whites, these twin issues must be addressed.

Black Americans have made tremendous progress in their quest to achieve the American dream. The black homeownership rate, both absolutely and as a percentage of the white homeownership rate, is at an all-time high. Yet, too many blacks still do not have the opportunity to become homeowners. The black homeownership rate is only where the white homeownership rate stood a century ago. And while homeownership does help create wealth for blacks, they still lag far behind the wealth acquired by white homeowners. The issues of residential segregation and blacks' access to credit must be addressed if the American dream is to mean true equality for blacks.

References

Conley, Dalton. 1999. *Being Black Living in the Red.* Berkeley: University of California Press.

Dedman, Bill. 1989. *The Color of Money.* Atlanta Journal Constitution, May 1–5.

Fannie Mae. 1994. *Fannie Mae National Housing Survey.* Washington, D.C.: Fannie Mae.

Freeman, Lance. 2005. "Black Homeownership: The Role of Temporal Changes and Residential Segregation at the End of the 20th Century" *Social Science Quarterly.* 86(2):403–27.

Freeman, Lance, and Darrick Hamilton. 2004. "The Changing Determinants of Inter-Racial Homeownership Disparities: New York City in the 1990's." *Housing Studies.* 19(3):301–323.

Harris, David R. 1999. Property Values Drop Move in, Because: Racial and Socioeconomic Determinants of Neighborhood Desirability. *American Sociological Review.* 64(3): 461–79.

Lax, Howard, Michael Manti, Paul Raca, and Peter Zorn. 2004. Subprime Lending: An Investigation of Economic Efficiency. Housing Policy Debate. 15(3): 533–572.

Massey, Douglas S., Gretchen A. Condran, and Nancy A. Denton. The Effect of Residential Segregation on Black Social and Economic Well-Being. *Social Forces* 66 (1): 29–56.

Munnell, Alicia H., Lynn E. Browne, James McEneaney, and Geoffrey M.B. Tootell. 1996. Mortgage Lending in Boston: Interpreting HMDA Data. *American Economic Review* 86(1):25–53.

Oliver, Melvin L., and Thomas M. Shapiro. 1995. *Black Wealth/White Wealth.* New York: Routledge.

Rohe, William, George McCarthy and Shannon Van Zandt. 2000. The Social Benefits and Costs of Homeownership. Washington, D.C.: Research Institute for Housing America.

Ruggles, Steven, Matthew Sobek, Trent Alexander, Catherine A. Fitch, Ronald Goeken, Patricia Kelly Hall, Miriam King, and Chad Ronnander. 2004. Integrated Public Use Microdata Series: Version 3.0 [Machine-readable database]. Minneapolis, MN: Minnesota Population Center [producer and distributor]. URL: http://www.ipums.org.

Schwartz, Alex. 1998. From Confrontation to Collaboration? Banks, Community Groups, and the Implementation of Community Reinvestment Agreements." *Housing Policy Debate.* 9(3): 631–662.

U.S. Bureau of the Census. 2005. Housing Vacancies and Homeownership: Annual Statistics. http://www.census.gov/hhes/www/housing/hvs/annual04/ann04t20.html.

Wachter, Susan M. and Isaac Megbolugbe. 1992. Racial and Ethnic Disparities in Homeownership. *Housing Policy Debate.* 3(2):333–70.

Weaver, Robert. 1948. *The Negro Ghetto.* New York: Harcourt, Brace and Company.

Wiese, Andrew. 2004. *Places of Their Own: African American Suburbanization in the Twentieth Century.* Chicago: University of Chicago Press.

The Racial Composition of American Jobs

by Darrick Hamilton

About 35 years ago Barbara Bergmann (1971) hypothesized that labor market discrimination against black males is manifest in a "crowding" effect, resulting in lower earnings for them. White employers' refusal to hire blacks in certain types of jobs forces them to cluster and creates crowding in less desirable jobs, which reinforces a condition of lower earnings in those occupations. The following provides an updated analysis of the relationship between black male occupational crowding and wages to see if the crowding phenomenon is still evident in contemporary labor markets.

Since 1959, when the data for Bergmann's study was collected, there has been persistent evidence of disparities between white and black men. For example, the percentage of college educated black males rose from 4 percent in 1959 to 16 percent in 2000, a 300 percent increase, while the ratio of college educated black to white males rose moderately from 0.37 to 0.47, a 27 percent increase over that same period. In terms of income, white male median income in 1960 was $21,294, and $29,696 in 2000; while it was $11,202 in 1960 and $21,659 in 2000 for blacks (all median income statistics are based on year 2000 constant dollars).[1] Disparities in unemployment rates reveal a similar pattern. For whites, males and females, the unemployment rate fell slightly from 4.5 percent in 1970 to 3.5 percent in 2000, and for blacks the rate was 9.4 percent in 1973 and 7.6 percent in 2000 (U.S. Statistical Abstract, 2001, Table 569). Undoubtedly, some of the ebbs and flows in earnings and employment disparity are related to economic business cycles, but nonetheless there is sustained evidence of disparity in educational attainment, income and employment between blacks and whites.

Bergmann's (1971) "crowding" theory provides a framework to understand this persistent disparity in labor markets. She argues that black workers are denied employment in more desirable occupations and crowded into less desirable occupations. The result of this oversupply of workers in black dominated sectors is a reduction in wages in those occupations. She goes on to state that black workers who are able to attain employment in the more lucrative white dominated sectors would be willing to accept relatively lower pay as a result of the implicit threat that their alternative employment would occur in the crowded labor sectors that are predominantly reserved for blacks.

Bergmann explains that there may be various reasons why employers refuse to hire black workers in some sectors. The reasons include a distaste for associating with blacks, a belief that blacks are less productive, and a fear of a negative reaction from their white customers or current white employees. Moreover, she claims that white employees fear that a desegregated labor force would reduce their wages by forcing them to compete with black workers for more desirable jobs.

Measuring Occupational Crowding

Based on data from the 1960 U.S. Population Census, Bergmann calculated the under/overrepresentation of black males in 29 selected occupations where the majority of workers had less than a high school diploma. Since white males far exceeded black males in educational attainment, Bergmann decided to control for the education factor by examining the proportion of low-skilled workers in low-skilled occupations. If an occupation was composed of more than 10 percent of the expected number of blacks, it was deemed overrepresented with blacks; alternatively, occupations with less than 10 percent of the expected number of blacks were considered underrepresented.

Of the 29 low skilled occupations, Bergmann found that eight had more blacks than expected, and 18 had fewer than expected. The 18 "deficit"

occupations offered more lucrative pay than the "surplus" occupations
that were overcrowded with black employees.

Gibson, Darity and Myers (1998) updated Bergmann's results and
revised her measure of occupational crowding. They analyzed 59 occupations in Allegheny County (Pittsburgh), Pennsylvania and Wayne County
(Detroit), Michigan, using the 1990, 5 percent U.S. Census Public Use
Micro Data Sample (PUMS). They computed an expected occupational
share of black workers based on their share with the prerequisite educational requirements for that occupation. Rather than simply focusing on
low skilled workers and occupations, they imposed a more stringent education criterion. Only black individuals with educational attainment
between the 25th and 90th percentiles of the educational attainment held
by all persons in a particular occupation were treated as eligible for the job.

The results presented below are based on the revised crowding measure designed by Gibson, Darity and Myers. The data used is a sample of
males between the ages of 25 and 64 (working age) derived from the
2000 five percent U.S. Census PUMS.[2] In addition, the analysis conducted on all 475 occupational categories defined in the 2000, 5 percent U.S.
Census PUMS, yield 475 occupations for which I was able to compute
crowding measures.[3]

Results

The full set of the 475 occupational crowding measures are listed in the
Appendix Table. For each measure the table includes the census occupational code, the number of black respondents used to compute the index,
the prerequisite 25th and 90th educational percentile cutoff values for
occupational eligibility, the average occupational wage, and the actual
crowding measure. Recall that the crowding measure estimates the ratio
of the share of blacks within an occupation relative to their share in the
population that meets the educational requirements for that particular
occupation. A crowding value of one indicates proportional representation, a value less than one indicates under representation (or "crowded-
out") and a value greater than one indicates overrepresentation (or
"crowded"). Following Bergmann (1971) and Gibson, Darity and Myers

(1998) occupations with less than 10 percent of the expected number of blacks are considered under represented (i.e., crowding measures less than 0.90), occupations with more than 10 percent of the expected number overrepresented (i.e., crowding measures greater than 1.10), and occupations where the expected number of blacks does not exceed nor is less than 10 percent are considered proportionally represented.[4]

Table 1 provides a summary of the crowding results. The table presents the number and share of occupations in which blacks are under represented (crowded-out), proportional represented (not crowded) and overrepresented (crowded) as well as the average wages for those occupations. The first panel of the table displays the results for all 475 occupations; subsequent panels present results for occupations disaggregated by seven groupings based, in large part, on census classifications.

The last column of the table presents bivariate linear regression coefficients of occupational wages measured in $10,000 increments regressed on occupational crowding in order to statistical test for a relationship between average occupational wages and occupational crowding. In other words, it measures the change in occupational crowding that is associated with a hypothetical $10,000 rise in average occupational wages. In addition, Appendix Figures 1–8 visually summarizes these relationships and their regression results.

Beginning with the first panel of all occupations, Table 1 indicates that occupations in the U.S. tend to be racially segregated. Only 14 percent (67 out of the 475) of the occupations exhibit no occupational crowding. In addition, the average wage ($30,661) measured across the 192 crowded occupations is about 74 percent lower than the average wage ($41,414) for 216 occupations in which blacks are "crowded-out." Furthermore, the regression coefficient estimate reveals that for every $10,000 increase in occupational wages, there is an associated 0.10 point decrease in occupational crowding. This suggests that occupations in which blacks are "crowded-out" pay wages that are at least $10,000 higher than those occupations where they have proportional representation; occupations where blacks are "crowded" offer wages that are at least $10,000 less than occupations with a proportionate representation of black males.[5]

Table 1

The Relationship Between Occupational Crowding and Wages

OCCUPATIONS	TOTAL	CROWDED OUT[a]	NOT CROWDED	CROWDED	REGRESSION COEFFICIENT[b,c]
ALL OCCUPATIONS					
Number of Occupations	475	216	67	192	-0.10*
Share		0.45	0.14	0.40	(0.01)
Mean Occupational Wages	36370	41414	36471	30661	
MANAGEMENT, PROFESSIONAL AND RELATED OCCUPATIONS					
Number of Occupations	167	92	23	52	-0.10*
Share within Occupation		0.55	0.14	0.31	(0.02)
Mean Occupational Wages	49576	53809	51014	41145	
SERVICE OCCUPATIONS					
Number of Occupations	59	14	8	37	-0.11
Share within Occupation		0.24	0.14	0.63	(0.08)
Mean Occupational Wages	24361	26601	29578	22386	
SALES AND OFFICE OCCUPATIONS					
Number of Occupations	68	20	3	45	-0.22*
Share within Occupation		0.29	0.04	0.66	(0.04)
Mean Occupational Wages	34110	45392	26620	29595	
FARMING, FISHING AND FORESTRY OCCUPATIONS					
Number of Occupations	7	5	2	0	0.01
Share within Occupation		0.71	0.29	0.00	(0.16)
Mean Occupational Wages	20749	22020	17570	NA	
CONSTRUCTION, EXTRACTION AND MAINTENANCE OCCUPATIONS					
Number of Occupations	67	45	12	10	-0.06
Share within Occupation		0.67	0.18	0.15	(0.05)
Mean Occupational Wages	28770	29910	27552	25100	
PRODUCTION, TRANSPORTATION AND MATERIAL MOVING OCCUPATIONS					
Number of Occupations	103	40	19	44	-0.17*
Share within Occupation		0.39	0.18	0.43	(0.04)
Mean Occupational Wages	29344	31446	30947	26722	
MILITARY SPECIFIC OCCUPATIONS					
Number of Occupations	4	0	0	4	-0.03
Share within Occupation		0.00	0.00	1.00	(0.03)
Mean Occupational Wages	36144	NA	NA	36.144	

[a] The respective column headings "Crowded Out", "Not Crowded" and "Crowded" indicates occupations where the proportion of blacks is either 10 percent less than, proportional to or 10 percent greater than the expected number of blacks that would be employed based on the number of blacks that meet the educational requirements for that occupation.

[b] Bivariate regression coefficients of the average occupational wages measured in $10,000 increments regressed on occupational crowding measures, the ratio of black employees in an occupation relative to the expected proportion black with the prerequisite educational requirements of the occupation.

[c] Regression coefficient standard errors are presented in parenthesis ()

* Indicates 99 percent level of statistical significance.

Next, we turn to the occupational crowding results. The first category, management, professional and related occupations, has the highest average occupational wage—about $50,000. Fifty-five percent of the occupations in this wage grouping have a disproportionately low number of black male employees, an indication that black males are "crowded-out" of high wage jobs.

Moreover, within managerial and professional jobs, blacks are "crowded" into occupations that have about 76 percent lower wages than the occupations from which they are "crowded-out" ($41,145 versus $53,809). Additional evidence of this inverse relationship between occupational crowding and wages is indicated by the regression coefficient for these jobs. It estimates that a $10,000 increase in the wage of a management, professional and related occupation is associated with 10 percent reduction in the proportion of black workers in that occupation.

Moving to the next panel, Table 1 displays the results for service occupations. Only 14 of the 59 occupations in this category are underrepresented by black males, while 37 (63 percent) are considered "crowded" with black workers. In contrast to management, professional and related occupations, these service occupations typically offer lower wages and are overrepresented with black employees. The regression coefficient in Table 1 for service occupations indicates an inverse relationship between crowding and occupational wages, though the relationship is not statistically significant.[6] Nonetheless, the highly "crowded" and low-wage yielding service sector is, undoubtedly, a major contributor to the statistically significant finding in support of the crowding theory across all occupations.

Only three out of the 68 (4 percent) sales and office occupations have a proportional representation of black workers, indicating a pattern of racial segregation. In addition, there are 45 sales and office occupations that are "crowded" with black workers and these jobs offer wages that are 65 percent lower than the 20 sales and office occupations that are deemed "crowded-out." This pattern of occupational crowding is further supported by the large and statistically significant regression coefficients that estimates a $10,000 increase in the occupational wage of sales and office jobs is associated with a strikingly large 22 percent reduction in the proportion of black workers in those jobs.

There are only seven farming, forestry and fishing occupations of which none are overrepresented with black workers. There are five occupations in which black males are largely "crowded-out." Nonetheless, these occupations offer relatively low wages, and hence do not exhibit an inverse relationship between occupational crowding and wages. This is probably best explained by the concentration of blacks in metropolitan areas and the concentration of farming, forestry and fishing occupations in rural areas.

Next, the categories of construction, extraction and maintenance, and production, transportation and material moving occupations are discussed together. These occupations typically have lower educational requirements and occupational wages than management, professional and related occupations as well as sales and office occupations. Given that black males have lower educational attainment than white males, there are a relatively large numbers of black males competing for jobs in these two occupational categories. About 67 percent of construction, extraction and maintenance occupations are characterized by black male "crowding-out," compared to about 39 percent of the production, transportation and material moving occupations being "crowded-out." However, within both of these occupational sectors, these "crowded-out" occupations have relatively higher wages than other occupations in their respective groupings.

Yet, with regards to the regression results, the estimated coefficient for construction, extraction and maintenance occupations is relatively small and statistically insignificant. The coefficient for production, transportation and material moving occupations is statistically significant and indicates that a $10,000 increase in occupational wages is associated with a 17 percent reduction in the crowding of black workers.[7]

The final category in Table 1, military specific occupations, is made up of only four occupations. In contrast to the theory that blacks are "crowded" into low wage occupations, military occupations offer relatively high wages, yet feature concentrations of black men that range from 30 to 140 percent higher than their expected proportions.

Discussion and Conclusion

This analysis finds considerable evidence that, 35 years after Bergmann espoused the theory that Black males are systematically "crowded" into lower earning occupations, occupational crowding is still relevant today. Using the 5 percent sample of the 2000 U.S. Census PUMS, I examine the relationship between concentrations of black males and wages for 475 different occupations. The results show a general pattern of exclusion in the most desired management, professional and related sector even for blacks that have the requisite educational qualifications. Furthermore, this relationship of black exclusion from management, professional and related occupations and earnings is statistically significant. This pattern also holds for sales and office occupations. Those groupings, like management, professional and related occupations, also require high levels of education and yield high wages.

Unlike management, professional and related occupations, service occupations offer some of the lowest wages. In contrast, most of these low-wage service occupations contain a disproportionately high concentration of blacks. Construction, extraction and maintenance, and production, transportation and material moving are two other occupation sectors that require less education and offer low wages. Given that most of the construction, extraction and maintenance occupations had low concentrations of blacks (67 percent), it appears as though low-skilled blacks have relatively greater access to the production, transportation, and material moving sector.

Finally, there are two examples of occupational categories that, on the surface, seems to run counter to the "crowding" theory. Farming, fishing, and forestry are low-pay occupations that are not well represented by blacks while military occupations pay reasonably well and are overrepresented by blacks. Exclusion from the farming, fishing and forestry sector appears to be the result of where most blacks live and, at least in modern history, the military seems to have less restrictions on blacks than other occupations with similar pay. Such opportunities in the military provide a compelling case for "crowding" in that sector.

The crowding theory initiated by Bergmann provides a useful framework to analyze disparities in labor market outcomes. However, the framework is limited in that it does not address "pre-market" disparities. For example, the Appendix Table indicates that blacks are close to proportionately represented in the fields of physician and surgeons. However, the Association of American Medical Colleges states that blacks, based on their population proportion, are highly underrepresented in these professions. These seemingly contradictory claims are reconciled by the fact that crowding measures only take account of educationally qualified black males.[8] In short, the crowding model simply takes educational (or skill) attainment as a given. However, as pointed out by W. Arthur Lewis (1985), blacks may be systematically denied access to skill acquirement so as to render them "non-competing" in the labor market. Similarly, blacks with the requisite educational attainment may be denied access (crowded-out) of the higher paying more desirable jobs. A challenge to scholars is to come up with new or additional theories that account for "pre-market" and "in-market" transactions simultaneously in order to better explain why both education and employment outcomes are so unevenly racially distributed.

Notes

[1]Both the education and income statistics are obtain from the U.S. Census Bureau (http://www.census.gov/).

[2]Although not included here, this analysis was performed for females as well. In the interest of space the entire female results will be presented in a subsequent paper. The pattern of black male crowding was not as evident for black females when compared to white females. However, when compared to both white males and females, black female crowding was negatively associated with occupational earnings. In addition, female crowding in general is negatively associated with occupational earnings when compared to males.

According to Mary King's (1993) "access" model, jobs are distributed based on a queuing system that puts white men at the top followed by black men and white women with black women on the bottom. If the "access" model is correct the relevant comparison is not black women to white women, but rather all groups in comparison to white men. Furthermore, if black females suffer from both racial and gender discrimination, a comparison among all females will not allow us to separate out the gender and racial components of wage disparities.

[3] The five percent sample of U.S. residents allows for enough observations to compute crowding measures for so many occupations at a very detailed level.

[4] Due to space limitation, a more detailed discussion of the crowding measures for specific occupations is not presented here, but will be presented in a subsequent paper. Instead, general trends of occupational crowding are discussed.

[5] I caution the reader that these bivariate regression coefficients do not necessarily indicate a causal relationship.

[6] Perhaps the lack of observations and variations of occupational wages in service jobs are the culprit for not detecting statistical significance.

[7] Similar to service occupation, perhaps the lack of observations and variations of occupational wages explains the inability to detect statistical significance in construction, extraction and maintenance jobs.

[8] Blacks comprised only 8 percent of students enrolled in medical school in 1997 (AAMC Data Book, 1998).

References

Bergmann, Barbara R. 1971. "The Effect on White Incomes of Discrimination in Employment" *Journal of Political Economy* 29(2):294–313.

Gibson, Karen, William Darity, Jr. and Samuel Myers, Jr. 1998. "Revisiting Occupational Crowding in the United States: A Preliminary Study" Feminist Economist 4(3):73–95.

Jolly, Paul and Dorothea M. Hudley. 1998. *AAMC Data Book: Statistical Information Related to Medical Education.* 1998. Association of American Medical Colleges, Section for Operational Studies.

King, Mary. 1993. "Black Women Breakthrough into Clerical Work: An Occupational Tipping Model" *Journal of Economic Issues* 27(4):1097–1127.

Lewis, W. Arthur. 1985. *Racial Conflict and Economic Development.* Cambridge, MA: Harvard University Press.

Ruggles, Steven, Matthew Sobek, Trent Alexander, Catherine A. Fitch, Ronald Goeken, Patricia Kelly Hall, Miriam King, and Chad Ronnander. 2004. Integrated Public Use Microdata Series: Version 3.0 [Machine-readable database]. Minneapolis, MN: Minnesota Population Center [producer and distributor]

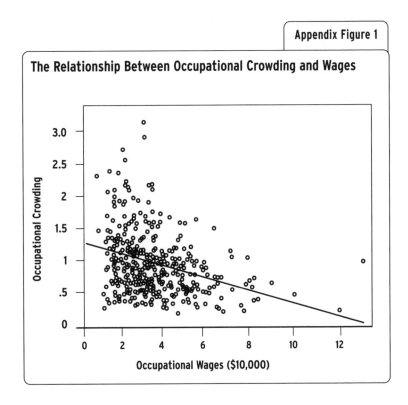

Appendix Figure 1

The Relationship Between Occupational Crowding and Wages

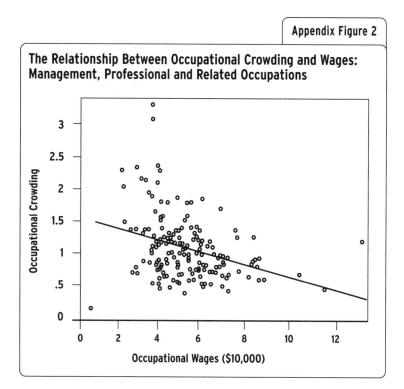

Appendix Figure 2

The Relationship Between Occupational Crowding and Wages: Management, Professional and Related Occupations

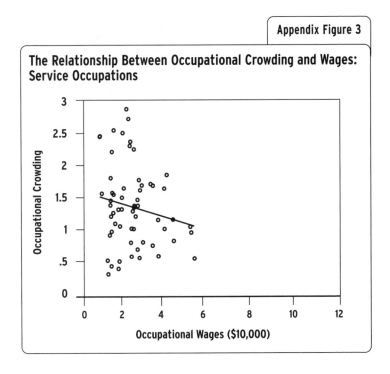

Appendix Figure 3

The Relationship Between Occupational Crowding and Wages: Service Occupations

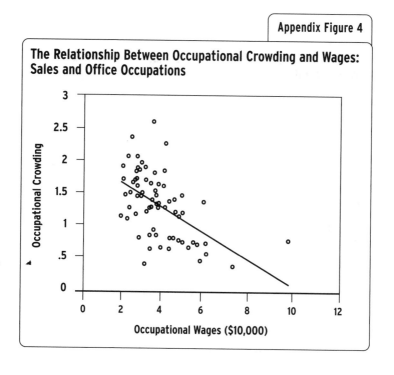

Appendix Figure 4

The Relationship Between Occupational Crowding and Wages: Sales and Office Occupations

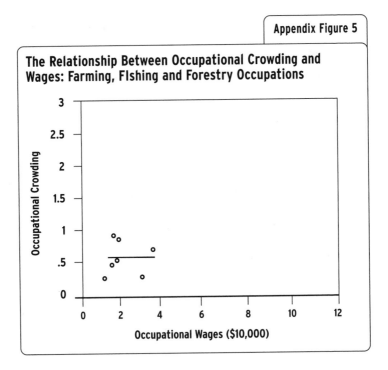

Appendix Figure 5

The Relationship Between Occupational Crowding and Wages: Farming, Fishing and Forestry Occupations

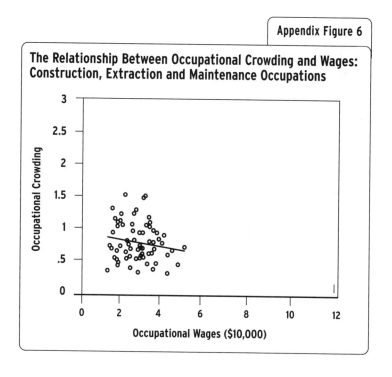

Appendix Figure 6

The Relationship Between Occupational Crowding and Wages: Construction, Extraction and Maintenance Occupations

The Relationship Between Occupational Crowding and Wages: Production, Transportation and Material Occupations

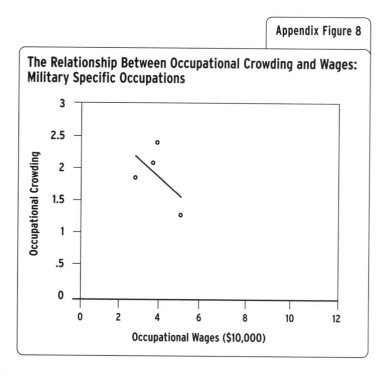

Appendix Figure 8

The Relationship Between Occupational Crowding and Wages: Military Specific Occupations

Appendix Table

3 Digit Code	Occupations	OBS	25th Percentile	90th Percentile	Occup.Ave	Crowding
	MANAGEMENT, PROFESSIONAL AND RELATED OCCUPATIONS					
21	Farmers and Ranchers	342	HS/GED	Bachelor's	3744.25	0.11
60	Cost Estimators	62	HS/GED	Bachelor's	48694.52	0.15
151	Nuclear Engineers	4	Bachelor's	Master's	70982.79	0.18
20	Farm, Ranch, and Other Agricultural Managers	237	HS/GED	Bachelor's	36316.25	0.23
1	Chief Executives	818	Some College	Master's	118839.40	0.24
164	Conservation Scientists and Foresters	19	Bachelor's	Master's	41505.47	0.25
304	Optometrists	9	Professional	Doctorate	58079.58	0.26
170	Astronomers and Physicists	11	Bachelor's	Doctorate	67734.25	0.26
145	Materials Engineers	37	Some College	Master's	57409.51	0.30
81	Appraisers and Assessors of Real Estate	72	Some College	Master's	35874.85	0.31
14	Industrial Production Managers	387	HS/GED	Bachelor's	58870.39	0.31
325	Veterinarians	20	Professional	Professional	62085.56	0.32
156	Surveying and Mapping Technicians	114	HS/GED	Assoc Occup	32891.32	0.32
300	Chiropractors	22	Professional	Doctorate	45591.14	0.32
22	Construction Managers	952	HS/GED	Bachelor's	45448.84	0.33
161	Biological Scientists	43	Bachelor's	Doctorate	43031.77	0.37
171	Atmospheric and Space Scientists	10	Assoc Occup	Master's	51209.80	0.38
30	Engineering Managers	145	Bachelor's	Master's	86212.19	0.38
143	Industrial Engineers, Including Health and Safety	232	Some College	Master's	53421.46	0.39
352	Opticians, Dispensing	25	Some College	Bachelor's	36012.53	0.40
36	Natural Sciences Managers	13	Bachelor's	Doctorate	88315.59	0.40
152	Petroleum, Mining and Geological Engineers, Including Mining Safety Engineers	22	Bachelor's	Master's	69863.51	0.42
5	Marketing and Sales Managers	957	Some College	Master's	80712.25	0.44

Appendix Table

3 Digit Code	Occupations	OBS	25th Percentile	90th Percentile	Occup.Ave	Crowding
320	Radiation Therapists	5	Some College	Master's	56833.79	0.45
263	Designers	515	Some College	Bachelor's	38557.32	0.45
52	Wholesale and Retail Buyers, Except Farm Products	190	HS/GED	Bachelor's	3996.48	0.45
4	Advertising and Promotions Managers	53	Some College	Master's	67925.43	0.46
33	Gaming Managers	37	HS/GED	Bachelor's	45815.50	0.47
2	General and Operations Managers	1210	Some College	Master's	7055172	0.48
284	Technical Writers	43	Assoc Occup	Master's	47595.41	0.49
120	Actuaries	14	Bachelor's	Professional	106030.66	0.49
174	Environmental Scientists and Geoscientists	75	Bachelor's	Professional	52722.08	0.49
326	Health Diagnosing and Treating Practitioners, All Other	5	Bachelor's	Professional	22511.25	0.49
260	Artists and Related Workers	223	Some College	Master's	24908.99	0.50
181	Market and Survey Researchers	49	Bachelor's	Master's	6437.33	0.50
131	Surveyors, Cartographers, and Photogrammetrists	42	Assoc Occup	Master's	38116.02	0.51
132	Aerospace Engineers	135	Bachelor's	Master's	62577.71	0.53
153	Miscellaneous Engineers, Including Agricultural and Biomedical	422	Assoc Occup	Master's	61316.30	0.53
11	Computer and Information Systems Managers	440	Some College	Master's	75959.85	0.54
101	Computer Programmers	872	Some College	Master's	55543.32	0.55
34	Lodging Managers	186	HS/GED	Bachelor's	35228.35	0.55
154	Drafters	366	Some College	Bachelor's	3604153	0.56
146	Mechanical Engineers	391	Assoc Occup	Master's	58560.61	0.56
144	Marine Engineers	18	Assoc Occup	Master's	5452719	0.57
165	Medical Scientists	41	Professional	Doctorate	5878612	0.57
130	Architects, Except Naval	207	Bachelor's	Master's	51320.08	0.57
176	Physical Scientists, All Other	106	Master's	Doctorate	55582.64	0.58
291	Photographers	161	Some College	Bachelor's	24260.84	0.59
141	Electrical and Electronics Engineers	471	Assoc Occup	Master's	64388.02	0.60

Appendix Table

3 Digit Code	Occupations	OBS	25th Percentile	90th Percentile	Occup.Ave	Crowding
283	Editors	107	Bachelor's	Master's	4247.35	0.61
160	Agricultural and Food Scientists	38	Assoc Occup	Doctorate	37073.91	0.61
43	Managers, All Other	2972	Some College	Master's	66234.35	0.62
301	Dentists	129	Professional	Professional	85198.69	0.62
15	Purchasing Managers	285	Some College	Master's	59686.12	0.64
53	Purchasing Agents, Except Wholesale, Retail, and Farm Products	311	Some College	Bachelor's	45376.80	0.64
285	Writers and Authors	110	Bachelor's	Master's	36947.82	0.64
136	Civil Engineers	382	Bachelor's	Master's	57955.18	0.64
340	Emergency Medical Technicians and Paramedics	188	Some College	Bachelor's	34597.26	0.66
85	Personal Financial Advisors	252	Bachelor's	Master's	82237.77	0.66
135	Chemical Engineers	89	Bachelor's	Master's	68317.24	0.67
142	Environmental Engineers	46	Bachelor's	Master's	55988.34	0.67
190	Agricultural and Food Science Technicians	53	HS/GED	Bachelor's	31322.53	0.68
193	Geological and Petroleum Technicians	36	HS/GED	Bachelor's	40122.14	0.68
271	Producers and Directors	202	Some College	Master's	55989.96	0.69
102	Computer Software Engineers	844	Bachelor's	Master's	68178.87	0.69
31	Food Service Managers	1102	HS/GED	Bachelor's	35086.20	0.69
286	Miscellaneous Media and Communications Workers	47	Some College	Master's	2829.36	0.70
182	Psychologists	85	Master's	Doctorate	44906.65	0.70
292	Television, Video, and Motion Picture Camera Operators and Editors	62	Some College	Bachelor's	39453.67	0.71
3	Legislators	21	Some College	Professional	50595.45	0.72
12	Financial Managers	898	Assoc Occup	Master's	83187.66	0.72
51	Purchasing Agents and Buyers, Farm Products	39	HS/GED	Bachelor's	35949.56	0.73
210	Lawyers	710	Professional	Professional	83861.85	0.73
155	Engineering Technicians, Except Drafters	1233	HS/GED	Bachelor's	39784.16	0.74
110	Network and Computer Systems Administrators	369	Some College	Master's	50662.41	0.75

Appendix Table

3 Digit Code	Occupations	OBS	25th Percentile	90th Percentile	Occup.Ave	Crowding
84	Financial Analysts	74	Bachelor's	Master's	8142.95	0.77
6	Public Relations Managers	63	Assoc Occup	Master's	65653.19	0.77
16	Transportation, Storage, and Distribution Managers	714	HS/GED	Bachelor's	43506.79	0.77
305	Pharmacists	196	Bachelor's	Professional	69850.58	0.79
312	Podiatrists	12	Professional	Professional	67615.11	0.79
71	Management Analysts	634	Bachelor's	Master's	66723.96	0.81
111	Network Systems and Data Communication Analysts	610	Some College	Master's	50806.76	0.83
41	Property, Real Estate, and Community Association Managers	603	Some College	Master's	48476.73	0.83
140	Computer Hardware Engineers	118	Assoc Occup	Master's	63396.16	0.83
100	Computer Scientists and Systems Analysts	1288	Some College	Master's	57198.93	0.83
91	Loan Counselors and Officers	437	Some College	Master's	56585.90	0.84
316	Physical Therapists	78	Bachelor's	Professional	54867.66	0.84
196	Miscellaneous Life, Physical, and Social Science Technicians, Including Social Science Research Assistants and Nuclear Technicians	279	HS/GED	Bachelor's	32200.55	0.85
186	Miscellaneous Social Scientists, Including Sociologists	39	Bachelor's	Doctorate	40861.12	0.85
315	Occupational Therapists	14	Bachelor's	Master's	46407.35	0.86
54	Claims Adjusters, Appraisers, Examiners, and Investigators	335	Some College	Bachelor's	42363.65	0.87
94	Tax Preparers	100	Some College	Master's	32357.56	0.89
220	Postsecondary Teachers	1212	Bachelor's	Doctorate	47730.84	0.91
10	Administrative Services Managers	195	Some College	Master's	56236.95	0.92
40	Postmasters and Mail Superintendents	81	Some College	Bachelor's	48874.82	0.94
191	Biological Technicians	31	Some College	Master's	34256.90	0.95
90	Financial Examiners	15	Bachelor's	Master's	62350.20	0.95
106	Database Administrators	113	Assoc Occup	Master's	5997.07	0.97
205	Directors, Religious Activities and Education	59	Some College	Master's	32725.03	0.97
50	Agents and Business Managers of Artists, Performers, and Athletes	62	Some College	Master's	49938.56	0.98

Appendix Table

3 Digit Code	Occupations	OBS	25th Percentile	90th Percentile	Occup.Ave	Crowding
240	Archivists, Curators, and Museum Technicians	39	Assoc Occup	Master's	35825.98	0.99
281	News Analysts, Reporters, and Correspondents	102	Bachelor's	Master's	4649725	1.00
122	Operations Research Analysts	153	Assoc Occup	Master's	56865.50	1.00
56	Compliance Officers, Except Agriculture, Construction, Health and Safety, and Transportation	202	Some College	Master's	47489.06	1.01
323	Speech-Language Pathologists	12	Master's	Master's	47105.24	1.03
232	Secondary School Teachers	869	Bachelor's	Master's	39492.42	1.03
104	Computer Support Specialists	853	Some College	Bachelor's	43712.57	1.03
243	Librarians	74	Bachelor's	Master's	3692195	1.04
280	Announcers	157	HS/GED	Bachelor's	34299.34	1.05
86	Insurance Underwriters	64	Bachelor's	Master's	6159412	1.06
332	Diagnostic Related Technologists and Technicians	262	Some College	Bachelor's	41960.53	1.06
306	Physicians and Surgeons	880	Professional	Professional	139743.44	1.07
124	Miscellaneous Mathematical Science Occupations, Including Mathematicians and Statisticians	40	Bachelor's	Doctorate	57652.45	1.08
172	Chemists and Materials Scientists	172	Bachelor's	Doctorate	55537.56	1.08
290	Broadcast and Sound Engineering Technicians and Radio Operators and Other Media and Communication Equipment Workers	297	Some College	Bachelor's	3660726	1.08
322	Respiratory Therapists	147	Some College	Bachelor's	4026.78	1.10
184	Urban and Regional Planners	38	Bachelor's	Master's	53328.05	1.11
32	Funeral Directors	165	Some College	Bachelor's	45945.01	1.12
192	Chemical Technicians	310	HS/GED	Bachelor's	41299.85	1.13
180	Economists	42	Master's	Doctorate	83213.99	1.13
331	Dental Hygienists	9	Assoc Occup	Professional	38394.49	1.14
95	Financial Specialists, All Other	81	Some College	Master's	7511915	1.14
80	Accountants and Auditors	1950	Bachelor's	Master's	54593.30	1.15

Appendix Table

3 Digit Code	Occupations	OBS	25th Percentile	90th Percentile	Occup.Ave	Crowding
270	Actors	82	Some College	Master's	33517.20	1.15
354	Other Healthcare Practitioners and Technical Occupations	188	Some College	Master's	42866.96	1.18
206	Religious Workers, All Other	119	Some College	Master's	27760.04	1.19
282	Public Relations Specialists	228	Some College	Master's	5373.66	1.21
215	Miscellaneous Legal Support Workers	230	Some College	Professional	40920.06	1.21
93	Tax Examiners, Collectors, and Revenue Agents	131	Some College	Master's	45319.35	1.24
13	Human Resources Managers	965	Some College	Master's	56558.95	1.24
211	Judges, Magistrates, and Other Judicial Workers	105	Bachelor's	Professional	74296.92	1.26
234	Other Teachers and Instructors	774	Some College	Master's	28934.66	1.26
73	Other Business Operations Specialists	550	HS/GED	Master's	44496.86	1.26
204	Clergy	1128	Assoc Occup	Professional	3064.177	1.26
275	Musicians, Singers, and Related Workers	522	HS/GED	Master's	21481.43	1.27
276	Entertainers and Performers, Sports and Related Workers, All Other	93	HS/GED	Bachelor's	24152.06	1.27
272	Athletes, Coaches, Umpires, and Related Workers	453	Some College	Master's	37530.62	1.29
313	Registered Nurses	663	Assoc Occup	Master's	47542.41	1.30
314	Audiologists	663	Assoc Occup	Master's	47542.41	1.30
70	Logisticians	139	Some College	Master's	51738.10	1.30
311	Physician Assistants	80	Assoc Occup	Professional	54850.24	1.32
244	Library Technicians	29	HS/GED	Bachelor's	18657.78	1.40
233	Special Education Teachers	83	Bachelor's	Master's	36736.28	1.44
62	Human Resources, Training, and Labor Relations Specialists	1664	Some College	Master's	4872.713	1.44
330	Clinical Laboratory Technologists and Technicians	404	Some College	Master's	36790.09	1.48
231	Elementary and Middle School Teachers	2631	Bachelor's	Master's	3741.86	1.51
42	Social and Community Service Managers	463	Some College	Master's	49964.75	1.51
214	Paralegals and Legal Assistants	213	Some College	Master's	33983.97	1.58
35	Medical and Health Services Managers	580	Assoc Occup	Professional	66558.62	1.64

Appendix Table

3 Digit Code	Occupations	OBS	25th Percentile	90th Percentile	Occup.Ave	Crowding
83	Credit Analysts	43	Assoc Acad	Master's	49770.76	1.74
82	Budget Analysts	77	Bachelor's	Master's	52034.36	1.75
255	Other Education, Training, and Library Workers	80	Bachelor's	Professional	40081.09	1.75
72	Meeting and Convention Planners	55	HS/GED	Bachelor's	36788.32	1.76
23	Education Administrator	1244	Bachelor's	Doctorate	57483.48	1.81
353	Miscellaneous Health Technologists and Technicians	193	Some College	Professional	44637.73	1.83
321	Recreational Therapists	19	Assoc Occup	Master's	32649.42	1.87
351	Medical Records and Health Information Technicians	73	HS/GED	Bachelor's	30663.82	1.92
274	Dancers and Choreographers	25	HS/GED	Bachelor's	17541.22	2.03
303	Dietitians and Nutritionists	66	HS/GED	Professional	34768.62	2.10
350	Licensed Practical and Licensed Vocational Nurses	454	Some College	Assoc Occup	29182.67	2.14
341	Health Diagnosing and Treating Practitioner Support Technicians	390	Some College	Bachelor's	26913.33	2.17
254	Teacher Assistants	540	HS/GED	Bachelor's	17329.24	2.32
202	Miscellaneous Community and Social Service Specialists	804	Some College	Master's	36264.50	2.32
230	Preschool and Kindergarten Teachers	65	Some College	Master's	24411.55	2.37
324	Therapists, All Other	106	Bachelor's	Master's	35000.22	2.40
200	Counselors	1674	Assoc Occup	Master's	32425.02	3.23
201	Social Workers	1196	Bachelor's	Master's	32354.14	3.48
	SERVICE OCCUPATIONS					
452	Miscellaneous Personal Appearance Workers	19	12th No Diploma	Assoc Occup	12850.29	0.25
454	Tour and Travel Guides	26	HS/GED	Bachelor's	17785.70	0.35
434	Animal Trainers	37	HS/GED	Bachelor's	14208.43	0.40
404	Bartenders	260	HS/GED	Bachelor's	17953.07	0.47
363	Massage Therapists	24	Some College	Master's	12430.69	0.49
372	First-Line Supervisors/Managers of Fire Fighting and Preventions Workers	107	Some College	Bachelor's	53098.98	0.52

Appendix Table

3 Digit Code	Occupations	OBS	25th Percentile	90th Percentile	Occup.Ave	Crowding
421	First-Line Supervisors/Managers of Landscaping, Lawn Service, and Groundskeeping Workers	312	HS/GED	Bachelor's	27690.18	0.53
441	Motion Picture Projectionists	9	HS/GED	Bachelor's	23636.65	0.55
430	First-Line Supervisors/Managers of Gaming Workers	85	HS/GED	Bachelor's	36426.54	0.56
440	Gaming Services Workers	129	HS/GED	Bachelor's	26689.20	0.69
432	First-Line Supervisors/Managers of Personal Service Workers	150	HS/GED	Bachelor's	33869.95	0.74
424	Pest Control Workers	219	HS/GED	Assoc Occup	23338.53	0.79
384	Miscellaneous Law Enforcement Workers	25	HS/GED	Bachelor's	29080.27	0.80
374	Fire Fighters	899	HS/GED	Bachelor's	43351.09	0.82
435	Nonfarm Animal Caretakers	136	HS/GED	Bachelor's	13553.19	0.92
371	First-Line Supervisors/Managers of Police and Detectives	401	Some College	Bachelor's	51566.19	0.95
425	Grounds Maintenance Workers	4668	9th Grade	Some College	14396.43	0.97
390	Animal Control Workers	37	HS/GED	Assoc Occup	24647.79	1.01
395	Lifeguards and Other Protective Service Workers	63	HS/GED	Bachelor's	23938.22	1.02
375	Fire Inspectors	75	Some College	Bachelor's	39064.10	1.02
382	Detectives and Criminal Investigators	386	Some College	Bachelor's	51357.60	1.03
411	Waiters and Waitresses	1038	HS/GED	Bachelor's	18100.79	1.05
451	Hairdressers, Hairstylists, and Cosmetologists	361	HS/GED	Assoc Occup	16215.27	1.11
391	Private Detectives and Investigators	173	Some College	Master's	36185.59	1.16
385	Police Officers	2518	Some College	Bachelor's	42986.52	1.18
413	Dining Room and Cafeteria Attendants, Bartender Helpers, and Miscellaneous Food Preparation and Serving Related Workers	421	5-8th Grade	Some College	14032.64	1.22
400	Chefs and Head Cooks	1037	HS/GED	Bachelor's	25605.58	1.22
465	Personal Care and Service Workers, All Other	87	HS/GED	Bachelor's	15211.33	1.28
362	Physical Therapist Assistants and Aides	56	Some College	Bachelor's	24295.84	1.31
443	Miscellaneous Entertainment Attendants and Related Workers	252	HS/GED	Bachelor's	17494.29	1.33

Appendix Table

3 Digit Code	Occupations	OBS	25th Percentile	90th Percentile	Occup.Ave	Crowding
415	Hosts and Hostesses, Restaurant, Lounge, and Coffee Shop	44	HS/GED	Bachelor's	18885.89	1.35
446	Funeral Service Workers	43	HS/GED	Bachelor's	25112.20	1.38
401	First-Line Supervisors/Managers of Food Preparation and Serving Workers	1142	HS/GED	Bachelor's	26378.96	1.39
406	Counter Attendants, Cafeteria, Food Concession, and Coffee Shop	81	12th No Diploma	Bachelor's	13519.26	1.40
403	Food Preparation Workers	871	9th Grade	Assoc Occup	14395.62	1.47
361	Occupational Therapist Assistants and Aides	7	Some College	Bachelor's	26663.79	1.48
422	Janitors and Building Cleaners	12093	11th Grade	Some College	19390.11	1.52
402	Cooks	5710	10th Grade	Some College	15435.88	1.58
414	Dishwashers	1106	5-8th Grade	Some College	9999.19	1.60
394	Crossing Guards	98	12th No Diploma	Some College	14373.12	1.60
405	Combined Food Preparation and Serving Workers, Including Fast Food	335	12th No Diploma	Assoc Occup	14699.87	1.62
420	First-Line Supervisors/Managers of Housekeeping and Janitorial Workers	963	HS/GED	Assoc Occup	27945.01	1.65
373	Supervisors, Protective Service Workers, All Other	513	HS/GED	Bachelor's	38837.02	1.68
442	Ushers, Lobby Attendants, and Ticket Takers	136	HS/GED	Bachelor's	20121.09	1.69
364	Dental Assistants	33	Some College	Professional	28470.28	1.74
380	Bailiffs, Correctional Officers, and Jailers	2502	HS/GED	Bachelor's	34100.01	1.74
455	Transportation Attendants	170	Some College	Bachelor's	32784.55	1.77
462	Recreation and Fitness Workers	481	Some College	Bachelor's	26939.33	1.82
461	Personal and Home Care Aides	314	HS/GED	Bachelor's	13952.38	1.87
370	First-Line Supervisors/Managers of Correctional Officers	384	HS/GED	Bachelor's	40058.39	1.91
423	Maids and Housekeeping Cleaners	1904	10th Grade	Some College	14537.62	2.29
365	Medical Assistants and Other Healthcare Support Occupations	581	HS/GED	Bachelor's	25004.62	2.32
464	Residential Advisors	115	HS/GED	Bachelor's	22942.42	2.39
392	Security Guards and Gaming Surveillance Officers	5680	HS/GED	Bachelor's	23407.63	2.46
450	Barbers	821	HS/GED	Some College	8887.62	2.55
412	Food Servers, Nonrestaurant	392	HS/GED	Assoc Occup	19546.48	2.61

Appendix Table

3 Digit Code	Occupations	OBS	25th Percentile	90th Percentile	Occup.Ave	Crowding
460	Child Care Workers	499	HS/GED	Bachelor's	15376.14	2.64
453	Baggage Porters, Bellhops, and Concierges	452	HS/GED	Bachelor's	22675.27	2.83
360	Nursing, Psychiatric, and Home Health Aides	2925	HS/GED	Bachelor's	21820.87	3.01
	SALES AND OFFICE OCCUPATIONS					
493	Sales Engineers	20	Assoc Occup	Master's	68922.88	0.24
475	Parts Salespersons	153	HS/GED	Assoc Occup	27895.97	0.29
485	Sales Representatives, Wholesale and Manufacturing	1289	Some College	Bachelor's	53916.53	0.33
471	First-Line Supervisors/Managers of Non-Retail Sales Workers	1295	HS/GED	Bachelor's	56650.83	0.46
470	First-Line Supervisors/Managers of Retail Sales Workers	3845	HS/GED	Bachelor's	39468.28	0.54
490	Models, Demonstrators, and Product Promoters	22	HS/GED	Bachelor's	30243.05	0.54
583	Desktop Publishers	10	Some College	Bachelor's	35248.18	0.56
492	Real Estate Brokers and Sales Agents	594	Some College	Master's	48598.61	0.56
481	Insurance Sales Agents	670	Some College	Bachelor's	52892.84	0.61
484	Sales Representatives, Services, All Other	872	Some College	Bachelor's	56504.94	0.63
496	Sales and Related Workers, All Other	223	Some College	Master's	45713.87	0.65
480	Advertising Sales Agents	228	Some College	Bachelor's	50787.84	0.65
482	Securities, Commodities, and Financial Services Sales Agents	446	Assoc Occup	Master's	9493O.13	0.68
520	Brokerage Clerks	9	HS/GED	Bachelor's	43758.99	0.69
515	Procurement Clerks	45	HS/GED	Bachelor's	39999.38	0.71
591	Proofreaders and Copy Markers	15	HS/GED	Master's	25159.74	0.72
560	Production, Planning and Expediting Clerks	524	HS/GED	Bachelor's	41575.73	0.73
476	Retail Salespersons	4206	HS/GED	Bachelor's	33298.25	0.76
483	Travel Agents	62	Some College	Bachelor's	30183.70	0.76
552	Dispatchers	453	HS/GED	Bachelor's	32080.28	0.86
513	Gaming Cage Workers	9	HS/GED	Bachelor's	19332.61	1.04

Appendix Table

3 Digit Code	Occupations	OBS	25th Percentile	90th Percentile	Occup.Ave	Crowding
495	Door-To-Door Sales Workers, News and Street Vendors, and Related Workers	366	HS/GED	Bachelor's	16487.04	1.08
533	Loan Interviewers and Clerks	65	Some College	Bachelor's	44040.36	1.09
474	Counter and Rental Clerks	182	HS/GED	Bachelor's	23469.97	1.13
523	Credit Authorizers, Checkers, and Clerks	41	Some College	Master's	45618.69	1.15
500	First-Line Supervisors/Managers of Office and Administrative Support Workers	2911	HS/GED	Bachelor's	42461.87	1.16
563	Weighers, Measurers, Checkers, and Samplers, Record keeping	259	HS/GED	Assoc Occup	28360.38	1.16
555	Postal Service Mail Carriers	1414	HS/GED	Bachelor's	37406.96	1.22
512	Bookkeeping, Accounting, and Auditing Clerks	833	Some College	Bachelor's	29907.25	1.23
472	Cashiers	1824	HS/GED	Bachelor's	20252.94	1.23
592	Statistical Assistants	45	Some College	Bachelor's	33959.50	1.25
511	Billing and Posting Clerks and Machine Operators	218	HS/GED	Bachelor's	30973.73	1.25
570	Secretaries and Administrative Assistants	558	Some College	Bachelor's	33453.42	1.29
524	Customer Service Representatives	2631	HS/GED	Bachelor's	34211.33	1.30
534	New Accounts Clerks	10	Some College	Bachelor's	55221.41	1.33
593	Office and Administrative Support Workers, All Other	608	Some College	Master's	39305.65	1.34
522	Court, Municipal, and License Clerks	88	HS/GED	Bachelor's	31100.03	1.36
584	Insurance Claims and Policy Processing Clerks	137	Some College	Bachelor's	41799.88	1.37
501	Switchboard Operators, Including Answering Service	48	HS/GED	Bachelor's	2626.36	1.42
550	Cargo and Freight Agents	95	HS/GED	Bachelor's	33399.04	1.43
561	Shipping, Receiving, and Traffic Clerks	3098	HS/GED	Assoc Occup	24471.71	1.44
530	Hotel, Motel, and Resort Desk Clerks	164	HS/GED	Bachelor's	18544.65	1.46
516	Tellers	110	HS/GED	Bachelor's	20569.94	1.47
586	Office Clerks, General	1119	HS/GED	Bachelor's	26527.22	1.48
541	Reservation and Transportation Ticket Agents and Travel Clerks	387	HS/GED	Bachelor's	32607.50	1.53
581	Data Entry Keyers	553	HS/GED	Bachelor's	24568.48	1.60
580	Computer Operators	713	Some College	Bachelor's	3624.74	1.60

Appendix Table

3 Digit Code	Occupations	OBS	25th Percentile	90th Percentile	Occup.Ave	Crowding
525	Eligibility Interviewers, Government Programs	72	Some College	Master's	34118.25	1.63
514	Payroll and Timekeeping Clerks	140	Some College	Bachelor's	30681.31	1.64
562	Stock Clerks and Order Filers	4674	HS/GED	Assoc Occup	22092.70	1.65
553	Meter readers, Utilities	309	HS/GED	Assoc Occup	28178.93	1.69
551	Couriers and Messengers	971	HS/GED	Bachelor's	23405.79	1.70
531	Interviewers, Except Eligibility and Loan	272	Some College	Master's	17299.59	1.72
540	Receptionists and Information Clerks	352	HS/GED	Master's	24197.23	1.72
503	Communications Equipment Operators, All Other	56	HS/GED	Bachelor's	32227.96	1.81
542	Information and Record Clerks, All Other	74	Some College	Master's	32362.01	1.83
554	Postal Service Clerks	677	HS/GED	Bachelor's	37170.27	1.85
526	File Clerks	364	HS/GED	Bachelor's	23506.01	1.86
535	Correspondence Clerks and Order Clerks	458	HS/GED	Bachelor's	25369.11	1.88
582	Word Processors and Typists	87	HS/GED	Bachelor's	24021.34	1.92
510	Bill and Account Collectors	430	HS/GED	Bachelor's	27895.69	1.93
532	Library Assistants, Clerical	97	Some College	Master's	17528.86	1.93
502	Telephone Operators	115	HS/GED	Bachelor's	26316.76	2.00
590	Office Machine Operators, Except Computer	186	HS/GED	Bachelor's	24285.11	2.10
494	Telemarketers	493	HS/GED	Bachelor's	19838.11	2.11
556	Postal Service Mail Sorters, Processors, and Processing Machine Operators	670	HS/GED	Bachelor's	37361.45	2.32
585	Mail Clerks and Mail Machine Operators, Except Postal Service	730	HS/GED	Assoc Occup	21650.50	2.43
536	Human Resources Assistants, Except Payroll and Timekeeping	132	Some College	Bachelor's	31610.43	2.69
	FARMING, FISHING AND FORESTRY OCCUPATIONS					
610	Fishing and Hunting Workers	118	11th Grade	Assoc Occup	12928.94	0.33
600	First-Line Supervisors/Managers of Farming, Fishing, and Forestry Workers	112	9th Grade	Bachelor's	29309.12	0.36
605	Miscellaneous Agricultural Workers, Including Animal Breeders	1938	5-8th Grade	Some College	15769.79	0.55

Appendix Table

3 Digit Code	Occupations	OBS	25th Percentile	90th Percentile	Occup.Ave	Crowding
612	Forest and Conservation Workers	51	10th Grade	Bachelor's	17881.30	0.61
601	Agricultural Inspectors	35	HS/GED	Bachelor's	34212.34	0.79
604	Graders and Sorters, Agricultural Products	72	5-8th Grade	Some College	18614.89	0.97
613	Logging Workers	876	10th Grade	Some College	16524.52	1.02
	CONSTRUCTION, EXTRACTION AND MAINTENANCE OCCUPATIONS					
736	Millwrights	143	HS/GED	Some College	41981.49	0.30
682	Earth Drillers, Except Oil and Gas	59	12th No Diploma	Some College	28875.49	0.31
643	Paperhangers	21	HS/GED	Assoc Occup	15045.60	0.33
684	Mining Machine Operators	125	HS/GED	Some College	35400.13	0.35
716	Automotive Glass Installers and Repairers	26	HS/GED	Some College	25646.03	0.37
724	Small Engine Mechanics	114	HS/GED	Some College	19646.32	0.41
670	Elevator Installers and Repairers	63	HS/GED	Assoc Occup	46758.61	0.44
722	Heavy Vehicle and Mobile Equipment Service Technicians and Mechanics	494	HS/GED	Some College	33048.20	0.44
620	First-Line Supervisors/Managers of Construction Trades and Extraction Workers	2310	HS/GED	Assoc Occup	36901.17	0.44
755	Manufactured Building and Mobile Home Installers	61	10th Grade	Some College	19962.21	0.46
623	Carpenters	3978	12th No Diploma	Assoc Occup	19514.70	0.50
754	Locksmiths and Safe Repairers	70	HS/GED	Assoc Occup	23787.03	0.52
694	Miscellaneous Extraction Workers, Including Roof Bolters and Helpers	112	11th Grade	Some College	28002.73	0.52
680	Derrick, Rotary Drill, and Service Unit Operators, and Roustabouts, Oil, Gas, and Mining	61	11th Grade	Some College	29399.98	0.52
624	Carpet, Floor, and Tile Installers and Finishers	643	11th Grade	Some College	18550.95	0.53
652	Sheet Metal Workers	437	HS/GED	Some College	31333.84	0.54
715	Automotive Body and Related Repairers	580	12th No Diploma	Some College	25260.37	0.56
731	Heating, Air Conditioning, and Refrigeration Mechanics and Installers	820	HS/GED	Assoc Occup	30202.15	0.56

Appendix Table

3 Digit Code	Occupations	OBS	25th Percentile	90th Percentile	Occup.Ave	Crowding
632	Miscellaneous Construction Equipment Operators	1358	12th No Diploma	Some College	3158.80	0.57
721	Bus and Truck Mechanics and Diesel Engine Specialists	1001	HS/GED	Some College	3158.81	0.57
700	First-Line Supervisors/Managers of Mechanics, Installers, and Repairers	1212	HS/GED	Assoc Occup	41993.77	0.58
743	Precision Instrument and Equipment Repairers	168	HS/GED	Bachelor's	33500.00	0.59
635	Electricians	2195	HS/GED	Assoc Occup	34898.79	0.60
732	Home Appliance Repairers	167	HS/GED	Assoc Occup	23315.56	0.62
633	Drywall Installers, Ceiling Tile Installers, and Tapers	665	10th Grade	Some College	19265.56	0.63
741	Electrical Power-Line Installers and Repairers	384	HS/GED	Assoc Occup	4402813	0.64
636	Glaziers	162	HS/GED	Some College	28663.46	0.65
733	Industrial and Refractory Machinery Mechanics	1809	HS/GED	Assoc Occup	36013.05	0.67
671	Fence Erectors	105	10th Grade	Some College	16759.58	0.67
751	Coin, Vending, and Amusement Machine Servicers and Repairers	136	HS/GED	Assoc Occup	25474.67	0.67
713	Security and Fire Alarm Systems Installers	127	HS/GED	Assoc Occup	30471.32	0.67
653	Iron and Steel Workers	318	HS/GED	Some College	3013.44	0.68
644	Pipelayers, Plumbers, Pipefitters, and Steamfitters	1993	HS/GED	Some College	30739.61	0.69
711	Electronic Equipment Installers and Repairers, Motor Vehicles	91	HS/GED	Assoc Occup	49770.62	0.70
712	Electronic Home Entertainment Equipment Installers and Repairers	155	HS/GED	Assoc Occup	20978.88	0.72
642	Painters, Construction and Maintenance	2193	10th Grade	Some College	16307.00	0.72
704	Electric Motor, Power Tool, and Related Repairers	141	HS/GED	Assoc Occup	29446.24	0.72
676	Miscellaneous Construction and Related Workers	135	12th No Diploma	Some College	24534.66	0.74
714	Aircraft Mechanics and Service Technicians	762	HS/GED	Assoc Occup	39419.17	0.76
666	Construction and Building Inspectors	252	HS/GED	Bachelor's	35527.47	0.77
621	Boilermakers	97	HS/GED	Some College	34062.68	0.78
720	Automotive Service Technicians and Mechanics	4622	12th No Diploma	Some College	23831.27	0.80
762	Other Installation, Maintenance, and Repair Workers, Including Commercial Drivers and Signal and Track Switch Repairers	993	HS/GED	Assoc Occup	27164.91	0.81

Appendix Table

3 Digit Code	Occupations	OBS	25th Percentile	90th Percentile	Occup.Ave	Crowding
710	Electrical and Electronics Repairers, Industrial, Utility, and Transportation Equipment	98	HS/GED	Assoc Occup	37906.43	0.82
702	Radio and Telecommunications Equipment Installers and Repairers	912	HS/GED	Assoc Occup	40322.99	0.88
651	Roofers	1180	10th Grade	Some College	17440.13	0.92
742	Telecommunications Line Installers and Repairers	729	HS/GED	Assoc Occup	37274.39	0.92
683	Explosives Workers, Ordnance Handling Experts, and Blasters	70	HS/GED	Assoc Occup	30825.52	0.92
734	Maintenance and Repair Workers, General	2172	HS/GED	Assoc Occup	29491.01	0.92
673	Highway Maintenance Workers	585	HS/GED	Some College	26394.24	0.95
703	Avionics Technicians	92	HS/GED	Assoc Occup	35620.97	0.96
626	Construction Laborers	6995	10th Grade	Some College	19534.06	1.01
730	Control and Valve Installers and Repairers	118	HS/GED	Assoc Occup	33764.56	1.02
735	Maintenance Workers, Machinery	150	HS/GED	Some College	32486.65	1.04
646	Plasterers and Stucco Masons	260	9th Grade	Some College	21715.64	1.04
630	Paving, Surfacing, and Tamping Equipment Operators	117	10th Grade	Some College	26112.45	1.05
726	Miscellaneous Vehicle and Mobile Equipment Mechanics, Installers, and Repairers	356	11th Grade	Some College	19958.48	1.08
675	Septic Tank Servicers and Sewer Pipe Cleaners	54	12th No Diploma	Some College	20669.86	1.10
761	Helpers--Installation, Maintenance, and Repair Workers	85	9th Grade	Some College	18390.54	1.13
701	Computer, Automated Teller, and Office Machine Repairers	945	Some College	Bachelor's	33442.82	1.16
622	Brickmasons, Blockmasons, and Stonemasons	1551	11th Grade	Some College	21112.45	1.21
640	Insulation Workers	293	11th Grade	Some College	26920.99	1.21
672	Hazardous Materials	146	12th No Diploma	Assoc Occup	27725.12	1.27
660	Helpers, Construction Trades	396	10th Grade	Some College	16874.15	1.29
756	Riggers	75	12th No Diploma	Assoc Occup	31165.35	1.47
674	Rail-Track Laying and Maintenance Equipment Operators	121	12th No Diploma	Some College	31825.12	1.49
625	Cement Masons, Concrete Finishers, and Terrazzo Workers	858	10th Grade	Some College	22871.14	1.50

Appendix Table

3 Digit Code	Occupations	OBS	25th Percentile	90th Percentile	Occup.Ave	Crowding
	PRODUCTION, TRANSPORTATION AND MATERIAL MOVING OCCUPATIONS					
813	Tool and Die Makers	156	HS/GED	Assoc Occup	43034.25	0.24
806	Model Makers and Patternmakers, Metal and Plastic	18	HS/GED	Assoc Occup	41826.44	0.25
903	Aircraft Pilots and Flight Engineers	127	Assoc Occup	Master's	79573.36	0.30
821	Tool Grinders, Filers, and Sharpeners	26	HS/GED	Some College	31194.69	0.34
876	Medical, Dental, and Ophthalmic Laboratory Technicians	62	12th No Diploma	Bachelor's	22446.87	0.37
931	Ship and Boat Captains and Operators	73	HS/GED	Bachelor's	41539.13	0.38
850	Cabinetmakers and Bench Carpenters	154	HS/GED	Assoc Occup	20001.88	0.38
952	Dredge, Excavating, and Loading Machine Operators	169	11th Grade	Some College	26505.58	0.43
801	Lathe and Turning Machine Tool Setters, Operators, and Tenders, Metal and Plastic	43	HS/GED	Some College	2767.07	0.43
965	Pumping Station Operators	61	HS/GED	Assoc Occup	32358.13	0.47
790	Computer Control Programmers and Operators	99	HS/GED	Assoc Occup	36756.38	0.49
803	Machinists	1343	HS/GED	Assoc Occup	33246.32	0.52
855	Miscellaneous Woodworkers, Including Model Makers and Patternmakers	91	HS/GED	Bachelor's	17936.55	0.53
892	Molders, Shapers, and Casters, Except Metal and Plastic	23	HS/GED	Bachelor's	25629.56	0.57
860	Power Plant Operators, Distributors, and Dispatchers	154	HS/GED	Assoc Occup	51242.88	0.62
833	Shoe and Leather Workers and Repairers	47	10th Grade	Assoc Occup	13583.87	0.62
796	Drilling and Boring Machine Tool Setters, Operators, and Tenders, Metal and Plastic	35	12th No Diploma	Some College	27496.60	0.65
956	Hoist and Winch Operators	43	11th Grade	Some College	30219.38	0.66
880	Packaging and Filing Machine Operators and Tenders	139	HS/GED	Bachelor's	29284.57	0.67
794	Rolling Machine Setters, Operators, and Tenders, Metal and Plastic	46	HS/GED	Some College	33654.34	0.67
933	Ship Engineers	26	HS/GED	Bachelor's	41165.05	0.67
825	Prepress Technicians and Workers	126	HS/GED	Bachelor's	31962.59	0.69

Appendix Table

3 Digit Code	Occupations	OBS	25th Percentile	90th Percentile	Occup.Ave	Crowding
835	Tailors, Dressmakers, and Sewers	107	9th Grade	Assoc Occup	22552.11	0.70
826	Printing Machine Operators	610	HS/GED	Some College	31806.19	0.70
851	Furniture Finishers	84	12th No Diploma	Assoc Occup	18292.66	0.71
893	Paper Goods Machine Setters, Operators, and Tenders	109	12th No Diploma	Bachelor's	24533.81	0.74
853	Sawing Machine Setters, Operators, and Tenders, Wood	298	10th Grade	Some College	20201.33	0.74
863	Miscellaneous Plant and System Operators	302	HS/GED	Assoc Occup	33581.18	0.75
814	Welding, Soldering, and Brazing Workers	2765	12th No Diploma	Some College	27742.82	0.75
834	Shoe Machine Operators and Tenders	19	9th Grade	Some College	18681.95	0.75
771	Aircraft Structure, Surfaces, Rigging, and Systems Assemblers	32	HS/GED	Assoc Occup	35837.32	0.77
792	Extruding and Drawing Machine Setters, Operators, and Tenders, Metal and Plastic	68	HS/GED	Some College	29934.64	0.81
923	Railroad Brake, Signal, and Switch Operators	46	HS/GED	Some College	40060.46	0.81
823	Bookbinders and Bindery Workers	93	HS/GED	Some College	29824.02	0.82
781	Butchers and Other Meat, Poultry, and Fish Processing Workers	1039	10th Grade	Some College	24217.75	0.82
770	First-Line Supervisors/Managers of Production and Operating Workers	4476	HS/GED	Bachelor's	41193.37	0.84
864	Chemical Processing Machine Setters, Operators, and Tenders	212	HS/GED	Assoc Occup	42390.33	0.87
810	Molders and Molding Machine Setters, Operators, and Tenders, Metal and Plastic	376	12th No Diploma	Some College	30188.69	0.87
883	Photographic Process Workers and Processing Machine Operators	782	11th Grade	Some College	26408.36	0.87
854	Woodworking Machine Setters, Operators, and Tenders, Except Sawing	185	11th Grade	Some College	22272.37	0.88
795	Cutting, Punching, and Press Machine Setters, Operators, and Tenders, Metal and Plastic	563	12th No Diploma	Some College	26833.06	0.91
904	Air Traffic Controllers and Airfield Operations Specialists	121	Some College	Bachelor's	61017.18	0.91
941	Transportation Inspectors	148	HS/GED	Bachelor's	41348.00	0.91
885	Cementing and Gluing Machine Operators and Tenders	116	HS/GED	Bachelor's	29840.49	0.92
773	Engine and Other Machine Assemblers	121	HS/GED	Some College	34930.29	0.94
840	Textile Cutting Machine Setters, Operators, and Tenders	52	9th Grade	Some College	22191.97	0.94

Appendix Table

3 Digit Code	Occupations	OBS	25th Percentile	90th Percentile	Occup.Ave	Crowding
774	Structural Metal Fabricators and Fitters	157	HS/GED	Some College	33037.82	0.95
800	Grinding, Lapping, Polishing, and Buffing Machine Tool Setters, Operators, and Tenders, Metal and Plastic	431	11th Grade	Some College	28301.23	0.95
845	Upholsterers	272	10th Grade	Some College	19411.81	0.95
872	Extruding, Forming, Pressing, and Compacting Machine Setters, Operators, and Tenders	440	11th Grade	Some College	23691.33	0.97
891	Etchers and Engravers	62	11th Grade	Some College	23683.53	0.98
822	Other Metal Workers and Plastic Workers, Including Milling, Planing, and Machine Tool Operators	2532	12th No Diploma	Some College	29087.26	0.99
951	Crane and Tower Operators	445	12th No Diploma	Some College	36755.15	0.99
861	Stationary Engineers and Boiler Operators	538	HS/GED	Assoc Occup	40466.99	1.01
824	Job Printers	350	HS/GED	Assoc Occup	28324.51	1.01
875	Jewelers and Precious Stone and Metal Workers	2374	HS/GED	Bachelor's	33542.05	1.02
913	Driver/Sales Workers and Truck Drivers	18898	12th No Diploma	Some College	27944.01	1.04
820	Plating and Coating Machine Setters, Operators, and Tenders, Metal and Plastic	138	10th Grade	Some College	26855.51	1.06
780	Bakers	467	11th Grade	Assoc Occup	20725.56	1.09
785	Food Cooking Machine Operators and Tenders	28	11th Grade	Some College	22247.29	1.10
920	Locomotive Engineers and Operators	308	HS/GED	Assoc Occup	49412.70	1.11
924	Railroad Conductors and Yardmasters	293	HS/GED	Assoc Occup	46935.96	1.11
815	Heat Treating Equipment Setters, Operators, and Tenders, Metal and Plastic	77	HS/GED	Some College	35112.90	1.13
775	Miscellaneous Assemblers and Fabricators	4450	12th No Diploma	Some College	26721.39	1.15
871	Cutting Workers	665	12th No Diploma	Some College	28855.10	1.17
936	Service Station Attendants	393	12th No Diploma	Some College	17016.66	1.18
894	Tire Builders	241	HS/GED	Some College	35272.44	1.18

Appendix Table

3 Digit Code	Occupations	OBS	25th Percentile	90th Percentile	Occup.Ave	Crowding
942	Miscellaneous Transportation Workers, Including Bridge and Lock Tenders and Traffic Technicians	98	HS/GED	Assoc Occup	32702.38	1.19
793	Forging Machine Setters, Operators, and Tenders, Metal and Plastic	111	12th No Diploma	Some College	31158.87	1.19
874	Inspectors, Testers, Sorters, Samplers, and Weighers	110	HS/GED	Some College	32097.86	1.20
772	Electrical, Electronics, and Electromechanical Assemblers	679	HS/GED	Assoc Occup	24974.04	1.20
896	Other Production Workers, Including Semiconductor Processors and Cooling and Freezing Equipment Operators	252	10th Grade	Some College	20995.17	1.23
865	Crushing, Grinding, Polishing, Mixing, and Blending Workers	376	HS/GED	Bachelor's	4061.46	1.25
873	Furnace, Kiln, Oven, Drier, and Kettle Operators and Tenders	251	12th No Diploma	Some College	28218.01	1.26
900	Supervisors, Transportation and Material Moving Workers	1201	HS/GED	Bachelor's	37004.64	1.26
975	Miscellaneous Material Moving Workers; Including Conveyor Operators and Tenders; Shuttle Car Operators; and Tank Car, Truck, and Ship Loaders	480	12th No Diploma	Some College	28538.40	1.27
804	Metal Furnace and Kiln Operators and Tenders	259	12th No Diploma	Some College	3021.09	1.27
862	Water and Liquid Waste Treatment Plant and System Operators	6821	12th No Diploma	Some College	27580.08	1.28
784	Food Batchmakers	258	11th Grade	Some College	24936.65	1.31
930	Sailors and Marine Oilers	185	HS/GED	Assoc Occup	28636.48	1.34
881	Painting Workers	956	10th Grade	Some College	21959.48	1.39
886	Cleaning, Washing, and Metal Pickling Equipment Operators and Tenders	98	10th Grade	Some College	23997.80	1.42
831	Pressers, Textile, Garment, and Related Materials	273	9th Grade	Some College	19251.48	1.42
964	Packers and Packagers, Hand	1116	9th Grade	Some College	17548.42	1.43
816	Lay-Out Workers, Metal and Plastic	79	HS/GED	Some College	30214.85	1.44
832	Sewing Machine Operators	882	5-8th Grade	Some College	18543.41	1.45
915	Miscellaneous Motor Vehicle Operators, Including Ambulance Drivers and Attendants	124	12th No Diploma	Assoc Occup	20602.33	1.45
830	Laundry and Dry-Cleaning Workers	682	11th Grade	Assoc Occup	16481.67	1.47
962	Laborers and Freight, Stock, and Material Movers, Hand	11428	12th No Diploma	Some College	22525.60	1.54

Appendix Table

3 Digit Code	Occupations	OBS	25th Percentile	90th Percentile	Occup.Ave	Crowding
846	Miscellaneous Textile, Apparel, and Furnishings Workers, Except Upholsterers	262	10th Grade	Some College	22853.44	1.63
895	Helpers-Production Workers	216	HS/GED	Some College	36195.99	1.67
963	Machine Feeders and Offbearers	320	11th Grade	Some College	23338.63	1.71
960	Industrial Truck and Tractor Operators	5025	11th Grade	Some College	24875.86	1.74
783	Food and Tobacco Roasting, Baking, and Drying Machine Operators and Tenders	74	12th No Diploma	Some College	25879.21	1.77
961	Cleaners of Vehicles and Equipment	2098	10th Grade	Some College	17113.07	1.78
841	Textile Knitting and Weaving Machine Setters, Operators, and Tenders	166	10th Grade	Some College	22563.72	1.85
926	Subway, Streetcar, and Other Rail Transportation Workers	106	HS/GED	Assoc Occup	36336.28	1.94
836	Textile Bleaching and Dyeing Machine Operators and Tenders	99	10th Grade	Some College	21939.44	2.08
914	Taxi Drivers and Chauffeurs	1864	HS/GED	Bachelor's	17109.47	2.11
842	Textile Winding, Twisting, and Drawing Out Machine Setters, Operators, and Tenders	182	10th Grade	Some College	22715.28	2.11
972	Refuse and Recyclable Material Collectors	1060	10th Grade	Some College	20492.59	2.12
935	Parking Lot Attendants	399	12th No Diploma	Assoc Occup	17526.77	2.19
912	Bus Drivers	2966	HS/GED	Assoc Occup	24597.89	2.32
	MILITARY SPECIFIC OCCUPATIONS					
980	Military Officer Special and Tactical Weapons Leaders/Managers	124	Assoc Occup	Master's	46592.34	1.30
982	Military Enlisted Tactical Operations and Air/Weapons Specialists and Crew Members	395	HS/GED	Bachelor's	27117.73	1.87
983	Military, Rank Not Specified (Census only)	884	HS/GED	Bachelor's	34504.56	2.10
981	First-Line Enlisted Military Supervisors/Managers	389	Some College	Master's	36362.96	2.41

Escaping the "Ghetto" of Subcontracting

by Mark D. Turner

In recent years, small minority-owned businesses (SMB) have firmly established a niche in the world of subcontracting—proffering competency, specialized expertise, and business acumen to larger and more lucrative prime contractors. The present burgeoning of SMBs is, arguably, a direct result of the unique opportunity that subcontracting offers—a significant lowering of the barrier to entry. Typically, SMBs possess less startup capital and lack established past performance histories.

Sole dependence on subcontracting, however, limits a company's opportunity for growth, financial independence, and self-determination. A prolonged dependence on revenues derived from subcontracting is not a sustainable approach to achieving long-term profitability. Guiding more small firms out of the subcontracting ghetto has become increasingly important as recent court decisions and procurement regulatory rules have diminished the incentives for utilizing Minority Business Enterprises (MBEs) and Women Business Enterprises (WBEs) as subcontractors.

This essay provides would-be entrepreneurs, small business owners, economic development officials, and policy makers with an overview of the prerequisites for the transition from sub- to prime contractor. Making this transition has become increasingly necessary.

The Ripple Effect of Growing Minority Firms

According to the U.S. Census Bureau, minorities and African Americans run 15.1 percent and 4.2 percent of businesses in the United States, respectively. Most U.S. firms are small; only 26 percent of non-

117

minority-owned firms, 20 percent of minority-owned firms, and 11 percent of black-owned firms had paid employees in 1997 (Lowery, 2005). The latest version of the Surveys of Minority- and Women-Owned Business Enterprises (SMOBE/SWOBE) indicated that there were 823,499 black-owned firms (3.96 percent of all firms), of which only 93,235 of these firms had employees (11.3 percent of all black-owned firms).

The benefits of growth for minority-owned firms go well beyond individual firm managers and investors. There is an abundance of empirical research that suggests minority-owned firms are more likely to hire minority employees and that minority-owned firms are more likely to use minority suppliers than non-minority firms (Policy Link, 2005).

Minority Firms Hire Minority Workers. In a study of Baltimore's blossoming biotech industry, Optimal Solutions Group LLC conducted a literature review on the propensity of minority businesses to hire minority employees (Turner and Leal 2004). In small firms, the hiring agent is typically the owner/manager. According to *Black Job Applicants and the Hiring Officer's Race*, firms with an African-American hiring agent are more likely to hire black applicants than establishments where the hiring agent is white. The authors assert that the hiring agent's race affects the racial composition of the workforce in the following ways (Stoll, Raphael, Holzer, 2004):

- Hiring agents may rely on social networks to recruit new hires; the racial composition of these networks is likely correlated to the race of the hiring agent;
- The race of the hiring agent may have an affect on the race of new hires if the hiring agent exhibits a preference for his/her own race;
- Minority hiring agents send the signal to other minorities that there is a potential for advancement within the firm, despite racial background; and,
- Firms with minority hiring agents are perceived as being less discriminatory, thus attracting a greater number of minority applicants, as opposed to a firm with a white hiring agent.

Moreover, a survey conducted in Los Angeles County regarding the hiring practices of minority-owned firms revealed that minorities have a tendency to hire workers within their own ethnic group. Key findings include (Romney, 1999):

- Nearly 75 percent of Hispanic business owners described their workforce as being Hispanic, 41 percent of black business owners hired within their own ethnic group, and nearly one-third of Asian firms reported having a predominately Asian workforce;
- No more than 3 percent of any minority group described their workforce as mostly white;
- African-American-owned businesses were the only firms likely to employ a predominately black workforce; only 1 percent of Hispanic firms, 3 percent of Asian firms, and 4 percent of white firms employed African Americans in any considerable numbers;
- Hispanics were the only ethnic group employed in large numbers by white-owned firms, indicative of the demographic profile of the area, where Hispanics comprise 41 percent of Los Angeles County's workforce, an even higher proportion than whites; and
- Employee recommendations are a key factor in the hiring process, especially for small companies that do not have human resource departments.

Minority Firms More Likely to Purchase from Minority Suppliers. Anecdotal evidence suggests that minority-owned businesses are more likely to purchase goods and services from other businesses within their ethnic and/or racial group. Most notably, Chinatowns in many American cities are archetypes of the financial nexus created within minority ethnic and racial communities.

With campaigns such as "Buy Black," that have given rise to the popular clothing-retailers like FUBU (For Us By Us) and Karl Kani, the African-American community has made significant strides toward creating and supporting black-owned businesses. The "Buy Black" campaign maintains that the African-American community benefits from starting its own businesses and supporting other black-owned enterprises.

According to the University of Georgia's Selig Center for Economic Growth, blacks represented 8.4 cents of every dollar spent nationally in 2005. In its latest report, the center says: "The Selig Center projects that the nation's black buying power will rise from $318 billion in 1990 to $590 billion in 2000, to $761 billion in 2005, to $1 trillion in 2010, up by 222 percent in 21 years. This overall percentage gain outstrips the 164 percent increase in white buying power and the 177 percent increase in total buying power (all races combined)."

Business pundits and advocates of the "Buy Black" movement predict a substantial economic upsurge in the greater African-American community if this buying power can be honed and shared with black-owned businesses. For companies such as FUBU and Karl Kani, clever marketing could produce high yields from African-American consumers, who, for example, spent roughly $23 billion on clothing goods in 2003.

Building Community Responsibility for Economic Prosperity, the maxim of the Black Dollar Task Force (BDTF) (BDTF, 2006), organized in Seattle, Washington, emphasizes empowerment through community responsibility. BDTF offers three strategies to achieve black economic self-sufficiency: self-help, institutional development, and reinvestment in the community. Fundamental to this endeavor is the belief that African-American "business growth and development must be a priority for all efforts to economically enhance [the] inner cities." When African-American consumers choose to financially buttress black businesses, it produces a ripple effect, enabling these businesses in turn to reinvest in the African-American community through job-creation. Direct spending by consumers creates a multiplier effect that will generate significant employment and returns for the community.

Reaping Profits

In competitive industries where the market sets the price of output there are two basic routes to profitability—efficiency and growth.

Efficiency. Throughout time, successful entrepreneurs have supplant-

120

ed competitors by coming up with innovations that reduced waste, as well as better utilized existing labor and/or equipment. From Henry Ford's assembly line to the leveraging of the Internet to increase productivity, increased efficiency has yielded profits.

Growth. Assuming that firms are not patently wasting their resources, as small firms grow they will achieve internal economies of scale and realize greater levels of profit. Internal economies of scale arise when the cost per unit falls as output increases. Why are economies of scale important? First, because a large business can pass on lower costs to customers and increase its share of a market. This poses a threat to smaller businesses in the same industry that can be "undercut" by the competition. Second, a business could choose to maintain its current price for its product and accept higher profit margins.

Principles of economics delineate four internal economies of scale:
- *Bulk-buying economies.* Business growth requires larger quantities of production inputs. For example, a growing IT system's integrator will order more computer equipment. As the order value increases, the IT system's integrator obtains more bargaining power with equipment suppliers. The IT system's integrator may then be able to obtain discounts and lower prices for computer equipment.
- *Technical economies.* Businesses with large-scale production can employ machinery that is more advanced or use existing machinery more efficiently. For example, many small and large firms require the use of a server and assistance from IT staff to maintain the server and other IT equipment. These IT costs are mainly fixed. Thus, as a business expands, it is able to spread IT costs over a wider range of products and sales—cutting the average IT costs per unit.
- *Financial economies.* Small businesses constantly face the challenge of securing adequate funding for their projects. Often small businesses do receive access to funds; however, the costs are substantially higher than for their larger business counterparts. Large businesses have the advantage of established records of accomplishments. Potential lenders regard smaller businesses as more risky.

Larger firms therefore enjoy greater ease in securing funding and can raise money at lower interest rates.

- *Marketing economies.* Every part of marketing has a cost, particularly promotional methods such as advertising and running a sales force. Many of these marketing costs are fixed-costs. Consequently, as a business gets larger, it is able to spread the cost of marketing over a wider range of products and sales, cutting the average marketing cost per unit.

Source: Tutor2u Limited, see www.tutor2u.net [2006]

Escaping the Subcontracting Ghetto

"Local governments are increasingly coming to the realization that true 'economic parity' for minority-owned businesses necessarily requires that they ultimately escape from the subcontracting 'ghetto' that traditional MBE subcontracting goals programs have too often relegated them to. MBEs must also join the ranks of competitive prime contractors if they are ever to become fully integrated into the economic mainstream. This new paradigm steadily advances as innovative race- and gender-neutral policies that boost competitive prime contract participation by small and minority-owned businesses rapidly gain favor across the country. At the end of the day, a successful MBE program should be measured according to its ability to produce an industry profile for minority-owned businesses that reflects the same mix of competitive primes and subs, of large firms and small firms, that any other business segment in the marketplace reflects."

Franklin M. Lee, Partner
Shapiro Sher Guinot & Sandler

A prolonged dependence on revenues derived from one or a limited number of prime contractors is not a wise strategy for sustainable profitability. Moreover, a prolonged dependence on subcontracting has become increasingly precarious. First, anecdotal evidence suggests that quite often, small firms do not have subcontract agreements that clearly delineate the scope of work, schedule of payments, and the terms and conditions for terminating contractual agreements. In some instances, they do not have anything in writing from the prime contractor. In these cases, disputes between the sub and prime contractors can result in costly litigation and possible non-payment.

For example, some agency-wide studies suggest that subcontractors identified during the bidding process are not utilized once the contract is awarded. In a recent study, the authors recommended that the agency should "closely monitor actual use of subcontractors and suppliers based on evidence of payments." The study goes on to say that the agency may find that, for some prime contractors committed to providing a certain percent of business to minority subcontractors during the bidding process, there is evidence of discrimination towards the subcontractors during the course of the contract (BBC Research and Consulting, 2005).

In addition, recent court decisions and procurement regulatory changes have diminished the incentives for utilizing Minority Business Enterprises (MBEs) and Women Business Enterprises (WBEs) as sub-contractors.

Subcontracting Dependency Should Be Temporary

According to the U.S. Small Business Administration (SBA), subcontracting or teaming with a larger firm can be a profitable experience as well as a growth opportunity but is not intended as the sole and/or sustainable source of revenue. The experience gained from performing as a subcontractor can assist small firms or larger firms entering a new market in responding to solicitations as a prime contractor.

Unfortunately, there is dearth of national statistics on how small firms revenues are generated, especially the proportion that are generated via subcontracting or prime contracting. However, anecdotal and agency-wide studies of government procurement practices suggest that minority-owned contractors over the past decade have made significant inroads in being awarded subcontracts but are still vastly under utilized as prime contractors.

For example, a 2005 disparity study for the Washington Suburban Sanitary Commission (WSSC) indicated that the utilization of MBEs/WBEs as subcontractors has increased significantly over the past five years. As a result, the authors of the study recommended that WSSC suspend the subcontracting goals program for goods and general services and professional services contracts, encourage MBE/WBEs to submit proposals as prime contractors, and retain an evaluation preference for MBE/WBE prime contractors in architecture and engineering and construction contracts.

The landmark Supreme Court cases, *Adarand Construction, Inc. v. Pena* and *Croson v. the City of Richmond* have reshaped race-targeted programs in contracting. In particular, the *Adarand* decision in 1995 imposed "strict scrutiny" standards on state and local procurement set-aside programs.

Strict scrutiny, the highest standard of judicial review, is applied when a constitutional right or policy is in conflict with the manner in which the interest is being pursued. To satisfy the strict scrutiny requirement, a law must neither be vague nor substantially over– or underinclusive. Because of such rigid requirements, critics say strict scrutiny amounts to "strict in theory, fatal in fact."

As a result of the higher standard, federal, state, and local governments have had to resort to innovative race- and gender-neutral approaches to enhance minority and women business enterprise participation. Many of these reforms are designed to ease the transition from subcontractor to prime contractor and to encourage government agencies to procure from small firms. Franklin Lee (2005), former Chief Counsel for the Minority Business Enterprise Legal Defense and Education Fund, Inc., (MBELDEF), outlines approaches that government agencies have undertaken to level the playing field post *Adarand*. He has drafted a list of "carrots" and "sticks" that government agencies have used to encourage the utilization of small businesses and SMBs:

Carrots

1 Revolving Working Capital Fund (provides a working capital financing vehicle for small government contractors; funded by banks and other private sector credit sources);

2 Small Business Enterprise program (provides subcontracting goals and/or prime contract set-asides for small businesses; "small" defined variously by annual sales, number of employees, owner net worth, and industry);

3 Small Local Business Enterprise program (provides subcontracting goals and/or prime contract set-asides for small local businesses; "local" defined by location of principal office or where significant number of employees are domiciled);

4 Technical Assistance Referral Network (provides an assessment of new small business vendors regarding technical assistance needs and issues referrals to existing community resources that provide such assistance);

5 E-commerce solutions (e.g., centralized bidder registration processes, bid rotations, small contract award rotations, industry-specific bidder outreach);

6 Procurement process reform (repackaging of smaller bid packages, multi-prime contracts, restrictive contract specification review, expedited payment of invoices;

7 Linked Deposit Programs (enhancing access to capital by linking government placement of deposits to a financial institution's policies and performance in issuing commercial loans to small and minority businesses);

8 Job Order Contracting (establishing competition among multiple, long-term prime contractors for additional work based, in part, on performance in the achievement of subcontractor diversity);

9 Capacity Development Programs (on-the-job-Training Demonstration Projects; Mentor-Protégé Programs, and Manufacturing Distributorship Supplier Development Programs); and

10 Wrap-around Bonding and Insurance Programs (where government owner purchase umbrella bonding and insurance policies providing coverage to all of its contractors at a standard rate).

11 Public-Private Strategic Partnership Models for development of long-term business relationships between major corporate players and minority suppliers (e.g., East Baltimore Biotech Park Minority Inclusion Agreement, Greater Baltimore Committee "Bridging the Gap" Initiative, NARUC's UMAP Initiative).

12 Promotion of "Best Practices" Principles to corporate community to

adopt internal audit procedures to identify, remove, and prevent procurement barriers and discriminatory practices disproportionately impacting minority suppliers.

13 Pilot Programs to encourage joint ventures and teaming agreements among MBEs and WBEs.

14 Tax credit programs to establish venture capital funds for M/WBE technology and manufacturing firms.

Sticks

1 Mandatory Small Business Set-Aside Program (requiring government agencies to set-aside a mandatory percentage of prime contracts for bidding exclusively by small businesses);

2 Commercial non-discrimination policies with administrative complaint, investigation, and enforcement processes (precluding the government from engaging in business with firms that discriminate in the solicitation, selection, or treatment of their subcontractors, suppliers, or commercial customers);

3 Prompt Payment provisions (requiring government purchasers and prime contractors to promptly pay supplier invoices to avoid penalties and interest charges); and

4 Purchasing Personnel Evaluation Criteria for Supplier Diversity (requiring annual review of government buyers' performance in conducting outreach to attract new bidders and to achieve greater diversity in contract awards as a condition of receiving salary increases and promotions).

Subcontracting can bring needed revenue, opportunities to learn from larger, more established competitors, and opportunities to build a successful track record. However, dependence on subcontracting opportunities subject small businesses to expanded levels of uncertainty and lack of control. Subcontracting has its advantages and disadvantages:

Advantages

- Lowers barrier to entry (e.g., startup capital, capital outlay, limited experience)

- Specialization and efficiency
- Gained insight about competitors

Disadvantages

- Financially dependent on relationship with prime contractor(s)
- Lack of direct contact with the client
- Client cannot directly evaluate subcontractor's performance
- Past performance evaluation dependent on prime contractor's performance
- Subcontractor and prime contractor may be competitors

"While the desire to grow is great, quite often small businesses don't have a template on how to transition from one phase to the next and what it takes to grow a business."

Paul Taylor, Executive Director
Small Business Resource Center, Baltimore, Maryland

Planning Your Escape

The ideal location for planning an escape from the subcontracting ghetto is behind enemy lines—as a subcontractor to industry leaders, with the mindset of gathering valuable insight and building a viable firm that can stand on its own. Large, well-established firms can provide a template for small firms. Below is a short list of prerequisite areas that need to be developed and refined:

- Corporate Structure and Legal Documentation
- Finance and Accounting

Corporate Structure and Legal Documents. An appropriate corporate structure and comprehensive legal documentation is necessary for entrepreneurs to build stable businesses.

Before entrepreneurs decide on an ownership structure, they must learn how each structure works. Below is a list of the most common forms of businesses:

- Sole proprietorship
- Partnership
- Limited partnership
- Limited liability company (LLC)
- Corporation (for-profit)
- Nonprofit corporation (not-for-profit)
- Cooperative

Local SBA representatives and attorneys can assist entrepreneurs in selecting the most appropriate corporate structure, taking into account of the following factors: legal liability, tax implications, cost of formation and ongoing administration, flexibility, and future needs (Entrepreneur.com, 2006).

Once entrepreneurs have identified the most appropriate corporate structure, they must then draft an operating agreement that addresses predictable as well as unpredictable issues. Below is a partial list:

- What is the initial capital contribution of each member?
- Will members be required to make additional contributions? If so, under what conditions?
- What happens if a member fails to make a required capital contribution?
- Are members allowed to withdraw their capital contributions? If so, under what circumstances?
- How are distributions to be divided among the members?
- How broad are the management powers of the manager?
- Are the members obligated to devote any particular amount of time to the company?
- What are the terms and conditions for buying out another member's interest?

Again, the SBA and an attorney should be consulted.

Comprehensive legal support and documentation is essential to any company's success. Legal documents, as well as contract templates covering such legal issues as the client's contract terms and conditions, sub-contractor agreements, vendor contracts, and employment contracts should be kept so that they are readily available.

An employee manual is also crucial to internal and external relations. In addition to providing a sense of community and common purpose in the workplace, a comprehensive employee manual establishes clear guidelines and spells out individual responsibility. The Society for Human Resource Management (SHRM) (2005) offers seven distinguishing and essential components covered by a good manual: benefits; compensation; employee relations; health, safety and security; selection and placement; technology; and training and development. The SHRM Web site, http://www.shrm.org, provides valuable information on developing an employee manual.

Finance and Accounting. Access to capital, either via personal savings, family, lines of credit at banks, and/or SBA-guaranteed loans is an invaluable resource for any business owner and for SMBs, in particular. The ability to secure funds from a variety of sources is conditioned upon accurate and auditable bookkeeping. Lending institutions consider a number of factors that small businesses should anticipate before seeking funding:

- Business type and corporate structure
- Management performance, planning, and integrity
- Market and business environment
- Industry status
- Industry competition
- Vulnerability

Developing and nurturing relationships with bankers, lending institutions, and potential investors can help to ensure access to adequate and timely financing to facilitate growth.

Conclusion

The penchant of black businesses for hiring and investing in minority employees, as well as supporting other black-owned enterprises, gives testimony to the direct link between the success of black businesses and the empowerment of the African-American community. These firms allow for the transfer of knowledge, wealth, and human capital to the community.

SMBs and their communities will only be poised to take full advantage of the economic momentum of America's 21st century if SMBs escape the ghetto of subcontracting. In order for this to happen, SMBs must begin the transition from sub to prime contractors. Subcontracting allows SMBs to learn from seasoned companies, accumulate revenue, and develop their economies of scale. It provides an opportunity to solidify a corporate structure that will provide for sustainable and competitive growth.

Even so, to view subcontracting as a permanent state is to jettison the prospects of future self-determination, economic empowerment, and actualized potential for both the individual SMB, as well as the greater community to which it belongs. Progress requires progressing to prime contractor status.

References

BBC Research & Consulting. (June 2005) "WSSC 2005 Disparity Study–Summary and Recommendations." June 2005. http://www.wssc.dst.md.us/business/slmbe/2005_Disparity_Study_final.pdf> (February 2005).

Black Dollar Days Task Force [BDTF]. (2006). "Mission Statement". www.Blackdollar.org/about.htm

Entrepreneur.com. (2006). "Choose Your Business Structure—Selecting a Business Entity." < http://www.entrepreneur.com/article/0,4621,287856-2,00.html>, retrieved February 2006.

Humphreys, Jeffrey M. "The Multicultural Economy 2005: America's Minority Spending Power." Selig Center for Economic Growth, Terry College of Business, University of Georgia (Third Quarter 2005, Volume 65, Number 3). http://www.selig.uga.edu/forecast/GBEC/GBEC053Q.pdf

Lee, Franklin (2005). Personal memorandum regarding Innovative Race / Gender-Neutral Approaches to enhancing M/WBE Participation.

Lowery, Ying, February 2005. "Dynamics of Minority-Owned Employer Establishments, 1997–2001: An Analysis of Employer Data from the Survey of Minority-Owned Business Establishments," February 2005. Small Business Administration, <http://www.sba.gov/advo/research/rs251tot.pdf>, retrieved February 2006.

Policy Link. "Minority Contracting." 2005.
    <http://www.policylink.org/EDTK/MinorityContracting/default.html> and
    <http://www.policylink.org/EDTK/MinorityContracting/Why.html> (February 2006)

Romney, Lee, (1999). L.A. County Small Business: Minority-Owned Firms Tend to Hire Within Own Ethnic Group. *Los Angeles Times.* September 18, 1999.

Society for Human Resource Management. (2005). "Sample Policies." SHRM Online Knowledge Center. < http://www.shrm.org/hrtools/policies_published/>, retrieved February 2006.

Stoll, Michael, Steven Raphael, & Holzer, Harry, (January 2004). Black job applicants and the hiring officer's race. Industrial and Labor Relations Review, 57.

Target Market News—The Black Consumer Market Authority. (2005). "Consumer Expenditure Data." The Buying Power of Black America. <http://targetmarket-news.com/buyingpowerstats.htm>, retrieved February 2006.

Turner, Mark and Leal, Monica. (December 2004). "Minority Suppliers for Baltimore's Biotech Industry." Empower Baltimore Management Corporation.

The State of Our Children

by Marian Wright Edelman

Dietrich Bonhoeffer, the great German Protestant theologian executed for opposing Hitler's holocaust, said the test of the morality of a society is how it treats its children.

The United States of America is flunking Bonhoeffer's test:

- A child is abused or neglected every 35 seconds, which comes to 906,000 a year;
- A child is born into poverty every 35 seconds; our 13 million poor children are the poorest age group in America;
- A baby is born without health insurance every 51 seconds; 90 percent of our 9 million uninsured children live in working families;
- A child or teen is killed by a firearm about every three hours—almost eight a day; a child dies from abuse or neglect every six hours;
- Every minute a baby is born to a teen mother and every 4 minutes to a mother who had late or no prenatal care. Every day a baby's mother dies in childbirth.

These statistics reflect children in every race, place, and family type. But minority children fare worse. Black babies are four times as likely as white babies to have their mothers die in childbirth. A black preschool boy born in 2001 has a one in three chance of going to prison in his lifetime; a black preschool girl has a one in 17 chance. Today, 580,000 black males are serving sentences in state or federal prison while fewer than 40,000 earn a bachelor's degree each year. One in three black men between 20–29 years old is under correctional supervision or control. Girls represent the fastest-growing group of detained juveniles. Black youths are 48 times more likely to be incarcerated than white youths for comparable drug offenses. More black children and teens have been killed by firearms over the past six years than all the black people of all ages that we lost in the history of lynchings.

Where is our voice?

Tougher sentencing guidelines, failing schools, zero tolerance school discipline policies—many inappropriately applied by black educators—poor, stressed, and often dysfunctional families; lack of adequate community health, mental health and other support services; too few positive alternatives to the streets and positive mentors and role models and an unequal playing field from birth all contribute to many poor black children being sucked into a Cradle to Prison Pipeline™ crisis.

This pipeline is destroying the hopes, dreams and lives of millions of children and must be dismantled if the clock of racial progress is not to turn backwards. Shamefully, the only thing our nation will guarantee every child is a juvenile detention or prison cell after s/he gets into trouble. States spend more than triple per prisoner than what they spend per public school pupil. What foolish investment priorities.

Where is our voice?

Nearly 70 percent of blacks in prison never completed high school. When black children do graduate from high school, they have a greater chance of being unemployed and a lower chance of going directly on to full-time college than white high-school graduates. According to a Harvard Civil Rights Project and Urban Institute report, only 50 percent of black students graduated from high school on time with a regular diploma in 2001; only 13 percent of black and 41 percent of white fourth graders are reading at grade level, and only 7 percent of black and 37 percent of white eighth graders perform at grade level in math. If we don't wake up and act to reverse these huge early childhood and educational gaps and incarceration trends, we are going to be headed back to slavery. These facts are not acts of God. These are our moral, political, and economic choices. We can and must change them through a 21st century transforming movement to put the social and economic underpinnings beneath the political and civil rights propelled by the Civil Rights Movement.

America's moral compass needs resetting. Hurricane Katrina ripped off the blinders of denial about the chronic, quiet but deadly twin tsunamis of poverty and race that have been snuffing out the lives and hopes of countless American children, especially poor children of color.

The whole world was horrified by the images of the desperate poor left behind in the hurricane. Americans expressed shock that people lacked the cars to escape. But they are the same poor children and adults America has left behind for decades to weather social and economic storms—faceless and voiceless—without help and just treatment in our rich nation. Before the hurricane, Mississippi was the poorest state for children, Louisiana the second poorest state, and Alabama the seventh poorest state.

Many of those left behind in New Orleans and then turned into "evacuees" after the storm hit were children and families. One in every three children in New Orleans lived in a household that didn't own a vehicle, and nearly all of those children were black. More than 98 percent of children in car-less households lived in minority households and 96 percent of them lived in black households. Not surprisingly, families that didn't own vehicles also were more likely to be poor. In a city where almost two in five children lived in poverty, bus or train tickets or taxis were just as unaffordable for many of their families as a car note or gas money. That's why we saw poignant pictures of them stranded on the roofs of their homes, highway exit ramps, or in the unspeakable conditions at the city's "shelters of last resort." And as we all know, there wasn't just one child left behind in New Orleans during the "mandatory evacuation," or just a few, but thousands.

The families that suffered in New Orleans were joined by the thousands of other families whose lives were devastated by Katrina across Alabama, Mississippi, and Louisiana. Many of these families were also poor before the storm and are poorer still after the storm, having lost everything they had. Now that the veil of neglect and inequality has been torn off showing the American empire was and still is unprepared to protect its children and families and vulnerable people from harm's way and to provide them health and mental health and housing and other survival supports to go on with their lives, it is time to act. Not to know is bad. To know and to do nothing is inexcusable.

The day after Hurricane Katrina hit, the U.S. Census Bureau released the latest data on American poverty showing that in 2004 poverty increased in our rich country for the fourth year in a row. The number of American children living in poverty has grown by 12.8 percent over the last four years, and is now more than 13 million. This means 1.5 million more children were poor in 2004 than in 2000. As these numbers were being released, was our government responding by announcing a federal emergency management plan to deal with increasing child and family poverty? Just the opposite: The Bush administration and Congress were sharing their recently-enacted plan to cut tens of billions of dollars from the budget for programs desperately needed by low and moderate income families and especially by Katrina evacuees. Worse, they proposed to cut billions from health and mental health care, foster care, food assistance, and other safety net programs in order to give tens of billions of dollars in additional tax cuts to powerful special interests. And the callousness has not stopped with more budget cuts being proposed in the new 2007 administration budget and efforts to make permanent the irresponsible tax cuts enacted earlier. The words have been eloquent but the budgets have been mean.

In an address to the nation from New Orleans 17 days after the storm hit, President Bush said, "Within the Gulf region are some of the most beautiful and historic places in America. As all of us saw on television, there is also some deep, persistent poverty in this region as well. And that poverty has roots in a history of racial discrimination, which cut off generations from the opportunity of America. We have a duty to confront this poverty with bold action. So let us restore all that we have cherished from yesterday, and let us rise above the legacy of inequality."

This is the same "deep, persistent poverty" the president spoke about in his first inaugural address, in January 2001, when he said, "In the quiet of American conscience, we know that deep, persistent poverty is unworthy of our nation's promise. And whatever our views of its cause, we can agree that children at risk are not at fault." As poverty has grown deeper and more persistent over the past four years, it is time for the administration, Congress, and all of us to translate words about the duty to confront this poverty into bold action. Health care for every child, not more tax cuts for every millionaire. Housing and jobs with living wages for those struggling for shelter, not more slashes in the Community Development Block Grant. An increase in the minimum wage, untouched at the federal level for eight years, not increased tax breaks and loopholes for powerful corporate interests.

Addressing the continuing post-Katrina chaos and human suffering still crying out for caring, competent and swift leadership and response at all levels so many months after the storm—with a new storm season on the way—is essential. Scattered across more than 40 states, tens— even hundreds—of thousands of Katrina's children and families still are without homes; without health and mental health care to treat their post-traumatic stress disorders; without schools; without child care and after-school programs; and without security in the present or hope for the future—living tentative, fragile lives. A teenage Katrina evacuee in Washington, D.C., wrote, "I don't believe anymore, but I want to." Our country needs to help her and the thousands like her believe that their country cares about them.

Dr. Bruce Perry, MD, Ph.D., Senior Fellow at the Child Trauma Academy in Houston, Texas, movingly warns us: "The real crisis of Katrina is coming … It will destroy a part of our country that is much more valuable than all of the buildings, pipelines, casinos, bridges and roads in all of the Gulf Coast. Over our lifetime, this crisis will cost our society billions upon billions of dollars. And the echoes of the coming crisis will haunt the next generation. This crisis is foreseeable. And, much of its destructive impact is preventable. Yet our society may not have the wisdom to see that the real crisis of Katrina is the hundreds of thousands of ravaged, displaced and traumatized children. And our society may not have the will to prevent this crisis. We understand broken buildings; we do not understand broken children."

This crisis was foreseeable, preventable, and yet our government is still dragging its feet. Thousands of mobile homes that cost hundreds of millions of taxpayers' dollars and that people needed for months have been sitting unused—inexplicably—in Hope, Arkansas. And thousands of New Orleans' people have been housed in trailer camps out in the boondocks of other cities without adequate support services—marooned out of sight, out of mind without transportation and critical services.

Families that have already struggled so hard to survive the trauma of Katrina's flooding now face extreme daily trauma and hardships. Many are being returned to shelters or turned out of hotels without a place to go. Many need counseling and health care. They need decent paying jobs and job training. They need a safe, stable place to live. They need good schools to send their children to. They need quality childcare and after-school programs when they work. They need safe and healthy communities. Failing schools, lack of health care, and loss of food stamps, after-school programs, and child care were crises before and after the storm not just for Katrina victims but for millions of children and working families across the nation hanging on the precarious razor's edge poverty creates. This time when God has troubled the waters, as our slave forebears sung, can and must become a time of hope and action to ensure access to opportunity for all Americans.

Our nation is making a terrible but typical mistake right now by arguing over whether to rebuild the destroyed buildings and levees and whether it was too soon to hold Mardi Gras while not discussing the critical underlying toll massive dislocation and poverty causes in the lives of so many, whose suffering will worsen the longer our political leaders dither.

The physical levees of New Orleans crumbled and left catastrophe in their wake, but the moral levees that have been crumbling for years in our nation's legal neglect and abuse of millions of children denied their most basic needs to survive and thrive are the greatest natural catastrophe. What are the values of a nation whose leaders relentlessly and repeatedly make budget and tax choices that widen the gulf between rich and poor and ask poor children to subsidize millionaires?

On March 31, 1968, the Sunday before his assassination, Dr. Martin Luther King, Jr. gave a sermon called "Remaining Awake Through a Great

Revolution" at Washington, D.C.'s National Cathedral. He reminded us of Jesus' parable about the rich man, Dives, and the beggar, Lazarus. "There is nothing in that parable that said Dives went to hell because he was rich ... Dives went to hell because he passed by Lazarus every day and he never really saw him. He went to hell because he allowed his brother to become invisible." Just as Dives didn't realize that his wealth was his opportunity, Dr. King warned that America could make the same mistake. He called for a Poor People's Campaign, a campaign he saw as "America's opportunity to help bridge the gulf between the haves and the have-nots. There is nothing new about poverty. What is new is that we now have the techniques and the resources to get rid of it. The real question is whether we have the will." This is still the real and urgent question for us today. How will we answer?

In 2005, the Senate rejected Senator Edward Kennedy's amendment to set a national goal to cut child poverty in half within a decade and to eliminate it entirely as soon as possible. At a time when all the nations of the world have set Millennium Development Goals (MDGs) to decrease global poverty, it is time for the richest nation on earth to lead by example and set MDGs for its own children and people. Poverty is the principal weapon of mass destruction driving the Cradle to Prison Pipeline™ crisis that wastes so many child lives. Keeping 13 million children in poverty costs taxpayers hundreds of billions of dollars in dependency and opportunity costs and lost future productivity. For less than the annual tax cut our leaders chose to give the top 1 percent of the wealthiest Americans, we could close the poverty gap for those 13 million children and put them on a path of hope and healing, towards productive adulthood rather than prison, and close rather than widen the gulf between Lazarus and Dives today, realize Dr. King's and America's dream, and save America's soul.

In the days following Dr. King's Cathedral sermon and before his assassination, he called his mother to tell her his next Sunday's sermon title at Ebenezer. It was "Why America May Go to Hell." What is it going to take to heed and act on his warning, the same warning of Isaiah, Amos, and of the New Testament child who Christians believe is God's messenger into history?

Where is our voice?

A Day in the Life of Black Children

Each Day in America for Black Children

3 children or teens are killed by firearms.

22 babies die before their first birthdays.

83 children are arrested for violent crimes.

92 babies are born to mothers who received late or no prenatal care.

103 children are arrested for drug abuse.

219 babies are born at low birthweight.

284 babies are born to teen mothers.

287 babies are born without health insurance.

372 babies are born to mothers who are not high school graduates.

506 high school students drop out.*

723 babies are born into poverty.

734 public school students are corporally punished.*

1,121 babies are born to unmarried mothers.

1,222 children are arrested.

5,798 public school students are suspended.*

Moments in America for Black children

Every 4 seconds a public school student is suspended.*

Every 34 seconds a public school student is corporally punished.*

Every 50 seconds a high school student drops out.*

Every minute a child is arrested.

Every minute a baby is born to an unmarried mother.

Every 2 minutes a baby is born into poverty.

Every 4 minutes a baby is born to a mother who is not a high school graduate.

Every 5 minutes a baby is born without health insurance.

Every 5 minutes a baby is born to a teen mother.

Every 7 minutes a baby is born at low birthweight.

Every 14 minutes a child is arrested for drug abuse.

Every 16 minutes a baby is born to a mother who received late or no prenatal care.

Every 17 minutes a child is arrested for violent crimes.

Every hour a baby dies before his first birthday.

Every 4 hours a child or teen dies in an accident.

Every 8 hours a child or teen is killed by a firearm.

* Based on calculations per school day (180 days of seven hours each).
  All calculations by the Children's Defense Fund.

ESSAY 5

Hurricane Katrina Exposed the Face of Poverty

by Maya Wiley

A s a nation, we face a rising tide. The floodwaters of poverty are eroding the shores of opportunity. The levees that broke in New Orleans, too weak to hold back the flood waters of the category 3 Hurricane Katrina, made this painfully clear. The flood waters of Lake Pontchartrain and the mighty Mississippi River reminded us that poverty, while it comes in all colors, is disproportionately black. It also reminded us that not everyone in this nation is equally able to protect herself or her family from the rising tide. Not everyone had a car, was healthy, or could pay for bus fare or a hotel room in some other city. The broken levees showed us something else. Our disinvestment in our public infrastructure harms us all, even if it does not harm us all equally.

The National Urban League's Equality Index continues to demonstrate that, on every indicator of well-being, whites are doing significantly better than blacks. In fact, whites are doing significantly better than almost every other person of color racial group. But the index, read properly, also demonstrates why blacks, despite important civil rights victories and tremendous resilience and perseverance in the face of 400 years of exclusion, have not achieved full social, economic and political inclusion. Our structural arrangements—the interaction and interrelationship of our institutions—create pathways to opportunity for some and block the path to success for others. Education, housing, healthcare, banking, transportation etc., are all systems and institutions that make up the structure of our society. They have never operated neutrally and work together to create and preserve pathways to opportunity for many whites while creating a labyrinth almost impossible to escape for many people of color. We have eliminated legalized racial discrimination against people of color, but have left the structures it produced intact. This is structural racism. The structures produced racialized outcomes—disparate poverty and exclusion for people of color and opportunities for whites. But they also produce racialized meaning. We often are blind to the existence of the structural racism that produces racialized poverty and weakens the middle class. We interpret the racial disparities we see as an indicator of inferiority, sometimes named as cultural, sometimes natural. But by it, we always imply the racial.

We remain blind at our peril. As Harvard Law Professor Lani Guinier has observed, black communities are our nation's miners' canary, likely to die if poisonous gases are in the mines. The structures that bar black, Latino, Native American and Asian achievement cast greedy nets that trap the unintended too. Across the nation the middle class is shrinking, quality educational opportunities are harder to find, jobs are less secure and we face a dwindling base of workers to support our aging population. Our structural arrangements may appear to work for those with good incomes living at the margins of our urban decay. But the opportunities privileged communities enjoy—high incomes, good schools and quality public services—are becoming ever more elusive. Moreover, wealthy communities are not self supporting, subsidized by poor urban residents.

Our ability to compete in a global economy, deliberately and steadily reduce poverty, strengthen and expand the middle class and create healthy, sustainable communities is at risk. The rising waters are also a rising tide of possibility—the possibility of pulling together, seeing our linked fate, investing in our communal strength and building boats to carry us all to the shores of the promised land—the land of opportunity. To build these boats, we must see that we need them. We must open our eyes to the very foundation of our national order and recognize the false god of racial hierarchy in its formation and the idolatry of coded racial meaning behind "deserving" and "undeserving" people or communities. We must recognize that our racial attitudes are also a product of our institutional formations. We must recognize that poverty and racial disparities are not the result of personal shortcomings or natural order, but are constructed. We must build new bulwarks against the rising tide to protect the most vulnerable if we are all to prosper.

Structural Racism Defined

U.S. society is like a large machine with many moving parts. We have schools, colleges and universities, employers, banks, housing developers, realtors and news media. Government serves, regulates and mediates these institutions as an integral set of pulleys, conveyor belts, ball bearings, axels and propane. All these parts move together or in reaction to the movement of another part.

Together these parts all affect our lives. Our machine was built, in part, on racism and poverty. Theft of the land of Native peoples, premised on their inferiority and dangerousness, black slavery,[1] and immigration laws that excluded all but those defined as "white"[2] are all part of the machine. Only whiteness allowed members of society to lay claim to belonging, even though the country was founded on the ideals of equality and opportunity. We have worked to rebuild the machine through constitutional amendments and civil rights laws, but have not yet remodeled it enough. This is, in part, because we are not always working on the parts that connect to the whole. This is what the structural racism lens helps us to see.

Structural racism has five primary characteristics: 1) it is not race neutral; 2) history matters in that the structure of our society has been constructed over time and racial hierarchy has been an integral part of that restructuring; 3) effects matter because they tell us how the structure operates so that intentional bad acts are irrelevant; 4) racial disparities are effects that show the structure does not operate neutrally; and 5) everyone is harmed by the structure, even if we see it most glaringly in majority people of color communities.

Structure matters because it helps to create opportunities or stifle them. Few would argue that slavery or segregation did not limit one's life chances. After all, both set up a structure that determined where blacks could live, whether they could work, what kind of work they were allowed to perform, whether they could receive an education and even if they could marry. These opportunities, denied overtly for more than 300 years from the 1600s until the 1960s, have created multi-generational deprivation. But blacks continue to be structurally barred from these opportunities in the post-civil rights era.

The structures have unevenly distributed the benefits and burdens of our public policies and private actions. For example, many outer-ring suburbs, which have become among the most opportunity-rich communities in most metropolitan areas, have received a much larger allocation of transportation infrastructure funds than their urban neighbors, despite their significantly lower share of the regional population compared to nearby cities. For example, in the Detroit metropolitan area, 80 per cent of the $1 billion spent on new highways between 1986 and 1995 went to one county that accounted for 26 percent of the population and was over 80 percent white.[3] When these wealthy suburbs are built, they have to create sewers, utility lines and, often build new schools. New suburban subdivisions do not pay for themselves. Inner-city tax dollars subsidize them.[4] The poor are paying for the rich. And often lower-income Blacks are paying to support better-off whites.

History matters. Our history and customs include racist and race neutral policies and practices that have had cumulative effects across generations and institutions in this country. For example, the New Deal of the 1930s created the middle class. The New Deal created Social Security to redistribute income from those with higher lifetime earnings to those with lower lifetime earnings to ensure retirement income. It had no overtly racist exclusions. Anyone who met the race-neutral eligibility requirements received benefits. Nonetheless, it excluded most blacks. Domestic and agricultural workers were ineligible for benefits. At least three-fifths of the black labor-force was denied these benefits. (The number is probably higher because it does not include sharecroppers.) Almost all (90 percent) of black women were domestic workers. They were not included in the program until the 1960s. As a direct result of their exclusion coupled with employment discrimination, they had nowhere to turn but the welfare rolls, for which they were publicly vilified.[5] Today, about 79 percent of white households have pension wealth, compared with 66 percent black and 46 percent of Latino households.[6]

While often even race neutral policies like those of the New Deal intended to exclude blacks, the intent becomes irrelevant, particularly given their current day impacts.[7] Today, most black workers are covered by social security, but still receive much lower benefits and pay a much higher proportion of their income into social security.[8] The program cannot better support blacks as long as black mortality rates remain as they are. Racial disparities, such as higher mortality rates or higher poverty rates are effects (or symptoms) of structural racism and therefore structural racism must be transformed to meaningfully impact racial disparities.[9]

The Eroding of the Middle Class

The U.S. middle class is shrinking. Two-thirds experienced downward mobility in the 1980s and 1990s.[10] Moreover, the poor are getting poorer and the rich are getting richer. In our globalized economy, entry-level jobs are disappearing and jobs are increasingly less secure. At the same time government investment in social programs has dwindled.[11] Under these conditions, generally speaking, the white middle class is closing ranks to protect itself by opposing black upward mobility and Latino and Asian immigration and membership in U.S. social, economic and political life. Opportunity posed by this rising tide of racial protectionism is the recognition that this reaction prevents our best efforts to reverse these trends. To reverse them, we must recognize that racial privilege—advantages one enjoys simply because he or she is white—has played a central role in the structural arrangements of our country and has led to racialized attitudes that stump our national growth and prosperity.

Consider the suburbs, a phenomenon of the second half of the 20th century. Government-created incentives targeting whites, subsidized their flight from the city, and their relocation to the suburbs.[12] New Deal legislation—the National Housing Act of 1934—created the Federal Housing Administration (FHA), which subsidized mortgages and insured private mortgages.

This program helped break up racially integrated communities and increased racial segregation, including segregation of blacks and Latinos from opportunities subsidized and encouraged in white communities. The

New Deal Home Owners' Loan Corporation (HOLC) developed a neighborhood quality rating system to determine risk for loans made to specific urban neighborhoods. HOLC rated central city, racially and ethnically mixed neighborhoods. It gave rated racially integrated working-class neighborhoods near black communities as high risk because they might attract, undesireables—black people.[13] This meant HOLC mortgage funds were directed away from black neighborhoods and integrated working-class neighborhoods.

These HOLC policies were the first redlining policies. Redlining policies, like HOLC's, devalued black and mixed neighborhoods. Whites had powerful disincentives and no incentives to locate to these communities. Federal policies also ensured that blacks would be barred from opportunities in the newly forming white suburbs. HOLC and the FHA often required new owners to incorporate racially restrictive covenants into their deeds.[14]

By the 1950s, the FHA and the Veterans Administration (VA) were insuring half the mortgages in the United States, but only in "racially homogenous" neighborhoods.[15] The FHA's underwriting manual required a determination about the presence of "incompatible racial or social groups ..."[16] People of color were literally classified as nuisances, to be avoided along with "stables" and "pig pens."[17] The FHA urged developers, bankers, and local government to use zoning ordinances and physical barriers to protect racial homogeneity.[18]

Transportation was another cog in the wheel that drove whites to opportunity and blacks to concentrated poverty. The transportation block grants of the 1980s allowed states to use mass transit dollars to serve those living in distant suburbs to commute by train to the financial city centers, while leaving thousands of city center residents, standing on city streets waiting for overcrowded buses.[19] Even in the 1990s, when certain federal highway funds were available on a flexible basis for states and regional localities to transfer from highway programs to public transit projects, only $4.2 billion of the $33.8 billion available, or 12.5 percent, was actually transferred.[20]

Federal housing and transportation policies have had a tremendous impact on where jobs are located and who can get to them. According to the 1995 Nationwide Personal Transportation Survey, in metropolitan areas more than half of commuters travel from home to work are suburb-to-suburb.[21] These travelers represent a broad mix of professional white collar, blue collar, sales and clerical workers.[22] Suburb-to-city commuters, on the other hand, tend to be white-collar workers. The smallest category of workers commute from city-to-suburb.[23]

Over time the federal programs and policies described in this section have been revised to remove racially explicit criteria. Yet the impacts persist because the structural arrangements remain in tact.[24] The machine produced increased racial segregation and the concentration of poverty and barriers to opportunity for blacks and the concentration of wealth and opportunity for whites. New Orleans provides a powerful and tragic example.

New Orleans was a racially and culturally vibrant and heterogeneous city, despite its poverty, in the first half of the 20th century. Until 1950, blacks and whites lived in close proximity and there were integrated communities. In the 1970s, New Orleans was a poor city, but its poor were not highly concentrated in hyper-segregated neighborhoods. That changed dramatically after 1970. By 2000, New Orleans ranked 29th in the country based on black/white racial segregation.

[25]The number of concentrated poverty neighborhoods in New Orleans actually grew by two-thirds between 1970 and 2000, even though the poverty rate stayed about the same (26–28 percent).[26]

When the levees broke in New Orleans, so did the nation's attitude toward poverty and race. Too many whites were poor, but their poverty was different from black poverty. Almost a third of black families in New Orleans lived below the federal poverty level, compared to just under 5 percent of white families. According to the Brookings Institution, blacks in New Orleans were so poor that almost 35 percent of the population had no car. A much lower percentage of whites—about 15—was in the same predicament.[27]

As these racial disparities suggest, New Orleans was neither healthy nor sustainable prior to the breaking of its levees. This trend, while among the most dramatic of major metropolitan regions in the country, is not unique. Many cities experienced similar trends as whites fled to suburbs, propelled by a history of incentive-laden federal policies traceable all the way back to the New Deal.

Building New Boats

Policies and actions driving racialized suburbanization have divided us as a nation. It has reduced our cross-racial interaction and, therefore, our ability to see ourselves as one community. It has fragmented our governmental structures between cities and suburbs, forcing our policy-makers to swim against the current of regional economic and social development. And it has made both city and suburbs, still critical in the globalizing economy and in the national consciousness, weak and unsustainable.

There is a way out. Research has shown that efforts to reduce central city poverty have led to an increase in regional wealth and a reduction of regional poverty. As Manuel Pastor, a noted economist, has pointed out, "Doing good and doing well [go] hand-in-hand for regions."[28] This work also makes clear that, as race is at the center of our broken national order, so racial equity must be at the center of our plan for national reinvigoration. We must cross lines and boundaries, real and imagined. We must cross urban and suburban governmental fragmentation, business and community group divisions, and racial group identities to work together and invest in the poorest people and their communities, to connect them to opportunities like jobs in growth sectors, training and educational opportunities, transportation and housing. The state of Black America is the state of the nation. We, black and white, single mother and two-parent household, citizen and undocumented, all of us are critical to the strengthening of our nation and the success of our democracy.

Notes

[1]Martinot, S., *The Rule of Racialization: Class, Identity, Governance*, Temple University Press (2003).

[2]Our first immigration law, the Naturalization Act of 1790, unanimously passed and limited citizenship to "free white persons." Foner, E., *The Story of American Freedom*, W.W. Norton & Co., New York: London (1998) at 39.

[3]Cashin, C., *The Failures of Integration: How Race and Class Are Undermining the American Dream*, Public Affairs New York (2004) at 180–181.

[4]Id. at 182.

[5]Brown, M. et. al., *White-Washing Race: The Myth of a Color-Blind Society*, Berkeley, CA: University of California Press (2003) at 28.

[6]Rakesh Kochhar, *The Wealth of Hispanic Households: 1996 to 2002*, Pew Hispanic Center (October 2004), available at http://pewhispanic.org/reports/report.php?ReportID=34

[7]Thompson, R. T., *The Boundaries of Race: Political Geography in Legal Analysis*, 107 Harv. L. Rev. 1841, 1844–45 (1994). According to Richard Thompson Ford, describing racism as structural recognizes that laws and institutions need not be explicitly racist in order to disempower communities of color, they need only perpetuate unequal historic conditions.

[8]See, C. Eugene Steuerle, Adam Carasso, Lee Cohen, *How Progressive Is Social Security and Why?* May 01, 2004, No. 37 in Series "Straight Talk on Social Security and Retirement Policy" available at http://www.urban.org/url.cfm?ID=311016 (finding less-educated, lower-income, and nonwhite groups benefit little or not at all from redistribution in the old age and survivors insurance (OASI) part of Social Security.) .

[9]See, *Applying A Structural Racism Framework: A Strategy for Community Level Research and Action*, The Aspen Institute Roundtable on Comprehensive Community Initiatives.

[10]See Barlow, A., *Between Hope and Fear: Globalization and Race in the United States* Rowman & Littlefield (2003) at 66-68.

[11]Id.

[12]See Aspen Institute, supra note 9, at 51.

[13]Douglas Massey, Nancy Denton, *American Apartheid: Segregation and the Making of the Underclass* Cambridg, MA: Harvard University Press (1993) at 51–52.

[14]See powell j.a., Graham K.M., Urban Fragmentation as a Barrier to Equal Opportunity, in *Rights at Risk: Equality in an Age of Terrorism. Report of the Citizens' Commission on Civil Rights*. Citizens Commission on Civil Rights 79-97 (2002).; Richard Thompson Ford, "The Boundaries of Race: Political Geography in Legal Analysis," 107 *Harvard Law Review* 449, 451 (1995).

[15]David Rusk, *Inside Game/OutsideGame: Winning Strategies for Saving Urban America*, (1999) at 86–88.

[16]See Michael H. Schill and Susan M. Wachter, "The Spatial Bias of Federal Housing Law and Policy: Concentrated Poverty in Urban America," 143 *University of Pennsylvania Law Review* 1285, 1286–90 (1995).

[17]See *The Boundaries of Race*, supra note 13, at 451 (citing Charles Abrams, *Forbidden Neighborhood: A Study of Prejudice in Housing*, at 231 (1955)).

[18]See *Inside Game/Outside Game*, supra note 14, at 87 (citing Irving Welfeld, *Where We Live: A Social History of American Housing* (1988)).

[19]See Bullard, D, Robert., Addressing Urban Transportation Equity in the United States, 31 *Fordham Urban Law Journal* 1183, 1196 (October 2004).

[20]See Robert Puentes, *Flexible Funding for Transit: Who Uses It?* Brookings Institution report: Survey Series of the Brookings Institution Center on Metropolitan Policy, at 1, 2 (available at <http://www.brook.edu/urban/flexfundingexsum.htm>) (May 2000).

[21]Frazier, et. al., *Race and Place: Equity Issues in Urban America* at 232 (Bouder, CO: Westview Press, 2003).

[22]Id.

[23]Id.

[24]See Urban Fragmentation, supra note 13, at 79–97.

[25]CensusScope http://www.censusscope.org/us/rank_dissimilarity_White_Black.html.

[26]Berube, et. al, Katrina's Window: Confronting Concentrated Poverty Across America, The Brookings Institution (Oct. 2005).

[27]See supra note 25 at 15.

[28]Pastor, M. et. al., Growing Together: Linking Regional and Community Development in a Changing Economy, *Shelterforce Online* January/February 1998. See www.nhi.org/online/issues/97/pastor.html.

Race, Poverty, and Healthcare Disparities

by Brian D. Smedley

"Of all the forms of injustice, injustice in health care is the most shocking and inhumane"

— *Martin Luther King, Jr.*

More than four decades have passed since Dr. King's observation that the racial and economic divide in healthcare most symbolized the brutality of state-sanctioned inequality and racial injustice. Today, healthcare for the poor and patients of color is less segregated and more accessible to a broader segment of the population than when Dr. King made this statement.[1] But a yawning chasm of healthcare inequality remains, often in ways that significantly limit health and life opportunities for many Americans.

The persistence of healthcare inequality is remarkable in a nation that has an abundance of healthcare resources. Americans spend nearly $2 trillion on healthcare annually, far more per capita than any other nation in the world. Still, the United States ranks 37th of 191 countries in a World Health Organization assessment of the world's health systems.[2] The United States fares poorly in large measure because of its marked inequality. The number of Americans without health insurance reached an all-time high of 45.8 million in 2004, and more than 80 million Americans lacked health insurance for all or part of 2002 and 2003.[3] While an increasing number of businesses are reducing or eliminating employee health benefits, for-profit specialty and "boutique" healthcare services are spreading in upper-income communities.[4] And despite growing awareness among policymakers of the phenomenon, patients' race, ethnicity and socioeconomic status still determines the timeliness and quality of his or her healthcare. These gaps threaten to worsen if some trends—such as the drive to privatize an increasing share of public healthcare programs—continue.

As with many other dimensions of American inequality, racial and poverty gaps in healthcare were never more evident than in the aftermath of Hurricane Katrina. Many poor African-American New Orleans residents lost what was already-precarious access to community-based healthcare as a result of displacement and damage to the city's infrastructure. And stark contrasts emerged in the differential treatment of patients in some of the city's main hospitals. At New Orleans' Charity Hospital, first opened in 1736 and whose primary mission is to treat impoverished southern Louisianans, doctors and patients waited for days for rescue in sweltering, fetid conditions, while across the street at better-resourced Tulane University Hospital, helicopters "ceaselessly evacuate[ed] insured patients from the roof."[5]

How has the Nation Fared in the Effort to Eliminate Healthcare Inequality?

Four years ago, a report by the Institute of Medicine—*Unequal Treatment: Confronting Racial and Ethnic Disparities in Health Care*—disclosed that people of color receive lower quality of health care even compared to whites with the same income, age, health condition and insurance status. It noted the prevalence of bias and stereotyping among health care providers. The study received front-page attention from *The New York Times*, *Los Angeles Times*, and other major newspapers, prompting debates about racial bias in healthcare delivery.[6] The attention was noteworthy, not only because inequality in healthcare has persisted without significant public debate for generations,[7] but also because of what was absent from the discussion—an examination of class-based inequality.[8] It nonetheless sparked Congressional attention, including a mandate that the U.S. Department of Human Services issue an annual report to measure progress toward reducing disparities. But the question remains: How is the nation faring in the effort to reduce healthcare inequality?

Evidence suggests that while some disparities in access to and the quality of care are narrowing, significant inequality remains.

A recent special issue of the *New England Journal of Medicine,* for example, examined trends in racial and ethnic healthcare disparities.

Among the findings:

- Between 1994 and 2002, African-American women deemed "ideal candidates" for reperfusion therapy and coronary angiography were less likely to receive these services than similar white women; these differences remained consistent over the period of study.[9]
- The racial gap in receipt of several high-cost surgical procedures (e.g., coronary-artery bypass grafting) increased significantly between 1992 and 2001 among Medicare beneficiaries.[10]
- While the overall quality of care for African-American and white Medicare beneficiaries enrolled in managed care plans improved between 1997 and 2003, and racial gaps narrowed in seven of nine measures of clinical performance, African Americans were still less likely than whites to receive care that met evidence-based standards.[11]

In January 2006, the U.S. Department of Health and Human Services released the third annual report of the state of healthcare quality and access for minority and low-income populations. The National Healthcare Disparities Report (NHDR) reviews a wide range of measures, including health care access (e.g., health insurance status, the frequency of physician visits), quality (e.g., use of evidence-based treatments) and outcomes (e.g., health outcomes after hospitalization, reductions in deaths from certain diseases). The report's assessment finds that healthcare disparities are narrowing slightly for many racial and ethnic minorities, but that low-income patients faced the largest disparities in measures of quality and access, regardless of race or ethnicity. Poor people received a lower quality of care than high-income (more than 400 percent of poverty) people in 11 of 13 measures, and in several areas, socioeconomic disparities in access and quality were found to be worsening. For example, low-income diabetic patients were found to be increasingly less likely than high-income diabetic patients to receive at least three recommended services, and measures of the timeliness of care for low-income people were found to be slipping relative to high-income groups.

Encouragingly, more indicators of racial disparities in quality of care were narrowing than were widening, and most racial disparities in access to care were narrowing for African Americans, Asians and American Indians/Alaska Natives. African Americans and Native Americans received poorer care than whites in about 40 percent of quality measures, but nearly 60 percent of these disparities have been narrowing over the past five years. These moderately positive trends were not true, however, among Hispanics, for whom the majority of disparities for both quality and access were growing wider. For example, the quality of diabetes care declined from 2000 to 2002 among Hispanic adults, while at the same time it improved among white adults.

The Policy Context: What Can Be Done to Improve Healthcare Equity?

Healthcare in the United States will face powerful winds of change in the next decade from economic, political, and social pressures. If the nation's priority is to create a comprehensive, equitable healthcare system that meets the needs of an increasingly diverse patient population, it must start with the goal of providing universal access to healthcare. A number of important policy developments in Washington, however, threaten to limit access to healthcare and deepen quality gaps. Congress has taken steps to curb the growth of Medicaid, the nation's largest healthcare program for low-income families. At the same time, Congress is entertaining means to promote "consumerism" in healthcare, under the theory that greater consumer cost-consciousness will improve quality and drive down costs. Preliminary evidence, however, suggests that consumer-driven healthcare may further "fragment" U.S. health systems along socioeconomic lines.

Curbing the Growth of Medicaid

Medicaid currently provides health insurance for more than 50 million people in the United States. Yet, the program's rapidly escalating price tag—average annual spending increased 10.2 percent from 2000 to 2003—has spurred federal and state efforts to significantly limit the program's growth.[12] On February 1, 2006, Congress passed budget reconciliation legislation that would allow states to impose higher cost-sharing requirements and/or charge premiums for certain Medicaid enrollees, and impose significant coverage reductions. In addition, this measure will impose a new mandate requiring that U.S. citizens receiving Medicaid prove their citizenship by submitting government-issued documentation.

These measures threaten to widen the socioeconomic gap in healthcare access. The Congressional Budget Office (CBO) estimates that if states impose new premiums allowed by the budget bill, as many as 45,000 Medicaid enrollees would lose coverage by 2010, and 65,000 would lose coverage by 2015. About 60 percent of those losing coverage would be children. And about one in five current Medicaid beneficiaries would receive reduced benefit packages, affecting an estimated 900,000 enrollees in 2010 and 1.6 million enrollees by 2015.[13] And while the CBO estimates that 35,000 current Medicaid enrollees will lose coverage as a result of the requirement that enrollees document their U.S. citizenship, a survey by the Center on Budget and Policy Priorities revealed that documentation problems may be far more widespread. About one in every 12 U.S.-born adults with incomes below $25,000 in this survey does not have a U.S. passport or birth certificate, suggesting that about 1.7 million U.S.-born adults may experience delays or denials of coverage. In addition, more than one in 10 U.S.-born adults with incomes below $25,000 who have children covered by Medicaid indicate that they do not have documentation for their children, suggesting that between 1.4 and 2.9 million children are in jeopardy of losing their Medicaid eligibility.[14]

Promoting "Consumerism" In Healthcare

Similarly, the trend toward consumer-driven health plans—touted by some policymakers as a means to lower healthcare costs and increase access to health insurance—may exacerbate racial, ethnic and socioeconomic healthcare gaps. Health savings accounts (HSAs) are an often-cited example of consumer-driven health plans. HSAs allow people to set aside money on a tax-free basis annually to pay for medical expenses. To qualify for the tax-free account, people must purchase a high-deductible health insurance policy. High-deductible plans are less expensive than more comprehensive, lower-deductible health insurance plans, but require high out-of-pocket payments if people have steep medical bills. Deductibles begin at $1,000 for individuals and $2,000 for families, but deductibles in some plans may be as high as $10,000.

About 3 million people are currently enrolled in HSAs, and this number is expected to rise as employers limit health benefits. But analyses by the Employee Benefit Research Institute (EBRI) and other groups find that HSAs do little to help the uninsured gain affordable health insurance, and will not contain healthcare costs. Moreover, they may exacerbate racial, ethnic, and socioeconomic disparities in access to and the quality of healthcare, for several reasons. One, HSA tax breaks disproportionately benefit wealthy Americans. A significant proportion of uninsured Americans—disproportionately people of color, immigrants, and the working poor—don't make enough money to pay taxes, so they would receive no benefit from the tax benefit of HSAs. Second, people with low incomes are less able to save enough, after taking into account housing, transportation, food, and other costs, to cover high deductibles typical of HSAs. High deductibles may prevent many people from getting care that they need if they cannot afford out-of-pocket costs, thereby increasing the risk that health problems that can be treated more cost-effectively at earlier stages will remain untreated until they are debilitating and costly. EBRI's 2005 survey, for example, found that about one-third of individuals enrolled in consumer-driven health plans such as HSAs reported delaying or avoiding seeking healthcare because of cost—a proportion nearly twice that of people enrolled in more comprehensive health insurance plans. These problems were more pronounced among individuals with health problems or incomes under $50,000. [15]

As a result, HSA's are likely to attract healthy and wealthier individuals who do not face high, on-going medical bills, and for whom the tax savings are substantial. A Government Accountability Office study of federal employees enrolled in HSAs finds strong support for this conclusion. [16]

The likely impact of this trend will be to make health insurance less affordable for those who need it most. Should HSA enrollment increase, healthy and wealthy individuals will be drawn away from traditional health insurance plans, which attempt to broadly spread risk among a large population. Traditional plans would then disproportionately serve lower-income, less healthy persons. Inevitably, premiums for these plans would increase, fewer employers will offer traditional health benefits, and fewer people will be able to afford health insurance.[17]

Creating a Universal Access, Equitable Healthcare System

Healthcare inequality must be tackled by state and federal efforts to develop a universally accessible, comprehensive, and equitable healthcare system. Access to healthcare can be expanded by:

- *Creating a "Medicare for all" national single-payer plan.* Medicare is more efficient than private plans because of its low administrative costs. And because Medicare is a federal program, subject to the Civil Rights Act of 1964 (which prohibits discrimination on the basis of race, ethnicity, language status, and other factors), it contains mechanisms of accountability that can be expanded and enhanced to ensure that inequitable health care is addressed. Allowing employers and individuals to buy into Medicare and expanding eligibility can be important initial steps toward a national single-payer plan.
- *Covering all children under a comprehensive health insurance plan.* The state and federal State Child Health Insurance Program (SCHIP) has improved access to healthcare for thousands of children whose families did not qualify for other sources of public insurance or who did not receive health benefits through employers. SCHIP should be fully funded and expanded to cover all uninsured children.

A national healthcare program will greatly reduce barriers to accessing healthcare, but universal access by itself will not eliminate gaps in healthcare quality. Government should ensure that the provision of healthcare is equitable and meets all patients' needs, regardless of race, ethnicity, gender, or language status. State and federal governments should also assess geographic disparities in healthcare resources, and create incentives to strengthen the healthcare infrastructure in medically underserved communities. Finally, the federal government should assist efforts to create culturally competent health systems by strengthening federal programs to increase the racial and ethnic diversity of healthcare professionals, and should build upon efforts to strengthen civil rights enforcement initiated at the U.S. DHHS Office of Civil Rights in the late 1990s.[18] Generally, cultural competence is defined as the knowledge and interpersonal skills that allows caregivers to understand, appreciate and work effectively with individuals from cultures other than their own.

Healthcare systems should take a number of steps, as outlined in the IOM Unequal Treatment report, to assess the needs of culturally and linguistically diverse patient populations and devise programs and ensure that they receive the highest quality of care:

- Hospitals and health systems should encourage the use of evidence-based clinical guidelines, to promote standardization of high-quality care for all patients.
- Hospitals and health systems should strive to provide culturally and linguistically competent services for an increasingly diverse nation, in accordance with the Cultural and Linguistic Access Standards (CLAS) developed by the U.S. Department of Health and Human Services.
- Health systems should regularly collect data on the race, ethnicity, and language skills of their patients, and provide information on healthcare access and quality along these dimensions to the federal government as a condition of participation in Medicare, Medicaid and SCHIP.[19]

Achieving an equitable, universal health system in the United States will not be easy, given the nation's long history of tacit (and sometimes explicit) tolerance of inequality in healthcare. Active partnerships between government, healthcare providers and institutions, health systems, and other important stakeholders—such as the business communi-ty, labor, faith groups, and others—will be necessary to create the politi-cal will to develop and sustain these policy goals. But the pressures for a more just, cost-effective, and fair healthcare system are mounting. We ignore them at our peril.

Notes

[1]Smith, DB. 1999. *Health Care Divided: Race and Healing a Nation.* Ann Arbor, MI: University of Michigan Press.

[2]Evans DB, Tandon A, Murray CJ, Lauer JA. 2001. Comparative efficiency of nation-al health systems: cross national econometric analysis. *British Medical Journal,* 323(7308):307–10.

[3]Families USA, "One in Three: Non-Elderly Americans Without Health Insurance, 2002–2003," (Washington, D.C.: Families USA, June 2004).

[4]Hurley RE, Pham HH, and Claxton G. 2005. A widening rift in access and quality: Growing evidence of economic disparities. *Health Affairs,* Dec 6; [Epub ahead of print].

[5]Berggren R. 2005. Unexpected necessities—Inside Charity Hospital. *The New England Journal of Medicine,* 353(15):1550–3.

[6]Institute of Medicine. 2003. *Unequal Treatment: Confronting Racial and Ethnic Disparities in Healthcare.* BD Smedley, AY Stith, and AR Nelson (Eds.). Washington, DC: National Academies Press.

[7]Byrd WM and Clayton LA. 2000. *An American Health Dilemma: A Medical History of African-Americans and the Problem of Race—Beginnings to 1900.* New York, NY: Routledge Press.

[8]Bloche MG. 2004. Health care disparities–science, politics, and race. *The New England Journal of Medicine,* 350(15):1568–70.

[9]Vaccarino V, Rathore SS, Wenger NK, Frederick PD, Abramson JL, Barron HV, Manhapra A, Mallik S, Krumholz HM. 2005. Sex and racial differences in the management of acute myocardial infarction, 1994 through 2002, *The New England Journal of Medicine,* 353(7):671–82.

[10]Jha AK, Fisher ES, Li Z, Orav EJ, and Epstein AM. 2005. Racial trends in the use of major procedures among the elderly. *The New England Journal of Medicine*, 353(7):683–91.

[11]Trivedi AN, Zaslavsky AM, Schneider EC, and Ayanian JZ. 2005. Trends in the quality of care and racial disparities in Medicare Managed Care. *The New England Journal of Medicine*, 353(7):692–700.

[12]The American Public Health Association. 2006. *Medicaid, Prevention and Public Health: Invest Today for Healthier Tomorrow*, Washington, D.C.: American Public Health Association.

[13]Congressional Budget Office. 2006. Letter to the Honorable John M. Spratt, Jr., Ranking Member, Committee on Budget, U.S. House of Representatives, January 27, 2006, regarding H.S. 4241, the Deficit Reduction Act of 2005.

[14]Ku L, Ross DC, Broaddus M. 2006. Survey Indicates Budget Reconciliation Bill Jeopardizes Medicaid Coverage for 3 to 5 Million U.S. Citizens. Washington, D.C.: Center on Budget and Policy Priorities.

[15]Fronstin P, Collins SR. 2005. *Early Experience with High-Deductible and Consumer-Driven Health Plans: Findings from the EBRI/Commonwealth Fund Consumerism in Health Care Survey*. Washington, DC.: Employee Benefit Research Institute.

[16]U.S. Government Accountability Office. 2006. *Federal Employees Health Benefits Program: First-Year Experience with High-Deductible Health Plans and Health Savings Accounts*. Washington, D.C.: U.S. Government Accountability Office.

[17]Families USA. 2005. *HSAs: Why High-Deductible Plans Are Not the Solution. Washington*, D.C.: Families USA.

[18]Institute of Medicine, 2003.

[19]Ibid.

The State of Civil Rights

by The Honorable Nathaniel R. Jones

The state of civil rights in America is most precarious.

Civil rights advocates may find themselves in the situation of the person who did not realize that his throat had been cut until he attempted to shake his head. This should come as no surprise to those who have been manning the barricades. The warning signs have been many.

The most ominous warning came from the late Justice Thurgood Marshall in the final dissenting opinion he wrote before retiring from the Supreme Court. Justice Marshall was disturbed at the way the Supreme Court majority had reversed itself in a death penalty case within a period of a few years. The majority had jettisoned the notion of *stáre decisis,* or precedent,—with no reasoned basis for doing so.

Justice Marshall wrote:

> Power, not reason, is the new currency of this court's decision making. ...neither the law nor the facts supporting Booth and Gathers underwent any change in the first four years. Only the personnel of this court did.

> In dispatching Booth and Gathers to their graves, today's majority ominously suggests that an even more extensible upheaval of this court's precedents may be in store ... [This opinion] sends a clear signal that scores of established constitutional liberties are now ripe for consideration.

One need only look at subsequent decisions of the Supreme Court on civil rights remedies, and in cases that impact on the rights of minorities and the poor, to know that Justice Marshall's warning is coming to pass.

Moreover, events surrounding the 2000 and 2004 presidential and congressional elections, followed by the way in which the federal judicial nominating process has been manipulated, have proven Justice Marshall prescient.

Those who oppose the expansion and enforcement of civil rights have cleverly masked their aims. They do not frontally attack civil rights—to the contrary—they preface their declarations with a reiteration of rhetoric about civil rights and equal opportunity for all. Then, they proceed to attack the means of implementing the remedies that give meaning to civil rights. They fail to concede that a right (which they profess to support) without a remedy is no right at all. Thus, to proclaim a belief in equal opportunity to educators and jobs while attacking affirmative action and enforceable consent decrees, is meaningless.

We know that voting rights are at the core of the people's right of self-determination. Hobbling the right to vote has an effect on the election of state and federal officials. When that ability is impaired, the officials who do get elected frequently dismiss or are deaf to the pleas of racial minorities. A recent example of this took place in the cynical way United States Senators turned a deaf ear to the protests raised by black and minority voters over Supreme Court nominees. Sadly, some Senators allowed their political partisanship and electoral cowardice to override their solemn duty. This was a classic instance of non-accountability that cries out for a renewal and expansion of the 1965 Voting Rights Act.

One's fitness to be a U.S. Supreme Court justice transcends what so many focused on during the recent confirmation process—stellar academic achievements and a degree of unquestioned professional competence. While such credentials are relevant, they should be the beginning of the scrutiny, not the end. The critical question is one of values, not competence.

To understand why this is true, consider the most wretched decision the Supreme Court ever handed down on the question of human rights,

Dred Scott v. Sanford. The author of that decision, Chief Justice Roger B. Taney, was undoubtedly highly qualified from a technical and professional standpoint, having been appointed by President Andrew Jackson after his service as Secretary of Treasury. Yet, when faced with the fundamental question of whether a one-time slave, Dred Scott, had standing to sue to retain his newly-acquired free status, Justice Taney wrote that black people—slaves—were not persons within the contemplation of the framers of the Constitution and were therefore powerless to sue. Had Chief Justice Taney been imbued with a different scale of values, our national history on race might have been considerably different.

Similarly, had those charged with wielding awesome judicial power at the time of the *Plessy v. Ferguson* case in 1896 understood that the 14th Amendment's guarantees were intended to include black people, America would have been spared a horrible chapter. Instead, Justice Henry Billings Brown and the Supreme Court majority stood the 14th Amendment on its head, thereby constitutionalizing and legitimizing racial discrimination.

The author of the majority opinion had all of the professional and academic equipment one customarily looks to in measuring one's fitness for service on the Supreme Court—academic credentials and prior judicial experience. Justice Brown had served on the Sixth Circuit Court of Appeals and was the holder of degrees from both Harvard and Yale. Yet, he lacked the values that sensitized him to understand why the 13th, 14th and 15th Amendments had to become a part of the Constitution. That responsibility fell to the lone dissenter, John Marshall Harlan, the son of Kentucky slave owners, a graduate of Centre College and Transylvania University. Justice Harlan offered an eloquent prophecy that the court and the nation would regret the doctrine it had imposed on the nation. At first glance, Justice Brown's academic and career credentials may have appeared more impressive than Justice Harlan's. But in the final analysis, it was Justice Harlan, with his superior values, who was unquestionably the finer judge. Clearly, if Justice Harlan's dissent had been the majority view, we would not be faced with the continuing struggles over race.

So pervasive did "separate but equal" become that many whites were freed of moral and legal guilt as they ghettoized blacks, denied them job opportunities, excluded them from places of public accommodation, relegated their children to inferior schools, denied them admission to colleges and universities, and operated a court system on an *apartheid* basis, with whites in control and blacks under control.

To those who quarrel with the view that the Supreme Court's "separate but equal" doctrine freed White America to harm and repress Black Americans, I cite the finding of the Kerner Commission. What White Americans have never fully understood—but what the Negro can never forget—is that white society is deeply implicated in the ghetto. White institutions created it, white institutions maintain it, and white society condones it.

When Charles Hamilton Houston launched his strategy to overturn the *Plessy v. Ferguson* decision, American law was firmly supportive of racial segregation. Houston and his colleagues, Thurgood Marshall and William Hastie, went from courtroom to courtroom challenging what they firmly believed to have been a hijacking of the 14th Amendment. Race was at the heart of these efforts because it was race that drove the Supreme Court to inject racism into the tributaries of this nation.

These giants had a profound belief in the Constitution's promise to establish justice, insure domestic tranquility and secure the blessings of liberty. Through the careful building of precedents, with much sacrifice and struggle, the Houston strategy resulted in the 1954 *Brown v. Board of Education* decision. That decision proved to be the launching pad for widespread attacks on racial discrimination.

Many other things operated in tandem with the litigation strategy that targeted that nation's racial affliction. At the beginning of World War II, organizations pressed President Franklin D. Roosevelt to issue an Executive Order that would require defense contractors to cease their discriminatory hiring practices. When he balked, A. Philip Randolph, founder of the Brotherhood of Sleeping Car Porters, and Walter White of the NAACP threatened a massive march on Washington. On the eve of the planned march, the president relented and issued an order banning discrimination in the defense industry and establishing a Fair Employment Practices Board.

After Harry Truman followed FDR as president, he issued a series of Executive Orders aimed to, among other things, end segregation in the Armed Forces. He broke ground with the appointment of William H. Hastie, the first African American to become a federal judge with lifetime tenure.

President Eisenhower renewed and extended the Truman orders covering government contracting and federal employment. He tapped his vice president, Richard Nixon, to oversee these programs aimed at ending racial discrimination in and by the federal government. During the Eisenhower administration, the first civil rights bill since Reconstruction was enacted in 1957 designed to deal with the barriers still existing that interfered with the ability of blacks to vote in the South.

Thereafter, John F. Kennedy introduced many other initiatives aimed at making the government more racially inclusive. Foremost among these actions was the appointment of minorities to sub-cabinet positions and, and in keeping with his campaign promise, appointing a number of blacks as district judges. He placed Thurgood Marshall on the Second Circuit and broke ground by appointing the first two blacks to serve as United States Attorneys–Cecil Poole and Merle M. McCurdy in Ohio.

I cite the foregoing to emphasize that race was at the heart of all of these activities. It should come as no surprise, then, that when the record, writings and views of a nominee appear to challenge the use of federal power to address the harmful vestiges of racist governmental policies, questions are raised and answers demanded. It should also come as no surprise that Black Americans and those who collaborated with us to effect change, are alarmed and wary that elevating such persons to the Supreme Court could result in an unraveling of the gains won at such a high price.

There is a tendency among persons who lack a sense of history to dismiss the claims raised by civil rights groups as nothing more than the whining of special interest groups. I'm old enough to know, firsthand, that such accusations are nothing new. In their day, Charles Houston, Thurgood Marshall, Martin Luther King, Jr., Medgar Evers and others who are now universally hailed as American heroes, were similarly accused of less-than-honorable motives. Yet, they kept their eyes on the prize and, through great sacrifice and commitment, pulled our nation back from the abyss. Their mission then and that mission now is not a "special interest"—it is the very core of our nation's creed. Mischaracterizing our concerns as irrelevant and cynical is simply wrong and an insult to the memory of those great Americans.

The legislative and judicial remedies aimed at ending the scourge of segregation do not belong to any particular party—they were the work of both Republicans and Democrats. The landmark *Brown v. Board of Education* opinion was authored by Chief Justice Earl Warren, a Republican who was appointed by a Republican president, Dwight D. Eisenhower. The most significant legislative accomplishments in the area of civil rights grew out of the leadership of President Kennedy and President Johnson but with the significant collaborative efforts of Republican Senators Everett Dirksen, Jacob Javits, John McCormack, Edward Brooke and Congressmen Emanuel Celler and William McColloch. These victories vindicated the faith of Black and White Americans, whose efforts were spearheaded by such pioneers as Clarence Mitchell, Jr. and Joseph Rauh, among others.

There is a daunting fear that as a result of the way federal judicial nominations were made and the confirmation process was conducted, that the ability of civil rights advocates to continue relying upon the federal courts to define and enforce remedies may have been seriously undercut.

Those who relied upon the jurisprudence developed and refined by Charles Hamilton Houston, Thurgood Marshall, William H. Hastie, and the civil rights bills enacted under the leadership of Clarence Mitchell, Whitney M. Young, Jr., Joseph Rauh and others, must be eternally vigilant and work to arouse the nation to the peril that confronts civil rights. As Justice Marshall warned, "scores of established constitutional liberties are now ripe for reconsideration." What was true when he wrote this is now, with the Supreme Court changed, even more true.

Racial Disparities Drive Prison Boom

by George E. Curry

"You could abort every Black baby in this country, and your crime rate would go down."

—*former Secretary of Education William Bennett*

Implicit in Bill Bennett's controversial 2005 comment on his syndicated radio program is the notion that black people are criminals and if you want to lower the U.S. crime rate, that could be accomplished by aborting all black babies. Of course, Bennett emphasized that he was speaking "hypothetically" and found such a prospect personally repugnant. Still, he made the assertion, a contention that he refused to back away from when later questioned about it.

If Bennett were interested in getting rid of practically all of our mass murderers, he could have proposed— "hypothetically," of course—that all white males be aborted. Then, we would not have had Charles Manson, the Boston Strangler (Albert De Salvo), Timothy McVeigh, Ted Bundy, the Son of Sam (David Berkowitz), the Unabomber (Ted Kaczynski), the University of Texas Sniper (Charles Whitman), Jeffrey Dahmer or John Wayne Gacy.

But he didn't mention white males—his comments where about all blacks as a race. In an attempt to contrast Bennett's "hypothetical" with American reality, I wrote a column that said, in part:

Even if one accepts Bennett's "hypothetical" assertion that if all Black babies were aborted, there would be a decline in the crime rate, that still would not provide a complete picture of what life would be like without Blacks.

If all African-American babies had been aborted, Whites might be crashing into one another at intersections. Garrett Morgan, a Black man, invented the first traffic signal. If the men survived the traffic, they might not have survived World War I. Morgan also invented the gas mask, which saved many lives in the war and today protects firemen and other emergency workers.

In Bill Bennett's world, even more people might be dying from heart attacks. Dr. Daniel Hale Williams, an African-American, performed the first open heart surgery in 1893.

Bennett would certainly be tired of walking up and down steps. Without Alexander Miles, the Black inventor of the elevator, that's what Americans would be left with. And if they didn't tire from climbing the steps, they might get tired of shifting gears in their automotive vehicles. Another Black man, Richard Spikes, invented the automatic gearshift.

Of course, an automatic gearshift wouldn't do them any good if they didn't have the spark plugs—invented by Edmond Berger, an African-American—under the hood.

A self-described family values person, Bennett couldn't imagine life without the baby buggy. Without the life of W.H. Richardson, an African-American, Bennett wouldn't have to imagine that kind of life—he would be experiencing it.

Life at home wouldn't be as pleasurable without the air conditioning unit invented by Frederick M. Jones, a Black man. Life without air conditioning would be bad enough, but to live without a refrigerator would be even worse. And that's what

Bennett would be doing if J. Standard, an African American, had been aborted.

If Bennett wanted to flee a burning apartment building, he would have to jump and take his chances. If Blacks hadn't been born, J.W. Winters would not have developed the fire escape ladder. Cutting the grass would be more of a chore, too. Bennett might have to utilize sling blades instead of using the lawn mower invented by L.A. Burr, an African American.

An educated person such as William Bennett can appreciate the need for an almanac and he can thank another African-American, Benjamin Banneker, for that. At some point, Bennett uses pencils. The pencil sharpener was invented by J. L. Love, an African-American. Even if the erudite Bennett prefers a fountain pen to a pencil, he would be out of luck if it had not been for Walter B. Purvis, the Black inventor.

From a pure entertainment perspective, can anyone really say they would have enjoyed watching professional sports without Jackie Robinson, Jim Brown, Bill Russell, Michael Jordan, Magic Johnson, Tiger Woods, Althea Gibson or Arthur Ashe?

Even the 2000 Republican National Convention in Philadelphia would have been souless without the appearances of Brian McKnight, Chaka Khan, the Temptations, Harold Melvin and the Blue Notes, the Delfonics and Aaron Neville, all of whom would have been aborted under Bennett's scenario.

Finally, Bill Bennett's Republican buddies—Retired Army General Colin Powell, Secretary of State Condoleezza Rice and HUD Secretary Al Jackson—would not have been in George W. Bush's administration—or any other one—if they had been aborted.

William Bennett is smart enough to know that all Blacks aren't criminals. And if all Black babies had been aborted, the nation would have lost far more than lawbreakers.[1]

Rather than focus on the numerous contributions African Americans have made, it is crime—or, at least the perception of it—that often colors the way African Americans are viewed in the United States.

The reality is that blacks are no more prone to crime than any other group.

"African Americans who use drugs are more likely to be arrested than other groups, and then to penetrate more deeply into the criminal justice system," according to a report by the Sentencing Project, a Washington, D.C.-based group that seeks alternatives to imprisoning non-violent drug offenders. "While African Americans constitute 13 percent of the nation's monthly drug users, they represent 35 percent of those persons arrested for drug crime, 53 percent of drug convictions and 58 percent of those in prison for drug offenses."[2] The report explained, "Higher arrest rates of African Americans generally reflect a law enforcement emphasis on inner-city areas, where drug sales are more likely to take place in open air drug markets and fewer treatment resources are available."

Racial disparities grow even wider in states with "three strikes and you're out" mandatory sentencing requirements. California, the nation's most populous state, is a case in point.

"Minorities tend to be arrested at higher rates than whites, then the dis-proportionality increases as they proceed through the system...African Americans constitute 6.5 percent of the state population but 21.7 percent of the felony arrests. Going deeper into the system, they constitute 29.7 percent of the prison population, 35.8 percent of second strikers and 44.7 percent of the third strikers.

"On the other hand, whites constitute 47.1 percent of the population but only 35.7 percent of felony arrests and 28.7 percent of the prison popula-tion. Whites constitute 26.1 percent of second strikers and 25.4 percent of third strikers. Thus, as cases move through the process into progressively harsher punishment, the proportion of whites diminishes while the pro-portion of African Americans increases."[3]

Figure 1

Race/Ethnicity of California's Population, Felony Arrests, Prison Population, and Strikers

Race/ Ethnicity	Population	Felony Arrests	Prison Population	Second Strikers	Third Strikers	All Strikers
Black	6.5%	21.7%	29.7%	35.8%	44.7%	37.4%
	2,222,816	92,312	46,250	12,700	3,334	16,034
Hispanic	32.6%	37.0%	35.9%	34.1%	25.6%	32.6%
	11,082,985	157,756	55,853	12,081	1,907	13,988
White	47.1%	35.7%	28.7%	26.1%	25.4%	26.0%
	16,047,989	152,099	44,756	9,245	1,896	11,141
Other	13.8%	5.6%	5.7%	4.0%	4.3%	4.1%
	4,689,408	23,658	8,863	1,436	321	1,757
California	100.0%	100.0%	100.0%	100.0%	100.0%	100.0%
	34,043,198	425,825	155,722	35,462	7,458	42,920

Source: Population: *Population Projections by Race/Ethnicity for California and Its Counties 2000-2005,* State of California, Department of Finance, Sacramento, California, May 2004. Online at: http://www.dof.ca.gov/HTML/DEMOGRAP/DRU_Publications/Projections/P-1_Tables.xls; Felony Arrests: "Adult Felony Arrests" as reported in *California Criminal Justice Profile–2002,* Table 22, California Attorney General, California Criminal Justice Statistics Center: Online at: http://justice.hdcdojnet.state.ca.us/cjsc_stats/prof02/index.htm; Prison Population: *Prison Census Data: Total Institution Population,* Table 4: Offenders by Ethnicity and Gender as of December 31, 2003, Data Analysis Unit, Estimates and Statistical Analysis Section, Offender Information Services Branch, California Department of Corrections, February 2004; Striker Data: *Second and Third Strikers in the Institution Population,* Table 3, Second and Third Strikers in the Institution Population by Gender, Racial/Ethnic Group and Type of Conviction, Data Analysis Unit, Estimates and Statistical Analysis Section, Offender Information Services Branch, California Department of Corrections, August 2004.

The United States imprisons more of its citizens than any country in the world. For years, the U.S. rate was higher than all industrialized nations and second only to Russia. However, Figure 2 shows, the United States incarcerates its citizens at a rate of 724 per 100,000 population, compared to 564 for Russia, 145 in England, 116 in Canada and 31 in India.

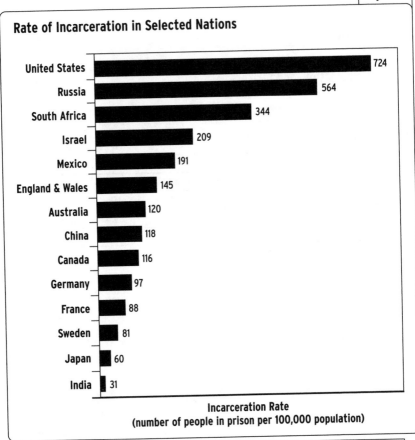

Rate of Incarceration in Selected Nations

Incarceration Rate
(number of people in prison per 100,000 population)

United States — 724
Russia — 564
South Africa — 344
Israel — 209
Mexico — 191
England & Wales — 145
Australia — 120
China — 118
Canada — 116
Germany — 97
France — 88
Sweden — 81
Japan — 60
India — 31

Source: Rate for the US from *Prisoners in 2004*; for all other nations, International Centre for Prison Studies available online at www.prisonstudies.org. Incarceration data were collected on varying dates and are the most current data available as of 2005.

The number of persons in jail and prison grew by 462,006 in the seven decades between 1910 and 1980. In the 1990s alone, that figure was almost doubled as the number of people in prison and jail increased by 816, 965.[4] The prison and jail population grew by almost 900 inmates a week between mid-2003 and mid-2004, reaching 2.1 million people or one in every 138 U.S. residents by last June.[5]

One study concluded, "The number of people behind bars not only dwarfs America's historical incarceration rates; it defies international comparisons as well. While America has about 5 percent of the world's population, almost one in four persons incarcerated worldwide are incarcerated in the U.S."[6]

That dramatic prison growth has been fueled primarily by harsher punishment for drug offenses.

"Responding to a perceived problem of high rates of drug abuse in the late 1970s, the Reagan administration and other political leaders officially launched a 'war on drugs' policy in 1982," recounts a report by the Sentencing Project. "Within a few years, both funding for drug law enforcement and a political focus on the drug war had increased substantially. As a result, there was a surge of arrests for drug offenses in the 1980s. The total of 581,000 arrests in 1980 nearly tripled to a record high of 1,584,000 by 1997 and continues to close at that level with 1,532,300 in 1999." [7]

Looking at it from a global perspective, the United States has 100,000 more persons behind bars *just for drug offenses* (458,131) than the European Union has *for all offenses* (356,626), even though the EU has 100 million more people than the U.S.[8]

The escalating arrest rates had another negative impact.

"As the number of arrests grew, so did the proportion of African Americans, from 24 percent of all drugs arrests in 1980 to 39 percent by 1993," says an October 1995 report from the Sentencing Project titled "Young Black Americans and the Criminal Justice System: Five Years Later." [9]

States followed the federal lead, enacting their own get-tough laws. Consequently, the federal government and every state now have mandatory sentencing laws, usurping the normal power of judges to use their discretion when considering a range of factors in determining prison terms. Most of the mandated laws cover drug-related drug offenses. [10]

Although the arrest numbers were up, most of them involved mid- to low-level dealers and users.

In 1992, the U.S. Sentencing Commission found that only 11 percent of federal drug defendants were high-level dealers. Another 34 percent were considered mid-level dealers and 55 percent were either street-level dealers or "mules," females used to transport drugs or money.[11]

Though perhaps unintended, the mandatory sentencing has had a disproportionate impact on Black youth and African-American women.

According to the Sentencing Project, 32 percent of all Black men between the ages of 20 and 29—were under some form of criminal justice system control in 1995, either in prison or jail or on probation or parole.[12]

As Figure 3 shows, almost 7 million Americans were either in jail, prison, or on probation or parole in 2004.

One study found that black youth were admitted to state public institutions for drug offenses at 48 times the rate for white youth.[13]

These numbers should not be viewed in a vacuum.

"An increasing numbers of young black men are arrested and incarcerated, their life prospects are seriously diminished. Their possibilities for gainful employment are reduced, thereby making them less attractive as marriage partners and unable to provide for children they father. This in turn contributes to the deepening of poverty in low-income communities."[14]

That's only half of the problem. As Figure 4 below shows, the fastest-growing segment of the prison population is black women, caught in the double-whammy of race and gender.

Figure 4

State Prisoners Incarcerated for Drug Offenses By Race/Ethnic Origin and Sex (1986 and 1991)

	1986		1991		% Increase	
	Male	Female	Male	Female	Male	Female
White (Non-Hispanic)	12,868	969	26,452	3,300	106%	241%
Black (Non-Hispanic)	13,974	667	73,932	6,193	429%	828%
Hispanic	8,484	664	35,965	2,843	324%	328%
Other	604	70	1,323	297	119%	324%
Total	35,930	2,370	137,672	12,633	283%	433%

Figure 3

Number of Persons Under Correctional Supervision

	Probation	Jail	Prison	Parole	Total
1980	1,118,097	183,988	319,598	220,438	1,842,100
1981	1,225,934	196,785	360,029	225,539	2,008,300
1982	1,357,264	209,582	402,914	224,604	2,194,400
1983	1,582,947	223,551	423,898	246,440	2,476,800
1984	1,740,948	234,500	448,264	266,992	2,690,700
1985	1,968,712	256,615	487,593	300,203	3,013,100
1986	2,114,621	274,444	526,436	325,638	3,241,100
1987	2,247,158	295,873	562,814	355,505	3,461,400
1988	2,356,483	343,569	607,766	407,977	3,715,800
1989	2,522,125	395,553	683,367	456,803	4,057,800
1990	2,670,234	405,320	743,382	531,407	4,350,300
1991	2,728,472	426,479	792,535	590,442	4,537,900
1992	2,811,611	444,584	850,566	658,601	4,765,400
1993	2,903,061	459,804	909,381	676,100	4,948,300
1994	2,981,022	486,474	990,147	690,371	5,148,000
1995	3,077,861	507,044	1,078,542	679,421	5,342,900
1996	3,164,996	518,492	1,127,528	679,733	5,490,700
1997	3,296,513	567,079	1,176,564	694,787	5,734,900
1998	3,670,441	592,462	1,224,469	696,385	6,134,200*
1999	3,779,922	605,943	1,287,172	714,457	6,340,800*
2000	3,826,209	621,149	1,316,333	723,898	6,445,100*
2001	3,931,731	631,240	1,330,007	732,333	6,581,700*
2002	4,024,067	665,475	1,367,547	750,934	6,758,800*
2003	4,144,782	691,301	1,392,796	745,125	6,936,600*
2004	4,151,125	713,990	1,421,911	765,355	6,996,500*

Note: The 2003 probation and parole counts are estimated and may differ from previously published numbers.
*Totals for 1998 through 2004 exclude probationers in jail or prison.
Source: Bureau of Justice Statistics Correctional Surveys (The Annual Probation Survey, National Prisoner Statistics, Survey of Jails, and The Annual Parole Survey.)

"...Justice Department data shows that between 1986 and 1991, the number of black, non-Hispanic women in state prisons for drug offenses nationwide increased more than eight-fold in this five-year period, from 667 to 6,193. This 828 percent increase was nearly double the increase for black non-Hispanic males and more than triple the increase for white non-Hispanic females."[15]

Contributing to that unprecedented growth are several factors unique to women.

In testimony before the Senate Judiciary Committee, Elaine Lord, the warden of New York State's maximum security prison for women, observed: "We need to be more honest with ourselves that the vast majority of women receiving prison sentences are not the business operatives of the drug networks. The glass ceiling seems to operate for women whether we are talking about legitimate or illegitimate business. They (women) are very small cogs in a very large system, not the organizers or backers of illegal drug empires."[16]

An often overlooked factor in the criminal justice system is the way consumption of certain drugs impacts prison sentences.

For example, there is a significant difference in the prison time given to those selling crack cocaine and powder cocaine, though each contain the same chemical mix. The U.S. Sentencing Commission has calculated that a person convicted of trafficking in five grams of crack with street value of $750 would receive the same sentence as a drug dealer selling 500 grams of powder cocaine valued at $50,000.[17]

"The harsher treatment of crack cocaine offenders may also be having a significant impact on young black women in particular since there are indications that women are more likely to use crack and are more likely to be involved in crack distribution relative to other drugs.

"U.S. Sentencing Commission data show that in fiscal year 1994 black women represented 82 percent of all women sentenced for drug offenses (trafficking and possession). Of black women sentenced for drug offenses overall, half were sentenced for crack offenses compared to 5 percent of all Hispanic women drug offenders and 7 percent of all white women."[18]

The warehousing of prisoners continues during a period in which crime rates have stabilized or decreased.

"America's fear of crime is driving our policies," says a report titled, "From Classrooms to Cell Blocks." The Justice Policy Institute study, written by Tara-Jen Ambrosio and Vincent Schiraldi, notes, "This fear of victimization, however, is unsubstantiated by the statistics. Over the last two decades crime rates in most categories have remained relatively stable (even though they may go up or down from year to year). Rape, robbery and aggravated assault have all shown yearly fluctuations but the overall trend has been stable or slightly downward. Murder, in particular, has remained remarkably stable since 1973, despite the enormous prison build-up."

The so-called drug war has not led to more violent offenders being locked up, as its sponsors had promised..

"Between 1980 and 1997, while the number of drug offenders entering prisons skyrocketed, the proportion of state prison space housing violent offenders declined from 55 percent to 47 percent," according to one report.[19]

From a financial perspective, money that would have normally gone to higher education has been diverted to prisons.

"Once a prison is built, the state will fill those cells with an increasing number of nonviolent offenders because there are simply not enough violent offenders to fill the cells," states one study. "These 'build-'em and fill-'em' policies are taking place at the expense of higher education. As more and more prison cells are built, fewer colleges are being constructed."[20]

The study also noted that throughout the 1980s, state spending for corrections increased by 95 percent while spending on higher education decreased by 6 percent.

As the data from *Cellblocks and Classrooms* in Figure 5 shows, the proportion of state and local spending on higher education decreased and spending for prisons dramatically increased.

Figure 5

In Most States, the Growth in funding for Prisons Dwarfed that for Higher Education. On Average, State Spending on Prisons Grew at 6 Times the Rate of Higher Education Funding (General Fund).

STATE	CHANGE IN STATE SPENDING ON HIGHER EDUCATION, 1985-2000	CHANGE IN STATE SPENDING ON CORRECTIONS, 1985-2000
AL	41%	107%
AK	-53%	45%
AR	32%	188%
AZ	50%	191%
CA	-16%	184%
CO	16%	366%
CT	37%	262%
DE	39%	156%
DC*	-7%	-5%
FL	88%	217%
GA*	93%	234%
HI	3%	164%
ID	64%	424%
IL	30%	110%
IN	39%	214%
IA	60%	107%
KS	30%	192%
KY	33%	164%
LA	6%	13%
ME	30%	75%
MD	37%	29%
MA	16%	273%
MI	27%	227%
MN	73%	148%
MS*	34%	185%
MO	52%	236%
MT	-14%	181%
NE	41%	148%
NV*	105%	107%

Figure 5

(continued)

STATE	CHANGE IN STATE SPENDING ON HIGHER EDUCATION, 1985-2000	CHANGE IN STATE SPENDING ON CORRECTIONS, 1985-2000
NH*	4%	138%
NJ	44%	137%
NM*	49%	48%
NY	-25%	137%
NC	8%	149%
ND	-17%	250%
OH	38%	211%
OK**	64%	128%
OR	64%	314%
PA	25%	413%
RI	-2%	188%
SC	29%	113%
SD	2%	214%
TN	22%	74%
TX*	47%	346%
UT	48%	195%
VT	-3%	179%
VA	42%	76%
WA	13%	138%
WV*	25%	139%
WI	29%	274%
WY*	-15%	110%
Average Percent Change of States	**29%**	**175%**

Source: National Association of State Budget Officers, State Expenditure Reports, 1985; 2000 (1987; 2001). *As some states did not publish fiscal data for 1985, we used the next available year for those states.

The *Cellblocks* study also stated: "The Post-Secondary Opportunities newsletter calculated that, in 1994, there were about 678,300 African-American males incarcerated in federal and state prisons and local jails, and 549,600 black males enrolled in higher education. Given what was known about government spending per full-time student in 1993, and the annual costs of incarceration, the researchers estimated that 'society now [1994] spends about $2.8 billion to higher educate black males, and $10 billion to lock them up.'"

What should be done?

Recommendations by the Sentencing Project and others include:

- Revise national spending priorities from two-thirds for law enforcement and one-third to treatment and prevention to strengthen the latter two categories;
- Repeal mandatory sentencing laws;
- Eliminate the sentencing disparities for those convicted of possessing crack cocaine and powder cocaine;
- Increase treatment options within the criminal justice system;
- Provide treatment programs that address the specific needs of women;
- Increase funding for public defender offices so that they can help divert substance-abusing defendants into treatment services;
- Approach drug abuse as primarily a community problem;
- Divert as many people from prison as possible, especially first-time, nonviolent offenders, without compromising public safety.

Conclusion

The so-called war on drugs has, in reality, been a war on U.S. citizens who find themselves ensnarled in the criminal justice system. The United States has the highest per capita incarceration rate in the world, even higher than the European Union, which has 1 million more citizens. Today, more than half of all prisoners are serving time on drug-related charges.

Amid an avalanche of bad news, however, are some encouraging signs of progress. Some states have begun experimenting with community corrections programs that can be operated more cheaply, and often more efficiently, than prisons. Citizens in some states are circulating ballot initiatives to allow judges more discretion in weighing all factors when handing down sentences. In 1994, Congress passed a "safety valve" to federal mandatory laws, permitting judges to sentence less than the mandatory terms if the offender has a limited prior record, is accused of a nonviolent offense, and is cooperating with the prosecutors.

Beyond the courtrooms and ballot boxes, America's future viability as a global competitor may rest on how it treats people at the margins of society.

The Metropolitan Center for Urban Education at New York University issued a report titled, "With All Deliberate Speed: Achievement, Citizenship and Diversity in American Education." The report stated, "We are losing ground and jobs to other countries—for example, China and India. Our nation's ability to sustain our long-term success increasingly depends on the very children we are not educating now."

It noted that only 31 percent of Latinos complete some college and 48 percent of African Americans, compared to 62 percent for whites and 80 percent for Asian Americans.

"According to the National Center on Education and the Economy, by the year 2020, the U.S. will need 14 million more college-trained workers than it will produce. Nowhere is college participation lower than among African-Americans and Hispanic youth; no where is the potential to meet our nation's need for college graduates greater."

And that requires making sure that we derail students on the brink of becoming mired in the prison-industrial complex. When we send them to college instead of prison, we strengthen them, their families and our country in the process.

NOTES

[1]Curry, George E., *Blacks are more than Criminals.* Column syndicated by the National Newspaper Publishers Association News Service for publication October 6, 5005. http://georgecurry.com/cgi-bin/news/search.cgi?category=1&keyword=Bennett

[2]*Drug Policy and the Criminal Justice System* (2001), a paper by the Sentencing Project, pp. 4–5.

[3]Scott Ehlers, Vincent Schiraldi and Eric Lotke, *Racial Divide: An Examination of California's Three Strikes Law on African Americans and Latinos*. Justice Policy Institute, October 2004. pp. 2–3

[4]Vincent Schiraldi, Barry Holman and Phillip Beatty, *Poor Prescription: The Costs of Imprisoning Drug Offenders in the United States*. Justice Policy Institute, July 2000. p. 2

[5]Bureau of Justice Statistics http://www.ojp.usdoj.gov/bjs/prisons.htm

[6]*Poor Prescription*, p. 3

[7]*Drug Policy and the Criminal Justice System*, p.1

[8]*Poor Prescription*, p.6

[9]By Marc Mauer and Tracy Huling, p. 9

[10]Bureau of Justice Assistance, 1966 National Survey of State Sentencing Structures, 1998, pp. 4–5.

[11]United States Sentencing Commission, Cocaine and Federal Sentencing Policy, 1955, p. 172.

[12]Mauer and Hauling, p.1.

[13]Michael Jones and Eileen Poe-Yamagata, *And Justice for Some?*, Building Blocks for Youth, Washington, D.C., April 2000

[14]*Young Black Americans*, p. 17.

[15]Ibid. pp. 19–20.

[16]Testimony before the Senate Judiciary Committee, June 1993. Quoted in *Young Black Americans*, p. 22.

[17]United States Sentencing Commission, *Cocaine and Federal Sentencing Policy,* February 1995, p. 175.

[18]*Young Black Americans,* p. 20.

[19]The Sentencing Project, Drug Policy and the Criminal Justice System," quoted in *Poor Prescription,* p. 3.

[20]*From Classrooms to Cell Blocks,* p. 3.

Sunday Morning Apartheid: A Diversity Study of the Sunday Morning Talk Shows

by Stephanie J. Jones

Concerned about the paucity of African Americans in the media venues that help to shape public opinion and influence policy, the National Urban League Policy Institute, the research, policy and advocacy arm of the National Urban League, last year undertook an in-depth study of the guest lineups of the Sunday morning political talk shows. In July 2005, the Institute released its preliminary findings, covering the five major cable and broadcast network Sunday morning talk shows for the period between January 1, 2004 and June 30, 2005. Among other things, the study concluded that 60 percent of the Sunday morning talk shows featured no black guests at all, either as interview subjects or roundtable participants and that 78 percent of the broadcasts contained no interviews with a black guest.

The National Urban League thereafter commissioned a more extensive follow-up study, covering the period from January 2004 through December 31, 2005. The findings of that study are detailed in this report.

Although the preliminary report was widely-publicized[1]—with the hope that networks would take it upon themselves to present a more diverse palette—the full two-year follow-up study showed no significant progress since publication of the initial study. Indeed, in some areas there has even been retrenchment.

For example, despite the extensive coverage of the preliminary report, the percentage of broadcasts with no black guests increased from 60 percent to 61 percent and the percentage of programs with no interviews with black guests went up from 78 percent to 80 percent.

In 1958, Dr. Martin Luther King, Jr. wrote: "It is appalling that the most segregated hour of Christian America is eleven o'clock on Sunday morning."[2] Today, nearly 50 years after Dr. King's incisive observation about America's churches, we are facing another form of Sunday Morning Apartheid—the Sunday morning network political talk shows.

Sunday morning talk shows are more than a mere source of news; they are a crucial staple in the public discussion, understanding and interpretation of politics and government and other public policy issues in the United States. Each Sunday, these programs signal what is considered important news and determine who are the newsmakers. Their selection and presentation of guests determine who are the experts on a topic and what voices and views will be considered authoritative. Sunday morning talk shows frame the perception and coverage of issues that have a substantial impact on the American public. Yet, with few exceptions, these programs consistently lack any African-American participation in the discussion of important issues—from the war in Iraq to judicial nominations to the economy to national security to foreign policy—and leave the impression that interest in and analysis of these topics are "for Whites only."

The exclusion of African-American voices is not unique to Sunday morning talk shows; with few exceptions, the television news outlets regularly fail to adequately include African Americans, other minorities and women in the vast majority of their news programming.[3]

The depth and breadth of the Sunday morning genre's influence was illustrated in December 2002 when Senate Majority Leader Trent Lott suggested during Strom Thurmond's 100th birthday celebration that the nation would have been better off if the segregationist had been elected president in 1948. Only two major news outlets, the *Washington Post* and ABC World News This Morning, briefly mentioned these remarks. However, the following Sunday, the Meet the Press roundtable discussion took up the incident. The next day, virtually every major newspaper and television network reported the story. Within a week, the story had escalated to the point where Sen. Lott was forced to resign his leadership position. By month's end, hundreds of stories had been published or broadcast about this incident.[4] While the extent of the influence of the Meet the

Press program cannot be accurately measured, there can be no doubt that its coverage put this story on the national media's radar screen," assuring that it would expand into a major news story.

As this example attests, the Sunday morning talk shows, which are watched by approximately 10 million viewers each week, have a significant impact upon the development of political and policy issues, public impressions and understanding of the news and political and policy events in Washington and across the nation. According to a recent study, 66 percent of African Americans rely upon the mainstream media for information about politics and the U.S. government.[5] Yet, when they turn to the main staple of news and analysis of issues of importance to them—the Sunday morning talk shows—politicians, journalists, opinion-makers, and viewers of all races are presented with a virtually all-white tableau:

- Ronald Reagan's death in June 2004 prompted the Sunday morning shows to devote their entire programs to his legacy. Of the nearly three dozen guests who appeared on talk shows that Sunday, only three were African-American—Secretary of State Colin Powell, National Security Advisor Condoleezza Rice, and Fox-TV commentator Juan Williams. On two of the five shows, the legacy of Reagan, a president who had an enormous effect on the black community, was assessed by all-white lineups.

- Throughout the second half of 2005, every Sunday morning talk show provided extensive coverage and discussion of the controversy over the use of the Senate filibuster, the death of U.S. Supreme Court Chief Justice William Rehnquist, the impending retirement of Justice Sandra Day O'Connor and the nominations of John Roberts and Samuel Alito to succeed them on the Supreme Court. These nominations were of great importance to African Americans, who were active and vocal in the speaking out about these issues.[6] Yet, not one Sunday morning talk show featured an interview with an African American about these topics.[7] Only one program—Fox News Sunday—included a black participant in its roundtable to discuss Supreme Court nominations and he was a regular commentator on the program.

- In September 2005, Sen. Barack Obama made his first Sunday talk show appearance since becoming a Senator eight months earlier; he was interviewed on This Week with George Stephanopoulos about race and poverty in the aftermath of Katrina. Sen. Obama's interview was followed by a roundtable discussion between columnists George Will and Fareed Zakaria, and former House Speaker Newt Gingrich, in which George Will, unchallenged, dismissed Sen. Obama's comments as being out of hand.

The value of diverse voices in the Sunday morning talk show political discussions was illustrated last fall after former Secretary of Education William Bennett claimed that "you could abort every Black baby in this country, and your crime rate would go down." Although the comments provoked a firestorm of controversy, the only Sunday morning roundtable to discuss these comments was the only Roundtable to feature a black participant: Fox News Sunday. During the lively colloquy, Fox commentator Juan Williams vigorously challenged the attempts to defend and downplay Bennett's remarks as misconstrued, irrelevant and inoffensive:

CHRIS WALLACE: Brit, is this much ado about something or about nothing?

BRIT HUME: Well, I think it's much ado, that's for sure. My sense is that it's much ado about not very much. It's not entirely clear to me what exactly his—the point he was making was if somebody argues is false—if somebody can help me with that, I might be able to comment better. What was false?

MARA LIASSON: False was saying that blacks are responsible for the crime rate.

HUME: Well, as a matter of fact, is it not the case that the per-capita crime rate among African Americans in this country is higher than other groups? If that's true, then it seems to me that's the point he was making.

The only thing I would think would be problematic about that is if it carries a suggestion that every black baby in the country is going to grow up and participate in crime at that same rate. That's an arguable point, it seems to me, at best.

LIASSON: I think the linking of race and crime in such a sweeping way is what caused the controversy. And everybody, from the White House on down, has separated themselves from those comments.

HUME: Right. But what is false here?

LIASSON: The linking of African-American babies and their later maturation as criminals.

HUME: I see.

...

JUAN WILLIAMS: You know, Brit, it really speaks to a deeply racist mindset to imagine America somehow as better off if we didn't have those black people around and all those racial issues and all these—you know, so many of these blacks end up in jail, as if they're criminals because they're black.

HUME: Juan, he didn't say that.

WILLIAMS: He certainly said it to me. That's what...

HUME: Excuse me.

WILLIAMS: ... I heard, Brit.

HUME: Excuse me. What he said was not that we should do that, but he said it would be morally reprehensible, impossible thing to do.

WILLIAMS: Right. Well, Brit...

HUME: He condemned that as an action.

WILLIAMS: Brit, if I'm sitting here on a national talk show and I say, you know, maybe if we killed off these white people, we wouldn't have so many mass murders in America, you'd say, Juan, are you out of your mind?

...

HUME: But here's the point about this. This is very important. There is a consensus in America, reached with great difficulty and after a long struggle over many years, that racial discrimination and especially, because of the history of this country, discrimination against African Americans, is a moral wrong.
The country agrees with that, which is why the charge of racist carries so much potential power against somebody. It is a potentially lethal weapon when wielded. And it is, in my view, a very reprehensible thing to do, to come along and take a man like Bill Bennett ... and suggest that because he does what clearly was a thought experiment, that he is racist. This is a cheap exploitation of the political circumstance in America which regards racism as utterly taboo and rightly so.

WILLIAMS: But he didn't just simply state it as a theory, Brit. I mean, when you have his standing in America, when you have a talk show, when you're speaking to an audience and make that suggestion out of the blue, as a non-sequitur to a question about Social Security, it strikes me as giving power to a deeply offensive idea and one that you point out, given our history in America with regard to race, has extraordinary power.

HUME: What the critics of him are doing is they're taking the hypothetical that he set up and condemned and denounced as if he had never condemned it. He did condemn it, and those words should have power, too.

WILLIAMS: No, I think what you're misunderstanding is it's the idea that he gave voice to this notion. If you were in a Nazi regime and said you know, gee, you know, a lot of these Jewish people have businesses and they dominate the academy, and therefore wouldn't it be better—that's not a good idea, Brit. Not a good idea to give voice to.

You could say, oh, it's my theory and it should be defensible as theory, but it has real power in a sociopolitical system.

HUME: It has power, but it doesn't have the kind of power you think it does. It has power to be used...

WILLIAMS: Well, as a black person, let me tell you, if you...

HUME: ... as a cudgel.

WILLIAMS: ... start talking about going after black people, it has power and impact on my life, Brit.[8]

We do not call for diversity in programming for diversity's sake, but because it will result in substantive benefits to the public. Broadening the pool of guests improves the tenor and quality of the debate, offers a richer and more varied array of information to viewers and helps fulfill the news outlets responsibility to educate its audience so that they will be better equipped to make informed political and policy choices. The National Urban League hopes the results of the Sunday Morning Apartheid Study will encourage the cable and network outlets to take positive and productive steps to provide their viewers a broader perspective of the public policy issues that impact us all.

EXECUTIVE SUMMARY

The Sunday Morning Apartheid study revealed, among other things, that during the two-year period studied:

- Sixty-one percent of all of the Sunday morning talk shows featured no black guests;
- Eighty percent of the broadcasts contained no interviews with black guests;
- Eight percent of the more than 2,800 guest appearances have been by black guests;
- One person—Juan Williams, a commentator for Fox News— accounts for 40 percent of all appearances by black guests;
- Three guests—Condoleezza Rice, Colin Powell, and Juan Williams— account for 65 percent of all appearances by black guests;
- The vast majority of interviews with black guests other than Rice and Powell focus on partisan political issues such as the 2004 Elections, rather than broader policy issues such as the economy, national security, and foreign affairs;
- Rice, Powell, and Williams have appeared almost twice as often as all other black guests.

The results of the Sunday Morning Apartheid study make clear that Sunday morning network and cable political talk shows, a significant source of information, analysis and opinion on government, politics, and social issues, consistently fail to include African Americans in their lineups.

METHODOLOGY

The National Urban League Policy Institute studied the five Sunday morning political network and cable talk shows—This Week with George Stephanopoulos (ABC), Face the Nation (CBS), Late Edition (CNN), Fox News Sunday (FOX) and Meet the Press (NBC)—reviewing and analyzing all programs broadcast between January 1, 2004 through December 31, 2005.

The study encompassed this particular genre for two reasons. First, unlike other network news and talk programs, the Sunday morning talk shows are generally similar in focus and format and, thus, offer consistent models for comparison. Second, Sunday morning talk shows play a unique and substantial role in the political discourse in America and, as such, deserve greater scrutiny.

In analyzing the data, the Institute examined several variables, including the:

- Number of programs with black guests v. number of programs with no black guests;
- Number of interviews with black guests v. number of interviews with no black guests;
- Number of roundtables with black participants v. number of roundtables with no black participants;
- Number of guest appearances by black guests v. guest appearances by non-black guests;
- Number of black guests v. non-black guests;
- Type of guest (Senator, House Member, Administration official, etc.);
- Frequency of appearances;
- Topics discussed by black guests

The study divided the programs into two segments: interviews and roundtable discussions.[9] For the purpose of our analysis, "guest" is defined as any individual who appeared on these programs one or more times, either as an interview subject or a roundtable participant. "Guest appearances" are defined as actual appearances by a guest. One guest could account for numerous guest appearances; for example, in determining the number of African Americans who have appeared as guests, Colin Powell is counted once. However, he has appeared 28 times during this period and, thus, accounts for 28 guest appearances. Therefore, the number black appearances, as limited as they are, are restricted to an even smaller pool of actual people.

FINDINGS

The study revealed, among other things, that during the two-year period studied:

- Sixty-one percent of all of the Sunday morning talk shows featured no black guests, either as interview subjects or roundtable participants;
- Eighty percent of the broadcasts contained no interviews with black guests;
- Eight percent of the more than 2,800 guest appearances have been by black guests;
- One person—Juan Williams, a commentator for Fox News— accounts for 40 percent of all appearances by black guests;
- Three guests—Condoleezza Rice, Colin Powell, and Juan Williams— account for 65 percent of all appearances by black guests;
- Rice, Powell, and Williams have appeared almost twice as often as all other black guests;
- The appearances by guests other than Rice, Powell and Williams account for less than 3 percent of all guest appearances;
- More than 750 people have appeared as guests once or more on the Sunday morning talk shows during the period studied. Thirty-six of them—fewer than 5 percent—were black;
- Three of the four programs presenting political roundtable discussions had no black participants in more than 80 percent of the shows broadcast;[10]
- While Senators and House Members appeared more than 712 times during the period, black representatives were featured only 16 times;
- Of the more than 113 Senators and House Members who appeared as guests, seven were black. Thirty-six of the 43 members of the Congressional Black Caucus never appeared on any of these programs during the 2-year period;
- Twenty-five administration officials appeared a total of 159 times during the period; Condoleezza Rice and Colin Powell were the only black administration officials to appear on any of these programs during the period covered;

- The vast majority of interviews with black guests other than Rice and Powell focused on partisan political issues such as the 2004 Elections, rather than broad policy issues such as the economy, national security, and foreign affairs;

- Only four African-American women—Donna Brazile, a political operative, Secretary of State Condoleezza Rice and journalists Gwen Ifill and Cynthia Tucker—appeared on any Sunday morning talk show during the period.

THIS WEEK WITH GEORGE STEPHANOPOULOS (ABC)
Generally

- Seventy-two percent of the broadcasts had no black guests, either as interview subjects or roundtable participants;

- Fifteen House members appeared, none of them were black.

Interviews

- More than 80 percent of the broadcasts contained no interviews with black guests;

- Nearly two-thirds—13—of the interviews with black guests were with Condoleezza Rice and Colin Powell;

- In 2004, Bishop Wilton Gregory, Barack Obama, Alan Keyes, and Rev. Floyd Flake were the only African Americans other than Colin Powell and Condoleezza Rice to be interviewed;

- In 2005, UN Secretary Kofi Annan, Sen. Barack Obama and New Orleans Mayor Ray Nagin were the only black guests other than Rice and Powell to be interviewed;

- Between January 2004 and June 2005, 60 percent of the broadcasts had no interviews with black guests; during the five months following the release of the preliminary report, the percentage of broadcasts with no interviews with black guests increased to 86 percent.

Roundtables

- Ninety percent of the roundtables had no black participants;

- In 2004, Donna Brazile, who appeared twice, was the only black guest to participate in a roundtable discussion until December, when Tavis Smiley and football player Darrell Green participated in a discussion about drugs in professional sports.

FACE THE NATION (CBS)

Generally

- Eighty-six percent of the broadcasts had no black guests;
- Senators appeared 108 times; Barack Obama, the lone black Senator, appeared once; he was interviewed on September 18, 2005 to discuss race and poverty in the aftermath of Katrina;
- House members appeared 15 times; the only black House member to participate , Rep. Charles Rangel, appeared once;
- In 2004, only three of 51 shows featured a black guest—Condoleeza Rice, Colin Powell and Barack Obama; each appeared once;
- Between January 2004 and June 2005, 84 percent of the broadcasts had no black guests; during the five months following the release of the preliminary study, the percentage of broadcasts with no interviews with black guests rose to 86 percent.

Interviews

- Ninety-one percent of the broadcasts had no interviews with black guests;
- In 2005, only six of 52 shows interviewed a black guest: Condoleezza Rice appeared twice, and Rep. Charles Rangel, Colin Powell, Rep. William Jefferson and Sen. Barack Obama each appeared once;
- Between January 2004 and June 2005, 87 percent of the broadcasts had no interviews with black guests; during the five months following the release of the preliminary study, the percentage of broadcasts with no interviews with black guests increased to 95 percent.

Roundtables

- 73 percent of roundtables had no black participants;
- *Washington Post* columnist Colbert King and author Stephen Carter were the only black guests to participate in the roundtables during the two-year period studied.
- Between January 2004 and June 2005, 40 percent of the broadcasts fea-

tured roundtables with no black participants; during the five months following the release of the preliminary study, the percentage of broadcasts with roundtable with no black participants rose to 83 percent.

LATE EDITION (CNN)

Interviews[11]

- Sixty-four percent of the broadcasts had no black guests;[11]
- Between January 2004 and June 2005, 60 percent of the broadcasts had no black guests; during the five-month period following the release of the preliminary study, the percentage of broadcasts with no black guests rose to 75 percent.

FOX NEWS SUNDAY (FOX)

Generally

- Ten percent of the broadcasts had no black guests;
- Absent Juan Williams, a regular Fox commentator, 86 percent of the broadcasts had no black guests;

Interviews

- Eighty-one percent of the broadcasts had no interviews with black guests;
- Throughout the two-year period studied, only four black guests other than Condoleezza Rice and Colin Powell were interviewed: Former Assistant Attorney General Eric Holder and Ohio Secretary of State J. Kenneth Blackwell were interviewed about the 2004 election, Bishop Wilton Gregory was interviewed about the Catholic Church abuse scandal and Washington, DC Mayor Anthony Williams, was interviewed about bringing professional baseball to the capital;
- Between January 30, 2005 and June 19, 2005, no black guests were interviewed;
- Between January 2004 and June 2005, 78 percent of the broadcasts had no interviews with black guests; in the six months following the release of the preliminary study, the percentage of broadcasts with no interviews with black guests increased to 90 percent.

Roundtables

- Ten percent of the roundtables had no black participants;[12]
- Throughout the two-year period studied, Juan Williams was the only black roundtable participant;
- On the nine Sundays that Juan Williams did not appear on a roundtable, he was either replaced by a white participant or not replaced at all.

MEET THE PRESS (NBC)

Generally

- Seventy-four percent of the broadcasts had no black guests;
- Of 93 House and Senate members that appeared, one—Rep. Charles Rangel—was black.

Interviews

- Eighty-five percent of the broadcasts had no interviews with Black guests;
- Throughout the two-year period studied, only four black guests other than Condoleezza Rice and Colin Powell were interviewed: Rep. Charles Rangel, Senator Barack Obama, UN Secretary General Kofi Annan, and New Orleans Mayor Ray Nagin.

Roundtables

- Seventy-five percent of the roundtables had no black participants;
- Only three black guests—journalists Gwen Ifill and Eugene Robinson and National Urban League President Marc Morial—participated in roundtables during the two-year period studied.

CONCLUSION

The results of the Sunday Morning Apartheid study make clear that Sunday morning network and cable political talk shows, a significant source of information, analysis and opinion on government, politics, and social issues, consistently fail to include African Americans in their lineups. We do no posit any theories or suggest any motivation for this exclusion, but simply present the numbers as they are.

And the numbers tell a stark story: unless an African American is a regular employee of one of the Sunday morning programs or sits in the highest level of the current administration, there is little chance of them appearing on these shows and even less chance that they will be asked to discuss anything beyond race, civil rights, partisan politics or sports.

According to the *Washington Post,* some network representatives responded to the Sunday Morning Apartheid preliminary report by suggesting that their selection of guests was driven by factors beyond their control:

> "Network officials said they rely on guests who are newsmakers, most of whom are white men in the top echelons of government.
>
> "'Face the Nation is a public affairs broadcast committed to booking the top newsmakers of the day,' said Donna Dees, a CBS News spokeswoman. 'Each week the broadcast strives to book guests who provide diverse opinions on the news topic of the day.'
>
> "Barbara Levin, senior communications director for NBC News, said that 'Meet the Press' interviews 'the same newsmakers who dominate the front pages and op-ed pages of every newspaper in America, including *The Washington Post.*'"[13]

The attempts to rationalize the failure to include Black guests on their Sunday morning programs by claiming to book "newsmakers who dominate the front pages and op-ed pages" ignores several salient points. First, the networks have the power to determine and often do determine who the newsmakers are, without need to rely upon the daily newspapers for guidance.

Second, the lack of diversity in the print media makes it an inadequate guide for determining who should be invited to appear on television talk shows.[14]

Third, the foregoing excuses do not explain the lack of minority journalists appearing on these programs, since it is journalists, not "newsmakers," who participate in roundtables and offer analysis and commentary about the news of the day Sunday after Sunday.[15] There are numerous African-American journalists, editorial writers and columnists working at major national newspapers such as the *New York Times*, *Washington Post*, *Los Angeles Times*, *Atlanta Constitution*, etc. In addition, outstanding black journalists write for the Black Press, local and regional papers across the country and could offer interesting and dynamic perspectives. African Americans also work in radio and TV and can be included in the roundtables.

Whatever is causing the dearth of African Americans on Sunday morning talk shows, lack of available qualified persons is not the problem. Yet, week after week, the Sunday morning talk shows continue to present their audiences with virtually all-white panels to deconstruct the issues of the day, even after being put on notice that this problem exists.

The National Urban League again urges the cable and broadcast networks to carefully consider these findings, assess their processes and aggressively work to diversify their on-air presentations.

It is time for Sunday Morning Apartheid to end.

Notes

[1] See, e.g., "Study: Few Blacks Seen on Talk Shows; Most Visits by Officials Such as Rice," *Washington Post*, July 31, 2005.

[2] *Stride Toward Freedom: The Montgomery Story*, 1958

[3] See, e.g., "Gender and Minority Representation in Network News," Center for Media and Public Affairs, February 2004; "Network Brownout 2003: The Portrayal of Latinos in Network Television News, 2002," National Association of Hispanic Journalists, December 2003; "Running in Place: Minorities and Women in Television," radio and television News Directors Association/Ball State University Annual Survey, 2005; "Who's Talking? An Analysis of Sunday Morning Talk Shows," The White House Project, December 2005.

[4] SOURCE: Lexis/Nexis

[5] "The Ethnic Media in America: The Giant Hidden in Plain Sight," Center for American Progress, LCCREF, New California Media, 2005

[6]See, e.g., "Civil Rights Groups, AFL-CIO Oppose Alito Confirmation," Associated Press, December 14, 2005; "Black Opposition to Alito Heats Up," BET, January 18, 2006,; see, also, e.g., Report on the Nomination of Samuel Alito, National Urban League Policy Institute, January 2006, Report on the Nomination of Samuel A. Alito, Jr., to the Supreme Court of the United States, NAACP Legal Defense and Educational Fund, Inc., December 2005.

[7]Sen. Barack Obama, during an interview on Katrina, Race and Poverty on the September 11, 2005 edition of This Week with George Stephanopoulos was asked to respond to a comment made by Democratic National Committee Chairman Howard Dean about postponing John Roberts' confirmation hearings in the wake of Hurricane Katrina, but was not otherwise interviewed about Supreme Court nominations.

[8]FOX News Sunday Transcript, October 2, 2005.

[9]Three of the five programs—This Week, Meet the Press and FOX News Sunday—regularly included political roundtable discussions. Face the Nation occasionally holds roundtable discussions. Late Edition does not feature roundtable discussions in its program.

[10]The fourth, FOX News Sunday featured a black roundtable participant on 95 out of 104 roundtables.

[11]Late Edition only presents interviews; it does not regularly feature roundtable discussions.

[12]Fox News Sunday is the only program to regularly feature a black roundtable participant, Juan Williams, who appeared in 95 out of 104 Roundtables.

[13]*Washington Post*, July 31, 2005.

[14]See, e.g., "News and Race: Models of Excellence," Poynter Institute, 2001.

[15]While many of the guest appearances on Sunday morning talk shows are by Senators, Members of Congress, Administration and foreign government officials, they comprise a minority of the guests who appear on these programs. The substantial majority—69 percent—of guests on these programs are journalists and non-federal government officials.

SUNDAY MORNING TALK SHOW GUESTS
JANUARY 2004-DECEMBER 2005

Black Guests:

1. Kofi Annan (2)
2. J. Kenneth Blackwell (1)
3. Donna Brazile (11)
4. Stephen Carter (1)
5. Clark Kent Ervin (1)
6. Floyd Flake (1)
7. Rep. Harold Ford, Jr. (2)
8. Darrell Green (1)
9. Bish. Wilton Gregory (2)
10. Grant Hill (1)
11. Eric Holder (2)
12. Gwen Ifill (7)
13. Rev. Jesse Jackson (3)
14. Rep. Jesse Jackson, Jr. (1)
15. Rep. William Jefferson (2)
16. Alan Keyes (2)
17. Colbert King (2)
18. Rep. Kendrick Meek (1)
19. Kweisi Mfume (3)
20. Marc Morial (1)
21. Mayor Ray Nagin (3)
22. Sen. Barack Obama (8)
23. Shaquille O'Neal (1)
24. Secy. Colin Powell (28)
25. Chief Charles Ramsey (1)
26. Rep. Charles Rangel (5)
27. Secy. Condoleezza Rice (29)
28. Eugene Robinson (6)
29. David Satcher (1)
30. Rev. Al Sharpton (4)
31. Tavis Smiley (1)
32. Lt. Gov. Michael Steele (1)
33. Rep. Bennie Thompson (2)
34. Cynthia Tucker (1)
35. Mayor Anthony Williams (1)
36. Juan Williams (95)

Non-Black Guests:

1. Amb. Paul Bremer (8)
2. Mahoud Abbas (1)
3. Adel Abdel-Mehdi (1)
4. Maumoon Abdul Gayoom (1)
5. King Abdullah (4)
6. Gen. John Abizaid (8)
7. Tim Adams (1)
8. Ahuma Adoduadji (1)
9. Hafez Al Mirazi (1)
10. Mithal Jamal Hussein Al-Alusi (1)
11. Madeleine Albright (11)
12. Buzz Aldrin (2)
13. Turki Al-Faisal (1)
14. Nail Al-Jubeir (1)
15. Adel Al-Jubeir (4)
16. Nasser al-Kidwa (1)
17. Iyad Allawi (3)
18. George Allen (10)
19. Mike Allen (5)
20. Thad Allen (8)
21. Rend Al-Rahim (3)
22. Mowaffak Al-Rubaie (6)
23. Muhammad Al-Sabah (1)
24. Farouk Al-Shara (1)
25. Ghazi al-Yawar (4)
26. John Lee Anderson (1)
27. Anonymous (1)
28. Jose Maria Anzar (1)
29. Nancy Aossey (1)
30. William Arkin (1)
31. Lance Armstrong (1)
32. Nan Aron (1)
33. Daniel Ayalon (2)
34. Whit Ayers (1)
35. Shaukat Aziz (2)
36. James Baker (4)
37. Rep. Tammy Baldwin (1)
38. Dan Balz (2)
39. Ki-Moon Ban (2)
40. Gov. Haley Barbour (4)
41. Fred Barnes (16)
42. John Barry (1)
43. Dan Bartlett (7)
44. Gary Bauer (3)
45. Sen. Evan Bayh (5)
46. Rand Beers (1)
47. Paul Begala (1)
48. Peter Beinart (1)
49. Carol Bellamy (2)
50. Sen. Robert Bennett (1)
51. Robert Bennett (1)
52. Bill Bennett (1)
53. Richard Ben-Veniste (8)
54. Sandy Berger (3)
55. Carl Bernstein (1)
56. John Berry (1)
57. Michael Beschloss (2)
58. Sen. Joseph Biden (50)
59. Hamad bin Jasim bin Al-Thanl (1)
60. Carmen bin Laden (1)
61. Bandar Bin Sultan (2)
62. Prime Min. Tony Blair (2)
63. Bradley Blakeman (1)
64. Hans Blix (1)
65. Rep. Roy Blunt (4)
66. Hal Bodler (1)
67. Thomas Bohlin (1)
68. Bono (1)
69. Gloria Borger (2)
70. Robert Bork (2)
71. Joseph Bottum (1)
72. Barbara Boxer (6)
73. Ben Bradlee (2)
74. Lakhdar Brahimi (2)
75. Sen. John Breaux (2)
76. Kristen Breitweiser (1)

77. Christine Brennan (1)
78. Stephen Breyer (1)
79. Doug Brinkley (1)
80. David Broder (18)
81. Tom Brokaw (4)
82. Albert Brooks (1)
83. David Brooks (10)
84. Soemadi Brotodiningrat (1)
85. Aaron Broussard (2)
86. Mark Malloh Brown (1)
87. Michael Brown (2)
88. Sen. Sam Brownback (5)
89. Ron Brownstein (15)
90. Zbignew Brzezinski (9)
91. Pat Buchanan (3)
92. John Buckley (2)
93. William F. Buckley, Jr. (1)
94. Elisabeth Bumiller (3)
95. Sen. Jim Bunning (1)
96. Anne Burke (2)
97. Deena Burnett (1)
98. Pres. George W. Bush (1)
99. Gov. Jeb Bush (1)
100. George H.W. Bush (2)
101. Laura Bush (2)
102. Diana Buttu (1)
103. Sen. Robert Byrd (2)
104. Thomas Cahill (1)
105. Mary Beth Cahill (2)
106. Charles Camarda (2)
107. Terry Campolo (1)
108. Jose Canseco (1)
109. Frank Carafa (1)
110. Andrew Card (5)
111. Jay Carney (1)
112. Brad Carson (1)
113. James Carville (5)
114. Steve Case (1)
115. George Casey (3)
116. Red Cavaney (1)
117. Sen. Lincoln Chafee (1)
118. Ahmad Chalabi (9)
119. Saxby Chambliss (3)
120. Dick Cheney (2)
121. Elizabeth Cheney (2)
122. Lynne Cheney (5)
123. Ron Chernow (1)
124. Michael Chertoff (7)
125. June Chwa (1)

126. Robert Clark (1)
127. Wesley Clark (10)
128. Richard Clarke (6)
129. Max Cleland (1)
130. Hillary Clinton (6)
131. Bill Clinton (4)
132. Sen. Tom Coburn (2)
133. Michael Cohen (1)
134. William Cohen (3)
135. Sen. Norm Coleman (2)
136. Sen. Susan Collins (6)
137. Eileen Collins (3)
138. Charles Colson (1)
139. Ceci Connolly (28)
140. Kent Conrad (1)
141. Charlie Cook (2)
142. Matthew Cooper (2)
143. Pete Coors (1)
144. Jeremy Copeland (1)
145. John Cornyn (7)
146. Jon Corzine (6)
147. Christopher Cox (7)
148. Catherine Crier (1)
149. Charles Curran (1)
150. Robert Dallek (1)
151. Sen. Tom Daschle (2)
152. Rep. Tom Davis (4)
153. Kevin Davis (1)
154. Lanny Davis (4)
155. John Dean (2)
156. Howard Dean (23)
157. Michael Deaver (1)
158. Tom DeLay (2)
159. Walter Dellinger (1)
160. Michael DeLong (2)
161. Justin DeMello (1)
162. Jim DeMint (1)
163. Jeremiah Denton (1)
164. Alan Dershowitz (1)
165. Tad Devine (9)
166. Giovanni di Stephano (1)
167. Larry Diamond (1)
168. Manny Diaz (1)
169. John Dickerson (2)
170. Joe DiGenova (1)
171. E.J. Dionne (13)
172. James Dobson (3)
173. Sen. Christopher Dodd (16)
174. Sen. Elizabeth Dole (2)

175. Robert Dole (8)
176. Sam Donaldson (7)
177. Sen. Byron Dorgan (2)
178. Steve Dorsey (1)
179. Linda Douglass (10)
180. Matthew Dowd (4)
181. Maureen Dowd (8)
182. Wayne Downing (2)
183. Rep. David Dreier (9)
184. Fr. Robert Drinan (2)
185. Ken Duberstein (4)
186. Tammy Duckworth (1)
187. Michael Duffy (5)
188. Richard Durbin (14)
189. Buddy Dyer (1)
190. Jim Dyke (1)
191. Lawrence Eagleburger (2)
192. Nina Easton (9)
193. Sen. John Edwards (22)
194. Elizabeth Edwards (2)
195. Jan Egeland (1)
196. Mohamed ElBaradei (3)
197. Joseph Ellis (2)
198. Rahm Emanuel (4)
199. Saeb Erakat (3)
200. Boomer Esiason (1)
201. Tucker Eskew (1)
202. Walter Eussenius (1)
203. Secy. Don Evans (2)
204. Jodie Evans (1)
205. Marty Evans (4)
206. Nabil Fahmy (1)
207. Steve Fainaru (1)
208. Richard Falkenrath (1)
209. Rev. Jerry Falwell (4)
210. Adib Farha (1)
211. Anthony Fauci (2)
212. Sen. Russ Feingold (10)
213. Sen. Dianne Feinstein (4)
214. John Feinstein (1)
215. Thomas Ferguson (1)
216. Brian Ferme (1)
217. Joseph Fessio (2)
218. Nathaniel Fick (1)
219. Dexter Filkins (1)
220. Harvey Fineberg (1)
221. Mark Fischetti (1)
222. Ellen Fitzpatrick (1)
223. Ray Flynn (2)

224. Stephen Flynn (2)
225. Rep. Mark Foley (2)
226. John Foley (1)
227. Steve Forbes (4)
228. Vicente Fox (2)
229. Hilary Franco (1)
230. Barney Frank (4)
231. Lois Frankel (2)
232. Al Franken (1)
233. Tommy Franks (2)
234. Louis Freeh (2)
235. Thomas Friedman (5)
236. Sen. Bill Frist (13)
237. Martin Frost (1)
238. David Frum (3)
239. Craig Fugate (1)
240. John Fund (1)
241. Terrance Gainer (1)
242. Joseph Galante (2)
243. Robert Gallucci (2)
244. Geoffrey Garin (1)
245. Bill Gates (1)
246. Marc Geller (1)
247. Francis Cardinal George (1)
248. Richard Gephardt (7)
249. Julie Gerberding (1)
250. Reuel Marc Gerecht (3)
251. David Gergen (5)
252. Jack Germond (1)
253. Shafeeq Ghabra (1)
254. Bobby Ghosh (1)
255. David Gibbs (1)
256. Paul Gigot (9)
257. Betty Gilbert (1)
258. Ed Gillespie (14)
259. Chester Gillis (2)
260. Newt Gingrich (15)
261. Manu Ginobili (1)
262. Ben Ginsberg (1)
263. Rudolph Giuliani (9)
264. John Glenn (1)
265. Dan Glickman (1)
266. Ed Goeas (1)
267. AG Alberto Gonzales (3)
268. Doris Kearns Goodwin (4)
269. Jamie Gorelick (1)
270. Sen. Slade Gorton (1)
271. Rep. Porter Goss (2)
272. Sen. Bob Graham (7)

273. Sen. Lindsey Graham (25)
274. David Graham (1)
275. Franklin Graham (1)
276. Gov. Jennifer Granholm (4)
277. Charles Grassley (1)
278. L. Patrick Gray (1)
279. C. Boyden Gray (4)
280. Andrew Greeley (1)
281. Judd Gregg (1)
282. David Gregory (4)
283. Michael Griffin (1)
284. Steve Grossman (1)
285. Grant Gullickson (1)
286. Richard Haass (3)
287. Stephen Hadley (7)
288. Sen. Chuck Hagel (23)
289. Alexander Haig (3)
290. Wayne Hale (2)
291. Mark Halperin (3)
292. Lee Hamilton (14)
293. Ned Handy (1)
294. Saad Hariri (1)
295. Sen. Tom Harkin (1)
296. Rep. Jane Harman (13)
297. Donald Harrington (1)
298. John Harris (3)
299. Peter Hart (1)
300. Thomas Hartman (1)
301. Bill Harwood (1)
302. John Harwood (15)
303. Speaker Dennis Hastert (4)
304. Sen. Orrin Hatch (8)
305. Stephen Hayes (4)
306. Rep. J.D. Hayworth (1)
307. Bernadine Healy (1)
308. Nathan Hecht (1)
309. Chris Heinz (2)
310. Seymour Hersh (10)
311. Issac Herzog (1)
312. Marvin Hier (1)
313. Carla Hills (1)
314. Richard Holbrooke (9)
315. Kip Holden (2)
316. A.J. Holloway (1)
317. Terry Holt (1)
318. Russel Honore (2)
319. David Horovitz (1)
320. Thomas Hoving (1)
321. Rep. Steny Hoyer (2)

322. Anthony Hsieh (1)
323. Reza Hslan (1)
324. Glen Hubbard (1)
325. Gov. Mike Huckabee (4)
326. Karen Hughes (3)
327. Brit Hume (80)
328. Jim Humphrey (1)
329. Al Hunt (1)
330. Duncan Hunter (8)
331. Billy Hunter (1)
332. John Hurley (1)
333. Sen. Kay Bailey Hutchison (5)
334. Pam Iorio (1)
335. Walter Isaacson (1)
336. Rep. Johnny Isakson (1)
337. Wolfgang Ischinger (3)
338. Feisal Istrabadi (1)
339. Bianca Jagger (1)
340. Faiza Janmohammad (1)
341. Steve Jarding (1)
342. Toni Jennings (1)
343. Rep. Bobby Jindal (2)
344. Haynes Johnson (1)
345. Robert Johnston (1)
346. Rep. Walter Jones (1)
347. Hamilton Jordan (1)
348. George Joulwan (7)
349. Hamid Karzai (4)
350. John Kasich (2)
351. Khurshid Kasuri (1)
352. Karim Kawar (1)
353. David Kay (4)
354. Katty Kay (4)
355. Thomas Kean (11)
356. Toby Keith (1)
357. Raymond Kelley (1)
358. James Kelly (1)
359. Ray Kelly (2)
360. Sen. Edward Kennedy (11)
361. Caroline Kennedy (1)
362. Bob Kerrey (7)
363. Sen. John Kerry (13)
364. Alexandra Kerry (1)
365. Teresa Heinz Kerry (1)
366. Vanessa Kerry (2)
367. Roula Khalaf (1)
368. Peter Khalil (1)
369. Zalmay Khalilzad (11)

370. Ziad Khassawneh (1)
371. Ghassan Khatib (1)
372. Rami Khouri (1)
373. Mark Kimmitt (1)
374. Rep. Peter King (1)
375. David Kirby (1)
376. Henry Kissinger (13)
377. Joe Klein (6)
378. Jack Klugman (1)
379. Douglas Kmeic (1)
380. Ed Koch (1)
381. Mort Kondracke (3)
382. Anne Kornblut (2)
383. Hal Koster (1)
384. Charles Krauthammer (10)
385. Bill Kristol (94)
386. Paul Krugman (3)
387. Laith Kubba (1)
388. Dennis Kucinich (2)
389. Howard Kurtz (1)
390. Sen. Jon Kyl (6)
391. Celinda Lake (1)
392. Richard Land (2)
393. Mitch Landrieu (1)
394. Sen. Mary Landrieu (6)
395. Tommy LaSorda (1)
396. Sen. Frank Lautenberg (1)
397. Bernard Cardinal Law (1)
398. Paul Laxalt (1)
399. Jim Leach (1)
400. Sen. Patrick Leahy (11)
401. Secy. Michael Leavitt (3)
402. John Lehman (5)
403. Carrie Lemack (2)
404. Carl Levin (29)
405. Jean-David Levitte (2)
406. Mara Liasson (67)
407. G. Gordon Liddy (1)
408. Sen. Joseph Lieberman (21)
409. Joe Lockhart (5)
410. Lara Logan (1)
411. Sen. Trent Lott (9)
412. Anne Graham Lotz (1)
413. Abbe Lowell (1)
414. James Loy (1)
415. Richard Lugar (24)
416. Mike Lupica (1)
417. Connie Mack (1)
418. Melissa Mahle (1)

419. Kanan Makiya (2)
420. Tom Malinowski (1)
421. Robert Manfred (1)
422. James Mann (1)
423. David Manning (2)
424. Mian Mansha (1)
425. Rosemary Mariner (1)
426. Rep. Ed Markey (1)
427. James Marks (2)
428. Liz Marlantes (1)
429. Paul Martin (1)
430. Robert Martin (1)
431. David Martin (1)
432. Mel Martinez (1)
433. Mary Matalin (8)
434. Ghulam Mattoo (1)
435. Garry Mauro (1)
436. Max Mayfield (3)
437. Terry McAuliffe (11)
438. Barry McCaffrey (2)
439. Sen. John McCain (36)
440. Theodore Cardinal McCarrick (4)
441. Sen. Mitch McConnell (18)
442. Patrick McCrummon (1)
443. David McCullough (1)
444. George McGovern (2)
445. Phil McGraw (1)
446. James McGreevey (1)
447. Brett McGurk (1)
448. Bill McInturff (2)
449. Hank McKinnell (1)
450. John McLaughlin (4)
451. Tony McPeak (1)
452. Morgan McPherson (1)
453. Jon Meacham (6)
454. Edwin Meese (2)
455. Ken Mehlman (9)
456. Gen. Montgomery Meigs (2)
457. Thomas Patrick Melady (1)
458. Jeralyn Merritt (1)
459. Jim Miklaszweski (1)
460. John Miller (3)
461. Sen. Zell Miller (2)
462. Hamid Mir (1)
463. George Mitchell (2)
464. Andrea Mitchell (4)
465. Michael Moore (1)
466. Stephen Moore (2)

467. Terry Moran (4)
468. Edmund Morris (1)
469. Amre Moussa (1)
470. Imad Moustapha (2)
471. Robert Moynihan (1)
472. Marwan Muasher (1)
473. Steve Murphy (1)
474. Rep. John Murtha (4)
475. Pervez Musharraf (3)
476. Lisa Myers (1)
477. Gen. Richard Myers (7)
478. David Nabarro (3)
479. Ralph Nadar (7)
480. Gov. Janet Napolitano (1)
481. Andrew Natsios (2)
482. Ahmed Nazif (2)
483. Ralph Neas (1)
484. Amb. John Negroponte (5)
485. Sen. Ben Nelson (1)
486. Sen. Bill Nelson (6)
487. Don Nelson (1)
488. Benjamin Netanyahu (1)
489. Gavin Newsom (1)
490. Greg Nickels (1)
491. Jack Nicklaus (1)
492. Don Nickles (1)
493. Peggy Noonan (3)
494. Michael Novak (1)
495. Robert Novak (4)
496. Sam Nunn (1)
497. Kate O'Beirne (6)
498. Margaret O'Brien Steinfels (1)
499. David O'Connell (3)
500. Van Odell (1)
501. Ehud Olmert (4)
502. Buster Olney (1)
503. John O'Neill (1)
504. Mary Aquin O'Neill (1)
505. Suze Orman (1)
506. Norm Ornstein (1)
507. Geneva Overholser (1)
508. Bill Owens (6)
509. Gen. Peter Pace (2)
510. Adnan Pachachi (7)
511. George Packer (1)
512. Susan Page (3)
513. Farah Pahlavi (1)
514. Reza Pahlavi (1)

515. Leon Panetta (4)
516. Gov. George Pataki (3)
517. Gov. Tim Pawlenty (1)
518. Rep. Nancy Pelosi (7)
519. Mike Pence (1)
520. Shimon Peres (1)
521. Tony Perkins (2)
522. Richard Perle (9)
523. Gov. Rick Perry (3)
524. David Petraeus (1)
525. Joseph Petro (1)
526. John Peter Pham (1)
527. Guy Phillipe (1)
528. Kasit Piromaya (1)
529. Byron Pitts (1)
530. Gary Player (1)
531. John Podesta (7)
532. Barbara Porchia (1)
533. Rep. Rob Portman (1)
534. Dana Priest (1)
535. Romano Prodi (1)
536. Mark Pryor (1)
537. Stephen Push (1)
538. Vladimir Putin (1)
539. Gerhard Putnam-
     Cramer (1)
540. Ashraf Qazi (1)
541. Jack Quinn (1)
542. Marc Racicot (11)
543. Martha Raddatz (4)
544. Howell Raines (1)
545. Rania (1)
546. Ed Rappaport (2)
547. Robert Ray (2)
548. Nancy Reagan (1)
549. Irwin Redlener (1)
550. Sen. Jack Reed (5)
551. Ralph Reed (1)
552. Thomas Reese (1)
553. Dana Reeve (1)
554. Robert Reich (8)
555. Sen. Harry Reid (6)
556. John Reid (2)
557. Gov. Ed Rendell (7)
558. James Reston, Jr. (1)
559. Tom Reynolds (2)
560. Frank Rich (1)
561. Barry Richard (1)
562. Gov. Bill Richardson (14)

563. Paul Rieckhoff (1)
564. Justin Rigali (1)
565. Sen. Pat Roberts (32)
566. John Roberts (1)
567. Cokie Roberts (23)
568. Rev. Pat Robertson (4)
569. Walter Robinson (1)
570. Sen. Jay Rockefeller (16)
571. Terje Roed-Larson (1)
572. Tim Roemer (3)
573. Ed Rollins (1)
574. Mitt Romney (3)
575. Steven Rosenberg (1)
576. Ileana Ros-Lehtinen (1)
577. Dennis Ross (1)
578. Karl Rove (2)
579. Alissa Rubin (1)
580. Robert Rubin (1)
581. Secy. Donald Rumsfeld (17)
582. Tim Russert (1)
583. Michael Ryan (1)
584. Mikhail Saakashvili (1)
585. William Safire (10)
586. Ken Salazar (1)
587. Zainab Salbi (1)
588. Barham Salih (4)
589. Bill Sammon (4)
590. Rep. Loretta Sanchez (1)
591. Gov. Mark Sanford (1)
592. Sen. Rick Santorum (7)
593. Dave Saunders (1)
594. Michael Scheuer (2)
595. Bobby Schindler (1)
596. David Schindler (1)
597. Doug Schoen (1)
598. Gary Schroen (2)
599. Catrin Schulte-Hillen (1)
600. William Schultz (1)
601. Chuck Schumer (18)
602. Gov. Arnold
     Schwarzenegger (3)
603. Brent Scowcroft (2)
604. Jay Sekulow (1)
605. Ronen Sen (1)
606. Dan Senor (3)
607. James Sensenbrenner (1)
608. Jeff Sessions (1)
609. Buthaina Shaaban (2)
610. Nabil Sha'ath (2)

611. John Shadegg (1)
612. Anthony Shadid (1)
613. Jeanne Shaheen (1)
614. Natan Sharansky (1)
615. Rep. Christopher Shays (4)
616. Cindy Sheehan (1)
617. Wendy Sherman (2)
618. Thaksin Shinawatra (1)
619. Claire Shipman (8)
620. Bob Shrum (3)
621. Muzammil Siddiqi (1)
622. Hugh Sidey (1)
623. Roger Simon (6)
624. Allen Sinai (1)
625. Secy. John Snow (6)
626. Sen. Olympia Snowe (1)
627. Mira Sorvino (1)
628. Larry Speakes (1)
629. Sen. Arlen Specter (20)
630. Gene Sperling (5)
631. Steven Spielberg (1)
632. Eliot Spitzer (1)
633. Barbara Springer (1)
634. Kenneth Starr (1)
635. Peter Steinfels (1)
636. David Stern (1)
637. Jessica Stern (1)
638. Stuart Stevens (1)
639. John Strynkowski (1)
640. Devinda Subasinghe (1)
641. Samir Sumaidaie (1)
642. Sen. John Sununu (4)
643. Ron Suskind (1)
644. Qubad Talabani (1)
645. Jalal Talabani (5)
646. Bill Taylor (1)
647. Stuart Taylor (1)
648. Inez Tenenbaum (1)
649. Norm Thagard (1)
650. Michael Thawley (1)
651. Rep. Bill Thomas (1)
652. Andy Thomas (1)
653. Evan Thomas (1)
654. James Thompson (1)
655. Fred Thompson (2)
656. Richard Thornburgh (3)
657. Sen. John Thune (4)
658. Mike Tidwell (1)
659. John Tierney (1)

660. Chuck Todd (1)
661. William Tomlinson (1)
662. Nina Totenberg (3)
663. Frances Townsend (3)
664. Stephen Trammell (1)
665. Laurence Tribe (1)
666. Joe Trippi (1)
667. Donald Trump (2)
668. Karen Tumulty (1)
669. Jonathan Turley (1)
670. Stansfield Turner (4)
671. Ivor Van Heerden (2)
672. Katrina Vanden Heuvel (2)
673. Gov. Tom Vilsack (4)
674. Rep. David Vitter (6)
675. Michael Waldman (2)
676. Mike Wallace (1)
677. Jim Wallis (2)
678. Mary Ann Walsh (1)
679. Gov. Mark Warner (1)

680. Sen. John Warner (11)
681. Rep. Debbie Wasserman-
      Shultz (1)
682. Rep. Henry Waxman (1)
683. George Weigel (1)
684. Jack Welch (2)
685. William Weld (1)
686. Curt Weldon (1)
687. Dave Weldon (2)
688. David Wessel (1)
689. Francis West (1)
690. Carlos Westendorp (1)
691. Stephen Whitcomb (1)
692. Bill White (1)
693. Tom White (1)
694. Christine Todd Whitman (2)
695. Elie Wiesel (1)
696. Lawrence Wilkerson (2)
697. George Will (77)

698. Pete Williams (1)
699. Joseph Wilson (4)
700. Rhonda Winfield (1)
701. James Wolfensohn (1)
702. Guy Womack (1)
703. Judy Woodruff (4)
704. Bob Woodward (5)
705. James Woolsey (2)
706. Robin Wright (6)
707. Sen. Ron Wyden (1)
708. David Yepsen (2)
709. Byron York (4)
710. Ronald Young, Jr. (1)
711. Fareed Zakaria (34)
712. Javad Zarif (2)
713. Hoshyar Zebari (5)
714. Gen. Anthony Zinni (2)
715. James Zogby (1)
716. Mort Zuckerman (2)

CONTACT INFORMATION FOR
SUNDAY MORNING TALK SHOW PRODUCERS

This Week with George Stephanopoulos (ABC)

1717 DeSales Street, NW

Washington, DC 20036

(202) 222-7100

Face the Nation (CBS)

2020 M Street, NW

Washington, DC 20036

(202) 457-4481

Late Edition (CNN)

One CNN Center

Box 105366

Atlanta, GA 30303

(404) 827-1500

Fox News Sunday (FOX)

400 North Capitol Street, NW

Washington, DC 20001

(202) 824-6400

Meet the Press (NBC)

4001 Nebraska Avenue, NW

Washington, DC 20016

(202) 885-4598

CHARTS AND FIGURES

Table 1

Broadcasts

	THIS WEEK	FACE THE NATION	LATE EDITION	FOX NEWS SUNDAY	MEET THE PRESS	OVERALL
Number of Broadcasts	102	103	102	104	103	514
Number of Broadcasts with No Black Guests	73	89	65	10	76	313
Percentage of Shows With No Black Guests	**72%**	**86%**	**64%**	**10%**	**74%**	**61%**

Table 2

Interviews

	THIS WEEK	FACE THE NATION	LATE EDITION	FOX NEWS SUNDAY	MEET THE PRESS	OVERALL
Number of Broadcasts with Interviews	102	101	102	104	102	511
Number of Broadcasts with No Interviews with Black Guests	82	92	63	84	87	408
Percentage of Broadcasts with No Interviews with Black Guests	**80%**	**92%**	**62%**	**81%**	**85%**	**80%**

Table 3

Guest Appearances (Interviews and Roundtables)

	THIS WEEK	FACE THE NATION	LATE EDITION	FOX NEWS SUNDAY	MEET THE PRESS	OVERALL
Total Number of Guest Appearances	548	251	855	724	450	2,828
Total Number of Appearances by Black Guests	32	14	45	113	29	233
Percentage of Guest Appearances by Black Guests	**6%**	**6%**	**5%**	**16%**	**6%**	**8%**

Table 4

Number of Appearances by Black Guests

	NUMBER OF APPEARANCES	PERCENTAGE OF APPEARANCES
Juan Williams	95	40.6%
Condoleezza Rice	29	12.4%
Colin Powell	28	12.0%
Donna Brazile	11	4.7%
Barack Obama	8	3.4%
Gwen Ifill	7	3.0%
Eugene Robinson	6	2.6%
Charles Rangel	5	2.1%
Al Sharpton	4	1.7%
Jesse Jackson	3	1.3%
Kweisi Mfume	3	1.3%
Ray Nagin	3	1.3%
Kofi Annan	2	0.9%
Harold Ford, Jr.	2	0.9%
Wilton Gregory	2	0.9%
Eric Holder	2	0.9%
William Jefferson	2	0.9%
Alan Keyes	2	0.9%
Colbert King	2	0.9%
Bennie Thompson	2	0.9%
Kenneth Blackwell	1	0.4%
Stephen Carter	1	0.4%
Clark Kent Ervin	1	0.4%
Floyd Flake	1	0.4%
Darrell Green	1	0.4%
Grant Hill	1	0.4%
Jesse Jackson, Jr.	1	0.4%
Kendrick Meek	1	0.4%
Marc Morial	1	0.4%
Shaquille O'Neal	1	0.4%
Charles Ramsey	1	0.4%
David Satcher	1	0.4%
Tavis Smiley	1	0.4%
Michael Steele	1	0.4%
Cynthia Tucker	1	0.4%
Anthony Williams	1	0.4%

Table 5

Number of Guests

	THIS WEEK	FACE THE NATION	LATE EDITION	FOX NEWS SUNDAY	MEET THE PRESS	OVERALL
Number of Guests	248	143	430	192	240	752
Number of Black Guests	13	6	6	7	10	36
Percentage of Black Guests	**5%**	**4%**	**1%**	**4%**	**4%**	**5%**

Table 6

Number of Black Roundtable Guests on This Week, Face the Nation and Meet the Press

	THIS WEEK	FACE THE NATION	MEET THE PRESS	OVERALL
Number of Roundtables	90	143	61	163
Number of Roundtables with No Black Guests	78	8	45	131
Percentage of Roundtables with No Black Guests	**87%**	**67%**	**74%**	**80%**

Table 7

Number of Appearances by Black Senators and Representatives

	THIS WEEK	FACE THE NATION	LATE EDITION	FOX NEWS SUNDAY	MEET THE PRESS	OVERALL
Number of Appearances by Senators and House Members	137	123	225	131	96	712
Number of Appearances by Black Senators and House Members	1	2	11	0	2	16
Percentage of Appearances by Black Senators and House Members	**0.7%**	**2%**	**5%**	**4%**	**2%**	**2%**

Table 8

Number of Black House and Senate Members Appearing as Guests

	THIS WEEK	FACE THE NATION	LATE EDITION	FOX NEWS SUNDAY	MEET THE PRESS	OVERALL
Number of House and Senate Members Appearing as Guests	64	123	78	55	58	113
Number of Black House and Senate Members Appearing as Guests	1	2	6	0	1	7
Percentage of Black House and Senate Members Appearing as Guests	2%	4%	8%	0%	2%	6%

| Table 9 |

Administration Officials Appearing as Guests

GUEST	NUMBER OF APPEARANCES
Condoleezza Rice	29
Colin Powell	28
Donald Rumsfeld	17
Paul Bremer	8
Dan Bartlett	7
Michael Chertoff	7
Stephen Hadley	7
Richard Myers	7
John Snow	6
Andrew Card	5
John Negroponte	5
George Casey	3
Alberto Gonzales	3
Karen Hughes	3
Michael Leavitt	3
Frances Townsend	3
Dick Cheney	2
Wayne Downing	2
Don Evans	2
Tommy Franks	2
Montgomery Meigs	2
Peter Pace	2
Karl Rove	2
Anthony Zinni	2
George W. Bush	1

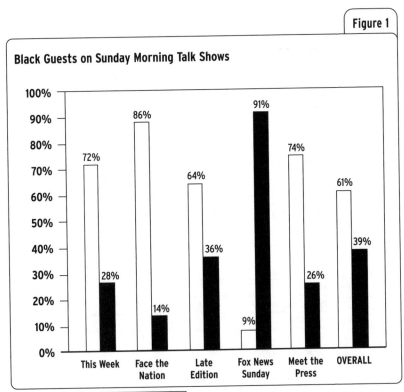

Figure 1

Black Guests on Sunday Morning Talk Shows

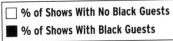

□ % of Shows With No Black Guests
■ % of Shows With Black Guests

Table 10

FULL STUDY (January 1, 2004 - December 31, 2005)

BY BROADCAST	THIS WEEK	FACE THE NATION	LATE EDITION	FOX NEWS SUNDAY	MEET THE PRESS	OVERALL
Number of Broadcasts	102	103	102	104	103	514
Number of Broadcasts with No Black Guests	73	89	65	9	76	312
Percentage of Shows with No Black Guests	**72%**	**86%**	**64%**	**9%**	**74%**	**61%**
Number of Broadcasts with One Black Guest (interviews and roundtables combined)	26	14	31	77	25	173
Percentage of Shows with One Black Guest	**25%**	**14%**	**30%**	**74%**	**24%**	**34%**
Number of Broadcasts with Two Black Guests (interviews and roundtables combined)	3	0	5	17	2	27
Percentage of Shows with Two Black Guests	**3%**	**0%**	**5%**	**16%**	**2%**	**5%**
Number of Broadcasts with More Than Two Black Guests (interviews and roundtables combined)	0	0	1	1	0	2
Percentage of Broadcasts with More Than Two Black Guests (interviews and roundtables combined)	**0%**	**0%**	**1%**	**1%**	**0%**	**0.4%**
GUEST APPEARANCES						
Total Number of Guest Appearances	548	251	855	728	450	2,832
Total Number of Appearances by Black Guests	32	14	45	114	29	234
Percentage of Guest Appearances by Black Guests	**6%**	**6%**	**5%**	**16%**	**6%**	**8%**
GUESTS						
Number of Guests	248	143	430	192	240	752
Number of Black Guests	13	6	6	7	10	36
Percentage of Black Guests	**5%**	**4%**	**1%**	**4%**	**4%**	**5%**

Table 10

FULL STUDY (January 1, 2004 - December 31, 2005, continued)

	THIS WEEK	FACE THE NATION	LATE EDITION	FOX NEWS SUNDAY	MEET THE PRESS	OVERALL
INTERVIEWS						
Number of Broadcasts with Interviews	102	101	102	104	102	511
Number of Broadcasts with No Interviews with Black Guests	82	92	63	84	87	408
Percentage of Broadcasts with No Interviews with Black Guests	**80%**	**91%**	**62%**	**81%**	**85%**	**80%**
Number of Interview Appearances	267	224	855	309	257	1,912
Number of Interview Appearances by Black Guests	21	11	45	19	15	111
Percentage of Interview Appearances by Black Guests	**8%**	**5%**	**5%**	**6%**	**6%**	**6%**
Number of Interview Guests	166	121	430	180	168	1,065
Number of Black Interview Guests	8	4	23	6	6	47
Percentage of Black Interview Guests	**5%**	**3%**	**5%**	**3%**	**4%**	**4%**
ROUNDTABLES						
Number of Roundtables	87	11		104	60	262
Number of Roundtables with No Black Guests	78	8		9	45	140
Percentage of Roundtables with No Black Guests	**90%**	**73%**		**9%**	**75%**	**53%**
Number of Roundtable Appearances	281	27		419	193	920
Number of Roundtable Appearances by Black Guests	11	3		95	14	123
Percentage of Roundtable Appearances by Black Guests	**4%**	**11%**		**23%**	**7%**	**13%**
Number of Roundtable Guests	82	22		12	72	188
Number of Black Roundtable Guests	5	2		1	12	20
Percentage of Black Roundtable Guests	**6%**	**9%**		**8%**	**17%**	**11%**

Table 10

FULL STUDY (January 1, 2004 - December 31, 2005, continued)

TYPE OF GUEST	THIS WEEK	FACE THE NATION	LATE EDITION	FOX NEWS SUNDAY	MEET THE PRESS	OVERALL
SENATORS						
Number of Senators	49	36	50	41	40	70
Number of Black Senators	1	1	0	0	0	1
Percentage of Black Senators Appearing as Guests	2%	3%	0%	0%	0%	1%
Number of Appearances by Senators	115	108	173	113	75	584
Number of Appearances by Black Senators	1	1	1	0	0	3
Percentage of Appearances by Black Senators	1%	1%	1%	0%	0%	1%
HOUSE MEMBERS						
Number of House Members	15	15	28	14	18	43
Number of Black House Members	0	1	6	0	1	6
Percentage of Black House Members Appearing as Guests	0%	7%	21%	0%	6%	14%
Number of Appearances by House Members	22	15	52	18	21	128
Number of Appearances by Black House Members	0	1	10	0	2	13
Percentage of Appearances by Black House Members	0%	7%	19%	0%	9%	10%
ADMINISTRATION OFFICIALS						
Administration Officials	16	9	16	16	17	25
Black Administration Officials	2	2	2	2	2	2
Percentage of Black Administration Officials Appearing as Guests	12%	22%	12%	12%	12%	8%
Number of Appearances by Administration Officials	32	20	39	40	28	159
Number of Appearances by Black Administration Officials	13	8	16	14	9	60
Percentage of Appearances by Black Administration Officials	41%	40%	41%	35%	32%	38%

Table 11

PRELIMINARY STUDY (January 2004 - June 2005)

	THIS WEEK	FACE THE NATION	LATE EDITION	FOX NEWS SUNDAY	MEET THE PRESS	OVERALL
BY BROADCAST						
Number of Broadcasts	77	77	78	78	78	388
Number of Broadcasts with No Black Guests	55	65	47	7	58	232
Percentage of Shows with No Black Guests	**71%**	**84%**	**60%**	**9%**	**74%**	**60%**
Number of Broadcasts with One Black Guest (interviews and roundtables combined)	19	11	26	56	19	131
Percentage of Shows with One Black Guest	**25%**	**14%**	**33%**	**72%**	**24%**	**34%**
Number of Broadcasts with Two Black Guests (interviews and roundtables combined)	3	0	5	14	1	23
Percentage of Shows with Two Black Guests	**4%**	**0%**	**6%**	**18%**	**1%**	**6%**
Number of Broadcasts with More Than Two Black Guests (interviews and roundtables combined)	0	0	0	1	0	1
Percentage of Broadcasts with More Than Two Black Guests (interviews and roundtables combined)	**0%**	**0%**	**0%**	**1%**	**0%**	**0.26%**
GUEST APPEARANCES						
Total Number of Guest Appearances	419	176	662	539	315	2111
Total Number of Appearances by Black Guests	25	11	36	87	21	180
Percentage of Guest Appearances by Black Guests	**6%**	**6%**	**5%**	**16%**	**7%**	**9%**
GUESTS						
Number of Guests	196	110	356	149	191	
Number of Black Guests	9	5	9	7	7	
Percentage of Black Guests	**5%**	**5%**	**3%**	**5%**	**4%**	

Table 11

PRELIMINARY STUDY (January 2004 - June 2005, continued)

	THIS WEEK	FACE THE NATION	LATE EDITION	FOX NEWS SUNDAY	MEET THE PRESS	OVERALL
INTERVIEWS						
Number of Broadcasts with Interviews	77	76	78	78	77	386
Number of Broadcasts with No Interviews with Black Guests	60	66	47	61	66	300
Percentage of Broadcasts with no Interviews with Black Guests	78%	87%	60%	78%	86%	78%
Number of Interview Appearances	196	164	662	219	184	1425
Number of Interview Appearances by Black Guests	18	9	36	16	12	91
Percentage of Interview Appearances by Black Guests	9%	5%	5%	7%	7%	6%
ROUNDTABLES						
Number of Roundtables	71	5	n/a	76	39	191
Number of Roundtables with No Black Participants	65	2	n/a	67	8	142
Percentage of Roundtables with No Black Participants	92%	40%		88%	21%	74%
Number of Roundtable Guest Appearances	199	10	n/a	322	120	651
Number of Black Roundtable Guest Appearances	7	2	n/a	71	9	89
Percentage of Black Roundtable Guest Appearances	4%	20%	n/a	22%	8%	14%

Table 12

POST-PRELIMINARY STUDY (August 2005 - December 2005)

	THIS WEEK	FACE THE NATION	LATE EDITION	FOX NEWS SUNDAY	MEET THE PRESS	OVERALL
Number of Broadcasts	21	21	20	21	20	103
Number of Broadcasts with No Black Guests	14	18	15	0	13	60
Percentage of Shows with No Black Guests	**67%**	**86%**	**75%**	**0%**	**65%**	**58%**
Number of Broadcasts with Interviews	21	20	20	21	20	102
Number of Broadcasts with No Black Interview Guests	18	19	15	19	17	88
Percentage of Shows with No Black Interview Guests	**86%**	**95%**	**75%**	**90%**	**85%**	**86%**
Number of Broadcasts with Roundtables	15	6	0	21	13	55
Number of Broadcasts with No Black Roundtable Guests	11	5	n/a	0	10	26
Percentage of Shows with No Black Roundtable Guests	**73%**	**83%**	**n/a**	**0%**	**77%**	**47%**

Table 13

TOPICS

BLACK INTERVIEW GUESTS	DATE	TOPIC
ABC - THIS WEEK WITH GEORGE STEPHANOPOULOS		
Colin Powell	12/25/05	Iraq
Ray Nagin	12/4/05	Katrina
Barack Obama	9/11/05	Race and Poverty
Condoleezza Rice	6/19/05	Iraq
Condoleezza Rice	3/13/05	Iraq
Condoleezza Rice	1/30/05	Iraq
Colin Powell	1/9/05	Iraq, Tsunami
Kofi Annan	1/2/05	Tsunami
Floyd Flake	11/28/04	Religion and Politics
Barack Obama	11/7/04	2004 Election
Condoleezza Rice	10/3/04	Iraq
Colin Powell	9/26/04	Iraq
Colin Powell	9/12/04	Iraq
Alan Keyes	8/15/04	2004 Election
Barack Obama	8/15/04	2004 Election
Condoleezza Rice	6/27/04	Iraq
Colin Powell	6/13/04	Iraq
Colin Powell	5/16/04	Iraq
Condoleezza Rice	4/18/04	Iraq
Colin Powell	3/14/04	Iraq
Wilton Gregory	1/4/04	Catholic Church Abuse Scandal
CBS - FACE THE NATION		
Barack Obama	9/18/05	Katrina
Wiliam Jefferson	9/4/05	Katrina
Charles Rangel	4/17/05	Social Security
Condoleezza Rice	3/13/05	Iraq
Condoleezza Rice	1/30/05	Iraq
Colin Powell	1/2/05	Iraq, Tsunami
Condoleezza Rice	9/12/04	Iraq
Barack Obama	7/25/04	2004 Election
Colin Powell	6/27/04	Iraq
Colin Powell	6/6/04	Iraq
Condoleezza Rice	4/18/04	Iraq
CNN - LATE EDITION		
Kendrick Meek	10/23/05	Hurricane Wilma
Eric Holder	10/9/05	2004 Election
Bennie Thompson	10/2/05	Katrina
Eugene Robinson	9/11/05	Katrina
David Satcher	9/4/05	Katrina
Bennie Thompson	9/4/05	Katrina
William Jefferson	9/4/05	Katrina
Ray Nagin	9/4/05	Katrina
Clark Kent Ervin	7/24/05	Homeland Security

Table 13

TOPICS (continued)

BLACK INTERVIEW GUESTS	DATE	TOPIC
Condoleezza Rice	6/19/05	Iraq
Jesse Jackson	4/3/05	Pope John Paul II
Colin Powell	4/3/05	Pope John Paul II
Grant Hill	2/20/05	NBA All-Star Game
Shaquille O'Neal	2/20/05	NBA All-Star Game
Condoleezza Rice	1/30/05	Iraq
Colin Powell	1/9/05	Iraq, Tsunami
Colin Powell	1/2/05	Iraq, Tsunami
JesseJackson	12/26/04	Religion and Politics
Charles Rangel	12/26/04	Social Security
Kweisi Mfume	12/5/04	Democratic Politics
Jesse Jackson, Jr.	11/21/04	Democrats and African Americans
Donna Brazile	11/7/04	2004 Election
Al Sharpton	10/31/04	2004 Election
Jesse Jackson	10/24/04	Religion and Politics
Condoleezza Rice	10/3/04	Iraq
Colin Powell	9/26/04	Iraq
Charles Rangel	9/19/04	Bush's National Guard Record
Condoleezza Rice	9/12/04	Iraq
Harold Ford, Jr.	9/5/04	2004 Election
Michael Steele	8/29/04	2004 Election
Donna Brazile	8/22/04	2004 Election
Alan Keyes	8/15/04	2004 Election
Condoleezza Rice	8/8/04	Iraq
Charles Ramsey	8/8/04	Homeland Security
Al Sharpton	8/1/04	2004 Election
Barack Obama	7/25/04	2004 Election
Harold Ford, Jr.	7/25/04	2004 Election
Charles Rangel	7/4/04	Social Security
Colin Powell	6/27/04	Iraq
Condoleezza Rice	6/13/04	Iraq
Colin Powell	6/6/04	Iraq
Colin Powell	4/11/04	Iraq
Al Sharpton	2/1/04	2004 Election
Donna Brazile	1/18/04	2004 Election
Donna Brazile	1/4/04	2004 Election
FOX - FOX NEWS SUNDAY		
Condoleezza Rice	12/18/05	Iraq
Condoleezza Rice	10/16/05	Iraq
Condoleezza Rice	6/19/05	Iraq
Condoleezza Rice	1/30/05	Iraq
Colin Powell	1/9/05	Iraq,Tsunami
Anthony Williams	12/19/04	Baseball in D.C.
J. Kenneth Blackwell	10/17/04	2004 Election/Voter Access
Eric Holder	10/17/04	2004 Election/Voter Access
Condoleezza Rice	10/10/04	Iraq

Table 13

TOPICS (continued)

BLACK INTERVIEW GUESTS	DATE	TOPIC
Colin Powell	9/26/04	Iraq
Colin Powell	9/12/04	Iraq
Donna Brazile	8/15/04	2004 Elections
Condoleezza Rice	6/27/04	Iraq
Colin Powell	6/13/04	Iraq
Condoleezza Rice	6/6/04	Iraq
Colin Powell	5/16/04	Iraq
Condoleezza Rice	4/18/04	Iraq
Colin Powell	3/14/04	Iraq
Wilton Gregory	2/29/04	Catholic Church Abuse Scandal
NBC - MEET THE PRESS		
Condoleezza Rice	12/18/05	Iraq
Condoleezza Rice	10/16/05	Iraq
Ray Nagin	9/11/05	Katrina
Condoleezza Rice	3/13/05	Iraq
Charles Rangel	2/13/05	Iraq, Social Security
Colin Powell	1/2/05	Iraq, Tsunami
Barack Obama	11/7/04	2004 Elections
Colin Powell	9/12/04	Iraq
Condoleezza Rice	8/8/04	Iraq
Barack Obama	7/25/04	2004 Elections
Colin Powell	6/13/04	Iraq
Colin Powell	5/16/04	Iraq
Kofi Annan	5/2/04	Iraq
Condoleezza Rice	3/14/04	Iraq
Charles Rangel	2/15/04	Social Security

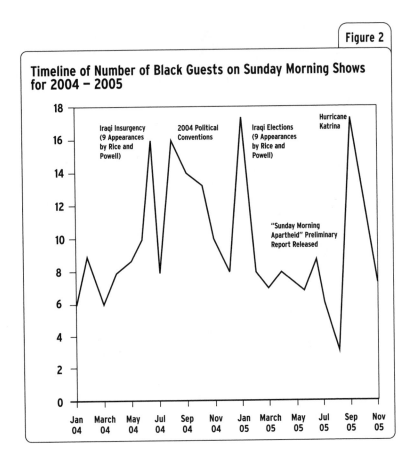

Figure 2

Timeline of Number of Black Guests on Sunday Morning Shows for 2004 – 2005

New Orleans Revisited
by Marc H. Morial

T he day after Katrina, pictures of New Orleanians stranded and suffering at both the Louisiana Superdome and the Ernest N. Morial Convention Center hit the national news.

Their faces, filled with so much pain and struggle, shocked both my wife and me. I was sad and angry, because I knew there was no reason that people should have been at the Superdome or the Convention Center, the landmark that bears my father's name, without food, water and medical supplies. Something had gone very, very wrong.

When I learned that breaks in the levees were the source of New Orleans' flooding, my heart sank. I told my wife, Michelle, a former TV anchor/reporter in New Orleans, that even one levee collapse would be a great impending catastrophe. I had spent enough hurricane seasons viewing computer modeling when I was mayor to know that the city would fill with water like a bathtub beneath a faucet. Hurricane Katrina had become the "worst case scenario." What became most distressing was the reaction of city, state and federal officials. Their response was weak, woeful and inadequate.

The phones at our house began to ring constantly. New Orleanians who were either stranded or looking for their family members could reach no one in their beloved hometown, so they reached out to us. As each day unfolded, the magnitude of what had become an international crisis, squarely hit me.

I called my childhood friend, Wynton Marsalis. We yearned to do something more than watch from the safety of New York City. We decided to act. With help from Michele Moore, our Senior Vice President for Marketing and Communications, we spoke to the key leaders at BET (Black Entertainment Television): Debra Lee, Chair and CEO; Reginald Hudlin, President, Entertainment and Nina Henderson-Moore, Executive Vice President for News and Public Affairs. It was immediately decided that we could do something and within 72 hours, a very successful television telethon was produced that ultimately raised $13 million for the American Red Cross to help people in immediate need.

When I visited New Orleans a few weeks later, I arrived to a city that was completely abandoned. There were few signs of life. On that first day back, I visited my old neighborhood, Pontchartrain Park. I knew earlier it had been completely covered by water. Now dry, it was gray and lonely.

I noticed that all of the grass along the once beautiful park had turned brown. There were abandoned cars everywhere, and once again, no signs of life. Slowly we drove towards Press Drive, my childhood home, and I could see the waterline along the side of the house. I had not lived in the house since 1972, when my family moved to my mother's present home on Harrison Avenue in the 7th Ward. But it was the house next door, the Dags' home, that caught my attention. The door had been jarred opened, so I went in to take a look. Inside, for the first time, I witnessed up-close the devastation of Hurricane Katrina. The house was topsy-turvy, with furniture turned over and the walls were covered with black mold. It was a sight no words could describe. Clearly, anyone stranded would have had a hard time coming out alive.

It was also clear that all of the houses in Pontchartrain Park had suffered such substantial damage that remediation, repairing and rebuilding would be difficult and indeed expensive.

But nothing could prepare me for the 9th Ward as I crossed the old, historic St. Claude Avenue Bridge. This bridge was near the man-made industrial canal where the levee broke.

The lower 9th Ward is special. Not only was it the home of Fats Domino, it formed an important part of the strong base that supported my father through four collective mayoral elections. It is an area that had long been forgotten, but I recalled as I drove there, one of my earliest commitments after being elected mayor was to hold the State of the City Address at the Martin Luther King Elementary School Library, which had been built as a result of a collaboration between the city and the state. I remember after that State of the City Address, we crossed the street to the Sanchez Community Center and dedicated a new gymnasium for the youth of the neighborhood.

While others had thought of the lower 9th Ward as an area that was unimportant and forgotten, it was a special part of the city to me. Both my father and I were determined through our terms as mayor to build schools, libraries, gymnasiums and repave the streets. I tried to help the neighborhood play catch up for many years of neglect and abandonment. Indeed, it was a strong neighborhood of homeowners, character, community and of families.

These memories made the devastation even more personal, even more heartbreaking. We sought to find the levee break itself and the closer we came, the more difficult the obstacle course before us. On Caffin Avenue, we looked to our left and saw the long white limousine that was a signature vehicle for the Glapion Funeral Home, had been carried two blocks by the sheer force of the water.

The gap in the levee was several city blocks long and the path it cut was like a powerful bomb, shattering every structure in its wake. There was rubble; people's homes and cars were scattered everywhere. The pain, the sadness, the sense of loss that came over all of us who were part of that trip was numbing. Despite it all, many homes were still standing. I came away believing that all of these neighborhoods could make a comeback. If the will of the people was there and with proper planning, resources and a commitment by the federal government to build a first-class levee system, it could be possible.

As we rode back across the St. Claude Avenue Bridge toward downtown New Orleans, we encountered a man walking swiftly with what appeared to be a large book. He recognized me and we embraced. He said that he had walked 55 blocks, defying the order to stay away from the lower 9th Ward area. He not only wanted to see his home, but retrieve his large family Bible. That was what he carried under his arm and he said it was one of the few things in his home that was not completely destroyed. Seeing his home had brought him to closure, and retrieving his treasured family Bible gave him the power and strength to move on.

His conviction and determination underscored the faith that I continue to have in the people of my beloved hometown. Faith that New Orleans can and must be rebuilt; not partially, but all of it. Its people must return and its soul and character must remain. It must become a better city.

I still love the Big Easy and all of its people. We are not perfect. We have suffered so greatly, but by the grace of God and the will of our spirit, New Orleanians will rebuild and live again.

New Orleans:
Next Steps on the Road to Recovery
by Donna L. Brazile

Do you know what it means to miss New Orleans
And miss it each night and day
I know I'm not wrong ... this feeling's gettin' stronger
The longer, I stay away.

Louis Armstrong

Somebody ought to circulate the lyrics of Louis Alter, made famous by the legendary jazz artist and famous New Orleans native, Louis Armstrong, "Do You Know What It Means to Miss New Orleans." Every member of my family, with roots in the bayou state since the mid-1800s, is now playing this 1947 song. We miss New Orleans—its smell, its weather, its culture, its people, its language and, most importantly, we miss our neighbors and our homes.

Last year will go down in my family's history book as the year of sorrow. Between August 28 and September, my family, like so many others residing in the Gulf Coast states of Louisiana, Mississippi, Texas and Alabama, were driven from their homes and into the caring, open arms of their fellow citizens across America. When they arrived, they were tired. Now, a half of a year later, they remain in limbo, waiting for a sign, any sign that help is truly on its way.

Hurricane Katrina was more than the worst natural disaster in American history. It was a defining moment, not only for me and my family, but for our country. Many of us watched in horror and sadness, television images of young children dying in their mothers' arms from dehydration amid reports of dead bodies floating down the flooded streets. Ordinary people were jumping off bridges, driven to suicide by overwhelming grief and the feeling of hopelessness. So far, there have been 1,310 confirmed deaths in Louisiana and Mississippi—and the number is still rising.

Although I was miles away from home, I will never forget the long hours that turned into days as we waited to hear from our loved ones. It would take days to hear from my siblings, my Dad, Lionel, and my other relatives. They had to be rescued.

As devastating images saturated the news, most of us wondered out loud how this could happen in America.

Hurricane Katrina shut down more than 80,000 small, medium and large businesses; it closed hospitals and schools, creating havoc for state and local governments. Hurricanes Katrina and Rita were equal opportunity destroyers. They showed us that nature wreaks havoc with impartiality. Their violent winds destroyed beautiful lakefront resorts, Gulf Coast mansions and profitable seaside casinos with the same gale force as those that ravaged the shotgun houses and public housing where some of America's poorest citizens lived.

I know I'm not wrong... this feeling's gettin' stronger.

Katrina struck my hometown in the early hours of the morning at the end of a long, hot month, when people living paycheck-to-paycheck are often without the resources to do more than just survive. Countless New Orleans residents, like my Dad and several of my siblings, were stuck in Katrina's path without cars, gas money, public transportation or credit cards to take them to higher ground. More than 1 million people were displaced in the days and months following Katrina, and less than half have returned. Some may never go back home.

Unfortunately, while nature may treat all of us equally, Katrina and Rita showed us that society does not. Blacks and whites did not even look at the disaster through the same set of lens. According to a report by the Pew Center for The People & The Press, two-thirds of African Americans polled said that if most victims had been white, there would have been a quicker government response. By an even larger margin—77 percent—whites said race played no part in the government response to the hurricanes.

Clearly, our country still has enormous problems with racial and economic inequality that are too easily brushed aside when the next news cycle rolls in. Now, more than ever, we must have a frank conversation about what it means to be poor in America and what we can do alleviate the pain and suffering of citizens who work two and three minimum-wage jobs to survive.

We owe it to the victims of hurricanes Katrina and Rita to once again summon this nation to eradicate poverty. We owe it to them to fight for justice. We owe it to them to increase economic opportunity for all Americans. We must never forget, as Coretta Scott King reminded us, that the "struggle is a never ending process. Freedom is never really won; you earn it and win it in every generation."

Members of our generation must now work together to end racism and poverty in America.

Race defines so much of what we do, where we live and where we go to school, but it should never define our government's response to fellow Americans stranded in water, trapped on their rooftop or corralled into a makeshift shelter without food or water.

Race is what placed so many victims in the lower areas of New Orleans and the surrounding region without the resources to get out of harm's way. I grew up one square block from the Mighty Mississippi and every time it rained, in every storm and after every winter, we feared the worst—the big one.

Like so many displaced families, my folks felt abandoned. They lacked adequate shelter and medical supplies. They struggled to find loved ones who had been evacuated at unknown times to unknown places. Even more inexcusable, they lacked information. These good Americans wanted nothing more than a chance to return home to pick up the pieces and to start rebuilding.

Unfortunately, most residents who were displaced by Hurricane Katrina have not yet been able to begin rebuilding their homes or their lives. Since Katrina, some members of my family have fallen back on hard times, using their modest assets and savings to survive in strange places while they awaited promising news from insurance companies or FEMA.

Do you know what it means to miss New Orleans

My sister, Lisa has returned to New Orleans, moved into a trailer, ripped out the mold in her red-tagged home, thrown out her destroyed belongings and waited for FEMA to deliver a blue tarp to patch up the roof. She still doesn't know whether she will be allowed to rebuild or whether enough people will come back to New Orleans to justify starting over there. Like so many others, her life has been on hold for six months.

With no binding commitment that the levees will be rebuilt to withstand another major storm, many residents and businesses are reluctant to rebuild, fearing their lives might be washed away for a second time. From near and afar, residents are waiting to see if they can return to the place they once called home.

Our first duty to the Gulf State residents must be to ensure that the devastation of last fall is not forgotten or pushed off the national agenda. This is not merely a Southern disaster, a poor disaster or a black disaster. We must show our fellow citizens the dignity they deserve and not forget about them when they need us the most.

We are going to need the continued support of the president and members of Congress to get the federal funding that states require. While billions of dollars flowed in at first, the administration is showing a reluctance to commit to long-term rebuilding without an adequate plan from state and local leaders. It's time for everyone to put aside partisan bickering and rebuild, rebuild, rebuild before the next storm season is upon us. We don't have long.

African-American voices should lead the debate in the rebuilding process since the burdens of poverty fall unevenly on us. Of the 37 million poor people in this country, 9 million are black. The effects of poverty became realized in the flooded ninth ward and the crowded Superdome. In a flood-prone area, expensive houses are built on dry land and cheaper houses are more vulnerable. Therefore, it is not surprising that a block-by-block analysis of census data and flood maps reveals that about half of the city's white residents experienced serious flooding, compared with three-quarters of African Americans.

It is not difficult to imagine why people without a lot of money will have a difficult time rebuilding. The simple laws of supply and demand are driving up housing prices along the Gulf Coast, especially in New Orleans. These costs will make it nearly impossible for many citizens to move back home unless we commit to providing these deserving Americans with the assets and the opportunities they need to return and rebuild. We must make sure that federal housing vouchers and targeted rental assistance are available to those that need them.

Providing a living wage is also critical. Since poor families are hurt when their members lack basic needs and standards of care, we must hold our government accountable for its pledge to promote strong and stable families. And people need more than a temporary raise in wages— they must be trained for quality jobs that will permanently increase their earning potential and continue to keep them and their families afloat. Getting the training needed to break into higher-paying jobs will interrupt the cycle of poverty.

Finally, as President Bush stated in his speech last year at Jackson square, "As we clear away the debris of a hurricane, let us also clear away the legacy of inequality. We have a duty to confront poverty with bold action." Let me add, we must also confront these problems with leadership at all levels, beginning at the top. If we are truly committed to rebuilding in a way that helps our most vulnerable, America must invest in building more affordable housing, schools and neighborhoods.

We do miss New Orleans where so many of us "left our hearts," our friends, our jobs, our schools and, not least, our culture which gave birth to America's soul and jazz.

Miss it each night and day

The National Urban League Katrina Bill of Rights

T he National Urban League believes that our nation cannot be whole again unless, and until, the lives of our neighbors in the Gulf Coast are finally made whole—in their homes, in their places of employment, in their schools, in their hospitals, in their businesses, and in revived vibrant and striving communities. The estimated two million American citizens displaced by hurricane Katrina, the 1,330 and possibly more who tragically lost their lives, and the thousands still unaccounted for deserve nothing less than our nation's total commitment to reaching this goal with deliberate speed.

Immediately after the storms hit and wreaked their havoc on whole cities and rural communities, the National Urban League and its affiliates went into immediate action. Urban League affiliates in cities throughout the country provided a wide range of direct recovery services to storm survivors evacuated to their cities. In a national policy address on the Katrina disaster held at Georgetown University Law Center on October 12, 2005, National Urban League President Marc Morial officially released the Katrina Bill of Rights to ensure that our nation rebuilds a treasured part of our country in a way that lives up to our highest ideals. These rights are:

1 The Right to Recover

The people of the Gulf Coast must be guaranteed the right to recover. To do that, they need immediate help to get back on their feet and rebuild their lives.

Congress should:

Provide extended unemployment assistance to the half a million hard-working Americans thrown out of a job because of the storm.

> *The National Urban League supports immediate action to extend and increase unemployment assistance to persons still unemployed as a result of hurricanes Katrina and Rita.*

Establish a Katrina ictims compensation fund. Within days after the terrorist attacks of September 11, 2001, Congress passed and the president signed legislation authorizing a 9/11 victims compensation fund, which eventually provided more than $7 billion in compensation. As it did then, Congress must now take immediate and decisive action to continue helping American citizens whose lives have been disrupted and whose livelihoods have been eliminated by this major national tragedy.

Establish an independent, non-partisan Commission to understand what went wrong in the response to this disaster.

> Despite oversight investigation of the federal response to hurricane Katrina by the House and Senate and a similar report by the White House, the National Urban League believes that only an independent, non-partisan commission can fully determine what went wrong, demand accountability, and from the lessons learned provide guidance on how to respond to future disasters.

2 The Right to Vote

We must secure the right to vote for the people of the Gulf Coast. Katrina may have knocked over buildings, but we must not let it weaken the foundation of our democracy.

Guarantee that citizens displaced by Katrina continue to have full voting rights in their home states. The ballot is the best way to ensure that our displaced citizens have the voice they want—and deserve—in the rebuilding of their communities. If we can establish national polling places for citizens of Iraq to vote in the U.S., certainly we can do the same for displaced citizens from New Orleans.

> The National Urban League strongly supports the Displaced Citizens Voter Protection Act of 2005 (H.R.3734/S.1867). The companion bills would ensure that victims of Hurricane Katrina and Rita have the right to vote by absentee ballot while temporarily displaced. The legislation would ensure that displaced citizens receive the same voting protections currently available to military and overseas voters.

3 The Right to Return

We must guarantee to every evacuee and every resident the right to return to their home. Every family should have the chance to come back to their hometown or neighborhood if they so choose.

Congress should:

Ensure home owners have the right of first refusal to reclaim property. These are their homes—washed out or not.

Institute a federal tax holiday for three years for returning gulf residents making less than $50,000 a year

Provide a 50 percent tax holiday to businesses that pay their workers a living wage. Nothing will do more to lift people out of poverty and help them rebuild than a good job at a good wage.

4 The Right to Rebuild

Every resident of the Gulf Coast has the right to rebuild and to have a say in the reconstruction of their damaged city.

Do not pay for rebuilding on the backs of the least fortunate. Rebuilding the Gulf Coast around the principle of equal opportunity for all means that as we rebuild, we must not tear down what has made us strong. We must not "pay for Katrina" by cutting Medicaid, education and job training programs, increasing Medicare premiums and gutting rural economic development efforts. Paying for the rebuilding on the backs of those whose lives are already ruined only adds insult to injury.

Break down the barriers to success for all gulf residents. We must rebuild the Gulf in a way that doesn't benefit only favored big contractors or major big real estate developers. We should turn New Orleans or other Gulf neighborhoods into gated communities. Rather, we should encourage programs, break down the barriers to success for all income groups.

Institute a moratorium on collections and deficiency judgments on real and personal properties. We should prohibit negative credit reporting or the omission of negative events from credit scores when the incidents were associated with Hurricane Katrina.

Encourage financial institutions to forebear On all loans and mortgages until people can move back—and live—in their homes. We must protect the people of the Gulf Coast from predatory lenders. And we should freeze all foreclosure proceedings against property in affected areas for a minimum of 12 months.

5 The Right to Work

Every Gulf Coast Resident must be assured of the right to work; there is no better anti-poverty program than a good job. With reconstruction and rebuilding, there will be many new jobs created in the region—and it's our duty to ensure that they first go to those from the Gulf region.

Give local residents first choice on recovery and reconstruction jobs and contracts. We should set a goal of 50 percent of all contracts for local contractors and 25 percent of all contracts to minority contractors.

Ensure that fair wages are paid and fairness in the workplace is upheld. Civil rights and equality of opportunity are not "red tape" to be cut when times are tough. They are who we are as a nation. Therefore, we should not suspend any such requirement now in effect.

Restore affirmative action and the Davis Bacon Prevailing Wage Laws. There should be no more federal contracts granted until these two guarantees are put back in place.

The Bush Administration reinstated the Davis-Bacon pre-
vailing wage law on November 8, 2005 in Louisiana,
Mississippi and selected other counties where President
Bush suspended it in the wake of Hurricane Katrina.

*Create a gulf coast economy that will sustain good-paying jobs for the
people of the region.* A vibrant economy and good-paying jobs will lift this
area out of the swamps of poverty.

The Katrina Bill of Rights cannot be fulfilled without a comprehensive
plan and a coordinated effort that will transcend the region's political bor-
ders and direct the rebuilding.

*The National Urban League calls on the President and Congress to
establish a gulf coast authority (CGA) with the charge and the power to
lead and implement this monumental rebuilding task.* The CGA must
have a dedicated budget, for in this current fiscal climate, with tax breaks
for the wealthy still being extended and commitments overseas seemingly unending, it is critical that we secure these funds separate from the federal budget to rebuild our towns and cities.

The National Urban League will closely monitor legislation in Congress
that can serve as important vehicles for implementing the provisions of
the National Urban League Katrina Bill of Rights.

> The National Urban League lends its unqualified support
> for the "Hurricane Katrina Recovery, Reclamation,
> Restoration, Reconstruction and Reunion Act of 2005
> (H.R.4197)" introduced by the Congressional Black
> Caucus. H.R.4197 includes many of the recommendations
> contained in the Katrina Bill of Rights, including voting
> rights guarantees, local resident hiring goals, and a victims'
> restoration fund modeled on the 9/11 fund that Congress
> authorized immediately after the 2001 terrorist attacks.
> Congress must take immediate and positive action to pass
> this important and historic legislation.

Rosa Parks: An Ordinary Woman, An Extraordinary Life

by Stephanie J. Jones

Rosa Parks just said "No" to Injustice.

It would have been so easy and so much safer for Rosa Louise McCauley Parks to move to the back of the bus as she was told on December 1, 1955. But she didn't. Now, more than 50 years later, the names of the bus driver who summoned the Montgomery Police Department when she refused to comply, the police officers who carted her off to jail, and the White Citizens Council members who fought to preserve white supremacy in Alabama are barely known. And in the rare cases their names are recalled, they are mentioned only to underscore the shameful behavior of those who trafficked in injustice.

But we all know Rosa Parks, whose name is forever a shining part of our history, our legacy, and our hearts. And when she died last October at the age of 92, the nation stopped to say goodbye and to pay tribute. In a bipartisan gesture, the United States Congress decreed that Parks should lie in honor in the Rotunda of the Capitol. She was the second African American and the first woman of any racial or ethnic group to be accorded that honor, a tribute bestowed to only 30 men in American history.

Tens of thousands of Americans stood in the long lines and cold for hours in order to get a glimpse of Parks' casket. Before they took their turn, Washington's power elite exerted its power by going first. All of the players were there: leaders of both Houses of Congress, present and former cabinet secretaries, federal judges and, of course, President George W. Bush and First Lady Laura Bush. The First Family entered the Rotunda early and waited, silently, 15 minutes for Parks' casket, accompanied by a military honor guard, to arrive.

To some, the quiet tributes in the Rotunda seemed like a long way from that December day in Montgomery. But it was America, not Rosa Parks, that had traversed history's long and rocky road. Throughout her life, she remained what she was in 1955—a quiet, dignified, respected and respectful woman.

In death, Parks has been vaulted into something approaching sainthood. This is not uncommon; one need only look at how Dr. Martin Luther King, Jr. was deified after he was assassinated. That's another characteristic of the United States—we have a tendency to canonize our heroes, turning them into sanitized icons they never were or wished to be. In an era of professed personal responsibility it absolves us—or so we think—of our responsibility to take bold, life-threatening action to eradicate injustice. In the meantime, we leave it up to the saints to do the saintly things and the heroes to perform the heroic acts, all on our behalf. And then we honor them for doing what we didn't have the temerity to do.

Tributes are often sincere and well-meaning. Yet, in a strange way, they diminish the legacy of those being honored. It was Rosa Parks' ordinariness that made her extraordinary. In many respects, she was an ordinary woman, with ordinary doubts, with ordinary fears and with ordinary faults.

Perhaps we fear her ordinariness because that makes her like us and us like her. And if we are indeed like her, that means that we, too, can and should perform courageous acts, both large and small. We also would be expected to say "no" when "yes" would be so much easier and safer.

Rosa Parks was a truly remarkable woman. But she was remarkable not because she was bigger than life. Rosa Parks was a quiet woman who had the courage to say "no" to injustice. When she said "no" to the bus driver, she said "yes" we can and must all be treated with decency and fairness. When she said "no" to degradation, humiliation and second-class treatment, Rosa Parks helped America save itself.

That's reason enough to honor her.

APPENDIX I

History of the National Urban League

T he National Urban League grew out of that spontaneous grass-roots movement for freedom and opportunity that came to be called the Black Migrations. When the U.S. Supreme Court declared its approval of segregation in the 1896 *Plessy v. Ferguson* decision, the brutal system of economic, social and political oppression the White South quickly adopted rapidly transformed what had been a trickle of African Americans northward into a flood.

Those newcomers to the North soon discovered that while they had escaped the South, they had by no means escaped racial discrimination. Excluded from all but menial jobs in the larger society, victimized by poor housing and education, and inexperienced in the ways of urban living, many lived in terrible social and economic conditions.

Still, in the North and West blacks could vote; and in that and other differences between living in the South and not living in the South lay opportunity—and that African Americans clearly understood.

But to capitalize on that opportunity, to successfully adapt to urban life and to reduce the pervasive discrimination they faced, they would need help. That was the reason the Committee on Urban Conditions Among Negroes was established on September 29, 1910 in New York City. Central to the organization's founding were two extraordinary people: Mrs. Ruth Standish Baldwin and Dr. George Edmund Haynes, who would become the Committee's first executive secretary. Mrs. Baldwin, the widow of a railroad magnate and a member of one of America's oldest families, had a remarkable social conscience and was a stalwart champion of the poor and disadvantaged. Dr. Haynes, a graduate of Fisk University, Yale University, and Columbia University (he was the first African American to receive a doctorate from the latter), felt a compelling need to use his training as a social worker to serve his people.

A year later, the Committee merged with the Committee for the Improvement of Industrial Conditions Among Negroes in New York (founded in 1906), and the National League for the Protection of Colored Women (founded in 1905) to form the National League on Urban Conditions Among Negroes. In 1920, the name was later shortened to the National Urban League.

The interracial character of the League's board was set from its first days. Professor Edwin R. A. Seligman of Columbia University, one of the leaders in progressive social service activities in New York City, served as chairman from 1911 to 1913. Mrs. Baldwin took the post until 1915.

The fledgling organization counseled black migrants from the South, helped train black social workers, and worked in various other ways to bring educational and employment opportunities to blacks. Its research into the problems blacks faced in employment opportunities, recreation, housing, health and sanitation, and education spurred the League's quick growth. By the end of World War I the organization had 81 staff members working in 30 cities.

In 1918, Dr. Haynes was succeeded by Eugene Kinckle Jones who would direct the agency until his retirement in 1941. Under his direction, the League significantly expanded its multifaceted campaign to crack the barriers to black employment, spurred first by the boom years of the 1920s, and then, by the desperate years of the Great Depression. Efforts at reasoned persuasion were buttressed by boycotts against firms that refused to employ blacks, pressures on schools to expand vocational opportunities for young people, constant prodding of Washington officials to include blacks in New Deal recovery programs and a drive to get blacks into previously segregated labor unions.

As World War II loomed, Lester Granger, a seasoned League veteran and crusading newspaper columnist, was appointed Jones' successor.

Outspoken in his commitment to advancing opportunity for African Americans, Granger pushed tirelessly to integrate recalcitrant trade unions, and led the League's effort to support A. Philip Randolph's March on Washington Movement to fight discrimination in defense work and in the armed services. Under Granger, the League, through its own Industrial Relations Laboratory, had notable success in cracking the color bar in numerous defense plants. The nation's demand for civilian labor during the war also helped the organization press with greater urgency its programs to train black youths for meaningful blue-collar employment. After the war those efforts expanded to persuading Fortune 500 companies to hold career conferences on the campuses of Negro Colleges and place blacks in upper-echelon jobs.

Of equal importance to the League's own future sources of support, Granger avidly supported the organization of its volunteer auxiliary, the National Urban League Guild, which, under the leadership of Mollie Moon, became an important national force in its own right.

The explosion of the civil rights movement provoked a change for the League, one personified by its new leader, Whitney M. Young, Jr., who became executive director in 1961. A social worker like his predecessors, he substantially expanded the League's fund-raising ability—and, most critically, made the League a full partner in the civil rights movement. Indeed, although the League's tax-exempt status barred it from protest activities, it hosted at its New York headquarters the planning meetings of A. Philip Randolph, Martin Luther King, Jr., and other civil rights and labor leaders for the 1963 March on Washington. Young was also a forceful advocate for greater government and private-sector involvement in efforts to eradicate poverty. His call for a domestic Marshall Plan, a ten-point program designed to close the huge social and economic gap between black and white Americans, significantly influenced the discussion of the Johnson Administration's War on Poverty legislation.

Young's tragic death in 1971 in a drowning incident off the coast of Lagos, Nigeria brought another change in leadership. Vernon E. Jordan, Jr., formerly Executive Director of the United Negro College Fund, took over as the League's fifth Executive Director in 1972 (the title of the office was changed to President in 1977).

For the next decade, until his resignation in December 1981, Jordan skillfully guided the League to new heights of achievement. He oversaw a major expansion of its social-service efforts, as the League became a significant conduit for the federal government to establish programs and deliver services to aid urban communities, and brokered fresh initiatives in such League programs as housing, health, education and minority business development. Jordan also instituted a citizenship education program that helped increase the black vote and brought new programs to such areas as energy, the environment, and non-traditional jobs for women of color—and he developed *The State of Black America* report.

In 1982, John E. Jacob, a former chief executive officer of the Washington, D.C. and San Diego affiliates who had served as Executive Vice President under Jordan, took the reins of leadership, solidifying the League's internal structure and expanding its outreach even further.

Jacob established the Permanent Development Fund in order to increase the organization's financial stamina. In honor of Whitney Young, he established several programs to aid the development of those who work for and with the League: The Whitney M. Young, Jr. Training Center, to provide training and leadership development opportunities for both staff and volunteers; the Whitney M. Young, Jr. Race Relations Program, which recognizes affiliates doing exemplary work in race relations; and the Whitney M. Young, Jr. Commemoration Ceremony, which honors and pays tribute to long term staff and volunteers who have made extraordinary contributions to the Urban League Movement. Jacob established the League's NULITES youth-development program and spurred the League to put new emphasis on programs to reduce teenage pregnancy, help single female heads of households, combat crime in black communities, and increase voter registration.

Hugh B. Price, appointed to the League's top office in July 1994, took its reins at a critical moment for the League, for Black America, and for the nation as a whole. The fierce market-driven dynamic known as "globalization," swept the world, fundamentally altering economic relations among and within countries, including the United States. Price, a lawyer by training, with extensive experience in community development and other public policy issues, intensified the organization's work in three broad areas: in education and youth development, in individual and community-wide economic empowerment, and in the forceful advocacy of affirmative action and the promotion of inclusion as a critical foundation for securing America's future as a multi-ethnic democracy.

In the spring of 2003, Price stepped down after a productive nine-year tenure, and Marc H. Morial, the former two-term Mayor of New Orleans, Louisiana, was appointed president and chief executive officer.

With the economic gains Black America had forged during the 1990s substantially evaporating under the post-9/11 stunning loss of jobs and an attendant, long-lasting "jobless recovery," Morial has aggressively guided the development of new programs he calls part of the "Empowerment Movement" for Black America. He has chosen to concentrate the League's efforts in five critical areas: in education and economic matters, in issues of civic engagement, in civil rights and racial justice; and in issues of health and quality of life. Although the League has long been active in these areas, Morial has pledged to substantially increase that involvement—and the contribution the League can make to improving conditions—within each. The entire campaign is driven by the urgency of the need for African Americans to build up their sense of self-reliance and entrepreneurial spirit, their financial literacy, and their material wealth in order to reduce the "equality gaps" that bedevil Black America and the nation. "Forty years ago," Morial said during his Keynote Address at the 2003 National Urban League Conference in Pittsburgh, his first as the organization's head, "a great generation of Americans led a movement that made America's present possible. The task for us, their beneficiaries, is to marshal the courage and conviction, the fortitude and the fight, the intelligence and the integrity they displayed to complete their work."

Roster of National Urban League Affiliates

AKRON, OHIO
Akron Community Service Center
and Urban League

ALEXANDRIA, VIRGINIA
Northern Virginia Urban League

ALTON, ILLINOIS
Madison County Urban League

ANDERSON, INDIANA
Urban League of Madison County, Inc.

ATLANTA, GEORGIA
Atlanta Urban League

AURORA, ILLINOIS
Quad County Urban League

AUSTIN, TEXAS
Austin Area Urban League

BALTIMORE, MARYLAND
Greater Baltimore Urban League

BATTLE CREEK, MICHIGAN
Southwestern Michigan Urban League

BINGHAMTON, NEW YORK
Broome County Urban League

BIRMINGHAM, ALABAMA
Birmingham Urban League

BOSTON, MASSACHUSETTS
Urban League of Eastern Massachusetts

BUFFALO, NEW YORK
Buffalo Urban League

CANTON, OHIO
Greater Stark County Urban League

CHAMPAIGN, ILLINOIS
Urban League of Champaign County

CHARLESTON, SOUTH CAROLINA
Trident Urban League

CHARLOTTE, NORTH CAROLINA
Urban League of Central
Carolinas, Inc.

CHATTANOOGA, TENNESSEE
Urban League Greater Chattanooga, Inc.

CHICAGO, ILLINOIS
Chicago Urban League

CINCINNATI, OHIO
Urban League of Greater Cincinnati

CLEVELAND, OHIO
Urban League of Greater Cleveland

COLORADO SPRINGS, COLORADO
Urban League of Pikes Peak Region

COLUMBIA, SOUTH CAROLINA
Columbia Urban League

COLUMBUS, GEORGIA
Urban League of Greater
Columbus, Inc.

COLUMBUS, OHIO
Columbus Urban League

DALLAS, TEXAS
Urban League of Greater Dallas and
North Central Texas

DAYTON, OHIO
Dayton Urban League

DENVER, COLORADO
Urban League of Metropolitan Denver

DETROIT, MICHIGAN
Detroit Urban League

ELIZABETH, NEW JERSEY
Urban League of Union County

ELYRIA, OHIO
Lorain County Urban League

ENGLEWOOD, NEW JERSEY
Urban League for Bergen County

FARRELL, PENNSYLVANIA
Urban League of Shenango Valley

FLINT, MICHIGAN
Urban League of Flint

FORT LAUDERDALE, FLORIDA
Urban League of Broward County

FORT WAYNE, INDIANA
Fort Wayne Urban League

GARY, INDIANA
Urban League of Northwest Indiana, Inc.

GRAND RAPIDS, MICHIGAN
Grand Rapids Urban League

GREENVILLE, SOUTH CAROLINA
The Urban League of the Upstate

HARTFORD, CONNECTICUT
Urban League of Greater Hartford

HOUSTON, TEXAS
Houston Area Urban League

INDIANAPOLIS, INDIANA
Indianapolis Urban League

JACKSON, MISSISSIPPI
Urban League of Greater Jackson

JACKSONVILLE, FLORIDA
Jacksonville Urban League

JERSEY CITY, NEW JERSEY
Urban League of Hudson County

KANSAS CITY, MISSOURI
Urban League of Kansas City

KNOXVILLE, TENNESSEE
Knoxville Area Urban League

LANCASTER, PENNSYLVANIA
Urban League of Lancaster County

LAS VEGAS, NEVADA
Las Vegas–Clark County
Urban League

LEXINGTON, KENTUCKY
Urban League of Lexington-Fayette
County

LONG ISLAND, NEW YORK
Urban League of Long Island

LOS ANGELES, CALIFORNIA
Los Angeles Urban League

LOUISVILLE, KENTUCKY
Louisville Urban League

MADISON, WISCONSIN
Urban League of Greater Madison

MEMPHIS, TENNESSEE
Memphis Urban League

MIAMI, FLORIDA
Urban League of Greater Miami

MILWAUKEE, WISCONSIN
Milwaukee Urban League

MINNEAPOLIS, MINNESOTA
Minneapolis Urban League

MORRISTOWN, NEW JERSEY
Morris County Urban League

MUSKEGON, MICHIGAN
Urban League of Greater Muskegon

NASHVILLE, TENNESSEE
Urban League of Middle Tennessee

NEW ORLEANS, LOUISIANA
Urban League of Greater New Orleans

NEW YORK, NEW YORK
New York Urban League

NEWARK, NEW JERSEY
Urban League of Essex County

NORFOLK, VIRGINIA
Urban League of Hampton Roads

OKLAHOMA CITY, OKLAHOMA
Urban League of Oklahoma City

OMAHA, NEBRASKA
Urban League of Nebraska

ORLANDO, FLORIDA
Metropolitan Orlando
    Urban League

PEORIA, ILLINOIS
Tri-County Urban League

PHILADELPHIA, PENNSYLVANIA
Urban League of Philadelphia

PHOENIX, ARIZONA
Phoenix Urban League

PITTSBURGH, PENNSYLVANIA
Urban League of Pittsburgh

PORTLAND, OREGON
Urban League of Portland

PROVIDENCE, RHODE ISLAND
Urban League of Rhode Island

RACINE, WISCONSIN
Urban League of Racine &
    Kenosha,Inc.

RALEIGH, NORTH CAROLINA
Triangle Urban League

RICHMOND, VIRGINIA
Urban League of Greater Richmond, Inc.

ROCHESTER, NEW YORK
Urban League of Rochester

SACRAMENTO, CALIFORNIA
Sacramento Urban League

SAINT LOUIS, MISSOURI
Urban League Metropolitan St. Louis

SAINT PAUL, MINNESOTA
St. Paul Urban League

SAINT PETERSBURG, FLORIDA
Pinellas County Urban League

SAN DIEGO, CALIFORNIA
Urban League of San Diego County

SEATTLE, WASHINGTON
Urban League of Metropolitan Seattle

SOUTH BEND, INDIANA
Urban League of South Bend
    and St. Joseph County

SPRINGFIELD, ILLINOIS
Springfield Urban League, Inc.

SPRINGFIELD, MASSACHUSETTS
Urban League of Springfield

STAMFORD, CONNECTICUT
Urban League of Southwestern
  Connecticut

TACOMA, WASHINGTON
Tacoma Urban League

TALLAHASSEE, FLORDIA
Tallahassee Urban League

TAMPA, FLORIDA
Tampa/Hillsborough Urban League, Inc.

TOLEDO, OHIO
Greater Toledo Urban League

TUCSON, ARIZONA
Tucson Urban League

TULSA, OKLAHOMA
Metropolitan Tulsa Urban League

WARREN, OHIO
Warren-Trumbull Urban League

WASHINGTON, D.C.
Greater Washington Urban League

WEST PALM BEACH, FLORIDA
Urban League of Palm Beach County, Inc.

WHITE PLAINS, NEW YORK
Urban League of Westchester County

WICHITA, KANSAS
Urban League of the MidPlains, Inc.

WILMINGTON, DELAWARE
Metropolitan Wilmington Urban
  League

WINSTON-SALEM, NORTH CAROLINA
Winston-Salem Urban League

Index of Authors and Articles 1987–2006

In 1987, the National Urban League began publishing *The State of Black America* in a smaller, typeset format. By so doing, it became easier to catalog and archive the various essays by author and article name.

The 2006 edition of *The State of Black America* is the twelfth to contain an index of the authors and articles that have appeared since 1987. The articles have been divided by topic and are listed in the alphabetical order of their authors' names.

Reprints of the articles catalogued herein are available through the National Urban League, 120 Wall Street, New York, New York 10005; 212/558-5316.

Affirmative Action

Special Section. "Affirmative Action/National Urban League Columns and Amici Brief on the Michigan Case," **2003**, pp. 225–268.

Afterword

Daniels, Lee A., "Praising the Mutilated World," **2002**, pp. 181–188

AIDS

Rockeymoore, Maya, "AIDS in Black America and the World," **2002**, pp. 123–146

An Appreciation

National Urban League, "Ossie Davis: Still Caught in the Dream," **2005**, pp. 137-138.

Jones, Stephanie J., "Rosa Parks: An Ordinary Woman, An Extraordinary Life," **2006**, pp. 245-246.

Black Males

Lanier, James R., "The Empowerment Movement and the Black Male," **2004**, pp. 143–148.

Lanier, James, "The National Urban League's Commission on the Black Male: Renewal, Revival and Resurrection Feasibility and Strategic Planning Study," **2005**, pp. 107–109.

Business

Emerson, Melinda F., "Five Things You Must Have to Run a Successful Business," **2004**, pp. 153–156.

Glasgow, Douglas G., "The Black Underclass in Perspective," **1987**, pp. 129–144.

Henderson, Lenneal J., "Empowerment through Enterprise: African-American Business Development," **1993**, pp. 91–108.

Price, Hugh B., "Beacons in a New Millennium: Reflections on 21st-Century Leaders and Leadership," **2000**, pp. 13–39.

Tidwell, Billy J., "Black Wealth: Facts and Fiction," **1988**, pp. 193–210.

Turner, Mark D., "Escaping the 'Ghetto' of Subcontracting," **2006**, pp. 117–131.

Walker, Juliet E.K., "The Future of Black Business in America: Can It Get Out of the Box?," **2000**, pp. 199–226.

Children and Youth

Comer, James P., "Leave No Child Behind: Preparing Today's Youth for Tomorrow's World," **2005**, pp.75–84.

Cox, Kenya L. Covington, "The Childcare Imbalance: Impact on Working Opportunities for Poor Mothers," **2003**, pp.197–224d.

Edelman, Marian Wright, "The State of Our Children," **2006**, pp. 133–141.

Fulbright-Anderson, Karen, "Developing Our Youth: What Works," **1996**, pp. 127–143.

Hare, Bruce R., "Black Youth at Risk," **1988**, pp. 81–93.

Howard, Jeff P., "The Third Movement: Developing Black Children for the 21st Century," **1993**, pp. 11–34.

McMurray, Georgia L. "Those of Broader Vision: An African-American Perspective on Teenage Pregnancy and Parenting," **1990,** pp. 195–211.

Moore, Evelyn K., "The Call: Universal Child Care," **1996**, pp. 219–244.

Scott, Kimberly A., "A Case Study: African-American Girls and Their Families," **2003**, pp. 181–195.

Williams, Terry M., and William Kornblum, "A Portrait of Youth: Coming of Age in Harlem Public Housing," **1991**, pp. 187–207.

Civil Rights

Archer, Dennis W., "Security Must Never Trump Liberty," **2004**, pp. 139–142.

Burnham, David, "The Fog of War," **2005**, pp. 123-127.

Jones, Nathaniel R., "The State of Civil Rights," **2006**, pp. 165–170.

Ogletree, Jr., Charles J., "Brown at 50: Considering the Continuing Legal Struggle for Racial Justice," **2004**, pp. 81–96.

Criminal Justice

Curry, George E., "Racial Disparities Drive Prison Boom," **2006**, pp. 171–187.

Drucker, Ernest M., "The Impact of Mass Incarceration on Public Health in Black Communities," **2003**, pp. 151–168.

Lanier, James R., "The Harmful Impact of the Criminal Justice System and War on Drugs on the African-American Family," **2003**, pp. 169–179.

Diversity

Bell, Derrick, "The Elusive Quest for Racial Justice: The Chronicle of the Constitutional Contradiction," **1991**, pp. 9–23.

Cobbs, Price M., "Critical Perspectives on the Psychology of Race," **1988**, pp. 61–70.

Cobbs, Price M., "Valuing Diversity: The Myth and the Challenge," **1989**, pp. 151–159.

Darity, William Jr., "History, Discrimination and Racial Inequality," **1999**, pp. 153–166.

Jones, Stephanie J., "Sunday Morning Apartheid: A Diversity Study of the Sunday Morning Talk Shows," **2006**, pp. 189-228.

Watson, Bernard C., "The Demographic Revolution: Diversity in 21st-Century America," **1992**, pp. 31–59.

Wiley, Maya, "Hurricane Katrina Exposed the Face of Poverty," **2006**, pp. 143–153.

Drug Trade

Lanier, James R., "The Harmful Impact of the Criminal Justice System and War on Drugs on the African-American Family," **2003**, pp. 169–179.

Economics

Alexis, Marcus and Geraldine R. Henderson, "The Economic Base of African-American Communities: A Study of Consumption Patterns," **1994**, pp. 51–82.

Bradford, William, "Black Family Wealth in the United States," **2000**, pp. 103-145.

———, "Money Matters: Lending Discrimination in African-American Communities," **1993**, pp. 109–134.

Burbridge, Lynn C., "Toward Economic Self-Sufficiency: Independence Without Poverty," **1993**, pp. 71–90.

Edwards, Harry, "Playoffs and Payoffs: The African-American Athlete as an Institutional Resource," **1994**, pp. 85–111.

Hamilton, Darrick, "The Racial Composition of American Jobs," **2006**, pp. 77-115.

Henderson, Lenneal J., "Blacks, Budgets, and Taxes: Assessing the Impact of Budget Deficit Reduction and Tax Reform on Blacks," **1987**, pp. 75–95.

———, "Budget and Tax Strategy: Implications for Blacks," **1990**, pp. 53–71.

———, "Public Investment for Public Good: Needs, Benefits, and Financing Options," **1992**, pp. 213–229.

Jeffries, John M., and Richard L. Schaffer, "Changes in the Labor Economy and Labor Market State of Black Americans," **1996**, pp. 12-77.

Malveaux, Julianne M., "The Parity Imperative: Civil Rights, Economic Justice, and the New American Dilemma," **1992**, pp. 281–303.

Morial, Marc H. and Marvin Owens, "The National Urban League Economic Empowerment Initiative," **2005**, pp. 111-113.

Myers, Jr., Samuel L., "African-American Economic Well-Being During the Boom and Bust," **2004**, pp. 53–80.

National Urban League Research Staff, "African Americans in Profile: Selected Demographic, Social and Economic Data," **1992**, pp. 309–325.

———, "The Economic Status of African Americans During the Reagan-Bush Era: Withered Opportunities, Limited Outcomes, and Uncertain Outlook," **1993**, pp. 135–200.

———, "The Economic Status of African Americans: Limited Ownership and Persistent Inequality," **1992**, pp. 61–117.

———, "The Economic Status of African Americans: 'Permanent' Poverty and Inequality," **1991**, pp. 25–75.

———, "Economic Status of Black Americans During the 1980s: A Decade of Limited Progress," **1990**, pp. 25–52.

———, "Economic Status of Black Americans," **1989**, pp. 9–39.

———, "Economic Status of Black 1987," **1988**, pp. 129–152.

———, "Economic Status of Blacks 1986," **1987**, pp. 49–73.

Shapiro, Thomas M., "The Racial Wealth Gap," **2005**, pp. 41–48.

Taylor, Robert D., "Wealth Creation: The Next Leadership Challenge," **2005**, pp. 119–122.

Tidwell, Billy J., "Economic Costs of American Racism," **1991**, pp. 219–232.

Turner, Mark D., "Escaping the 'Ghetto' of Subcontracting," **2006**, pp. 117-131.

Watkins, Celeste, "The Socio-Economic Divide Among Black Americans Under 35," **2001**, pp. 67-85.

Webb, Michael B., "Programs for Progress and Empowerment: The Urban League's National Education Initiative," **1993**, pp. 203-216.

Education

Allen, Walter R., "The Struggle Continues: Race, Equity and Affirmative Action in U.S. Higher Education," **2001**, pp. 87-100.

Bailey, Deirdre, "School Choice: The Option of Success," **2001**, pp. 101-114.

Bradford, William D., "Dollars for Deeds: Prospects and Prescriptions for African-American Financial Institutions," **1994**, pp. 31–50.

Comer, James P., Norris Haynes, and Muriel Hamilton-Leel, "School Power: A Model for Improving Black Student Achievement," **1990**, pp. 225–238.

Comer, James P., "Leave No child Behind: Preparing Today's Youth for Tomorrow's World," **2005**, pp.75–84.

Dilworth, Mary E. "Historically Black Colleges and Universities: Taking Care of Home," **1994**, pp. 127–151.

Edelman, Marian Wright, "Black Children In America," **1989,** pp. 63–76.

Freeman, Dr. Kimberly Edelin, "African-American Men and Women in Higher Education: 'Filling the Glass' in the New Millennium," **2000**, pp. 61–90.

Gordon, Edmund W., "The State of Education in Black America," **2004**, pp. 97–113.

Guinier, Prof. Lani, "Confirmative Action in a Multiracial Democracy," **2000**, pp. 333–364.

Journal of Blacks in Higher Education (reprint), "The 'Acting White' Myth," **2005**, pp.115–117.

McBay, Shirley M. "The Condition of African American Education: Changes and Challenges," **1992**, pp. 141–156.

McKenzie, Floretta Dukes with Patricia Evans, "Education Strategies for the 90s," **1991**, pp. 95–109.

Robinson, Sharon P., "Taking Charge: An Approach to Making the Educational Problems of Blacks Comprehensible and Manageable," **1987**, pp. 31–47.

Rose, Dr. Stephanie Bell, "African-American High Achievers: Developing Talented Leaders," **2000**, pp. 41–60.

Ross, Ronald O., "Gaps, Traps and Lies: African-American Students and Test Scores," **2004**, pp. 157–161.

Sudarkasa, Niara, "Black Enrollment in Higher Education: The Unfulfilled Promise of Equality," **1988**, pp. 7–22.

Watson, Bernard C., with Fasaha M. Traylor, "Tomorrow's Teachers: Who Will They Be, What Will They Know?" **1988**, pp. 23–37.

Willie, Charles V., "The Future of School Desegregation," **1987,** pp. 37–47.

Wilson, Reginald, "Black Higher Education: Crisis and Promise," **1989**, pp. 121–135.

Wirschem, David, "Community Mobilization for Education in Rochester, New York: A Case Study," **1991**, pp. 243-248.

Emerging Ideas

Huggins, Sheryl, "The Rules of the Game," **2001**, pp. 65-66.

Employment

Anderson, Bernard E., "African Americans in the Labor Force,: **2002**, pp. 51-67

Darity, William M., Jr., and Samuel L.Myers, Jr., "Racial Earnings Inequality into the 21st Century," **1992**, pp. 119–139.

Hamilton, Darrick, "The Racial Composition of American Jobs," **2006**, pp. 77–115.

Hammond, Theresa A., "African Americans in White-Collar Professions," **2002**, pp. 109–121

Thomas, R. Roosevelt, Jr., "Managing Employee Diversity: An Assessment," **1991**, pp. 145–154.

Tidwell, Billy, J., "Parity Progress and Prospects: Racial Inequalities in Economic Well-being," **2000**, pp. 287–316.

Tidwell, Billy J., "African Americans and the 21st- Century Labor Market: Improving the Fit," **1993**, pp. 35–57.

———, "The Unemployment Experience of African Americans: Some Important Correlates and Consequences," **1990**, pp. 213–223.

———, "A Profile of the Black Unemployed," **1987**, pp. 223–237.

Equality

Raines, Franklin D., "What Equality Would Look Like: Reflections on the Past, Present and Future, **2002**, pp. 13-27.

Equality Index

The National Urban League Equality Index, **2004**, pp. 15-34.

The National Urban League Equality Index, **2005**, pp. 15-40.

The National Urban League Equality Index, **2006**, pp. 13-60.

Families

Battle, Juan, Cathy J. Cohen, Angelique Harris, and Beth E. Richie, "We Are Family: Embracing Our Lesbian, Gay, Bisexual, and Transgender (LGBT) Family Members," **2003**, pp. 93-106.

Billingsley, Andrew, "Black Families in a Changing Society," **1987**, pp. 97–111.

———, "Understanding African-American Family Diversity," **1990**, pp. 85–108.

Cox, Kenya L. Covington, "The Childcare Imbalance: Impact on Working Opportunities for Poor Mothers," **2003**, pp. 197-224d.

Drucker, Ernest M., "The Impact of Mass Incarceration on Public Health in Black Communities," **2003**, pp. 151-168.

Hill, Robert B., "Critical Issues for Black Families by the Year 2000," **1989**, pp. 41–61.

Hill, Robert B., "The Strengths of Black Families' Revisited," **2003**, pp. 107-149.

Rawlston, Vanessa A., "The Impact of Social Security on Child Poverty," **2000**, pp. 317–331.

Scott, Kimberly A., "A Case Study: African-American Girls and Their Families," **2003**, pp. 181-195.

Shapiro, Thomas M., "The Racial Wealth Gap," **2005**, pp. 41-48

Stafford, Walter, Angela Dews, Melissa Mendez, and Diana Salas, "Race, Gender and Welfare Reform: The Need for Targeted Support," **2003**, pp. 41-92.

Stockard (Jr.), Russell L. and M. Belinda Tucker, "Young African-American Men and Women: Separate Paths?," **2001**, pp. 143-159.

Teele, James E., "E. Franklin Frazier: The Man and His Intellectual Legacy," **2003**, pp. 29-40

Thompson, Dr. Linda S. and Georgene Butler, "The Role of the Black Family in Promoting Healthy Child Development," **2000**, pp. 227–241.

West, Carolyn M., "Feminism is a Black Thing"?: Feminist Contribution to Black Family Life, **2003**, pp. 13-27.

Willie, Charles V. "The Black Family: Striving Toward Freedom," **1988**, pp. 71–80.

From the President's Desk

Morial, Marc H., "The State of Black America: The Complexity of Black Progress," **2004**, pp. 11-14.

Morial, Marc H., "The State of Black America: Prescriptions for Change," **2005**, pp. 11–14

Morial, Marc H., "The National Urban League Opportunity Compact," **2006**, pp. 9–11.

Health

Christmas, June Jackson, "The Health of African Americans: Progress Toward Healthy People 2000," **1996**, pp. 95–126.

Leffall, LaSalle D., Jr., "Health Status of Black Americans," **1990**, pp. 121–142.

McAlpine, Robert, "Toward Development of a National Drug Control Strategy," **1991**, pp. 233–241.

Nobles, Wade W., and Lawford L. Goddard, "Drugs in the African-American Community: A Clear and Present Danger," and **1989**, pp. 161–181.

Primm, Annelle and Marisela B. Gomez, "The Impact of Mental Health on Chronic Disease," **2005**, pp. 63–73.

Primm, Beny J., "AIDS: A Special Report," **1987**, pp. 159–166.

———, "Drug Use: Special Implications for Black America," **1987**, pp. 145–158.

Smedley, Brian D., "Race, Poverty, and Healthcare Disparities," **2006**, pp. 155–164.

Williams, David R., "Health and the Quality of Life Among African Americans," **2004**, pp. 115-138.

Housing

Calmore, John O., "To Make Wrong Right: The Necessary and Proper Aspirations of Fair Housing," **1989**, pp. 77–109.

Clay, Phillip, "Housing Opportunity: A Dream Deferred," **1990**, pp. 73–84.

Freeman, Lance, "Black Homeownership: A Dream No Longer Deferred?," **2006**, pp. 63–75.

James, Angela , "Black Homeownership: Housing and Black Americans Under 35," **2001**, pp. 115-129.

Leigh, Wilhelmina A., "U.S. Housing Policy in 1996: The Outlook for Black Americans," **1996**, pp. 188–218.

In Memoriam

National Urban League, "William A. Bootle, Ray Charles, Margo T. Clarke, Ossie Davis, Herman C. Ewing, James Forman, Joanne Grant, Ann Kheel, Memphis Norman, Max Schmeling," **2005**, pp. 139–152.

National Urban League, "Renaldo Benson, Shirley Chisholm, Johnnie Cochran, Jr., Shirley Horn, John H. Johnson, Vivian Malone Jones, Brock Peters, Richard Pryor, Bobby Short, C. Delores Tucker, August Wilson, Luther Vandross, and NUL members Clarence Lyle Barney, Jr., Manuel Augustus Romero;" **2006**, pp. 279–287.

National Urban League, "Ossie Davis: Still Caught in the Dream," **2005**, pp. 137–138.

Jones, Stephanie J., "Rosa Parks: An Ordinary Woman, An Extraordinary Life," **2006**, pp. 245–246.

Military Affairs

Butler, John Sibley, "African Americans and the American Military," **2002**, pp. 93-107

Music

Brown, David W., "Their Characteristic Music: Thoughts on Rap Music and Hip-Hop Culture," **2001**, pp. 189–201

Bynoe, Yvonne, "The Roots of Rap Music and Hip-Hop Culture: One Perspective," **2001**, pp. 175–187.

Op-Ed

Archer, Dennis W., "Security Must Never Trump Liberty," **2004**, pp. 139–142.

Burnham, David, "The Fog of War," **2005**, pp. 123–127.

Covington, Kenya L., "The Transformation of the Welfare Caseload," **2004**, pp. 149–152.

Emerson, Melinda F., "Five Things You Must Have to Run a Successful Business," **2004**, pp. 153–156.

Journal of Blacks in Higher Education (reprint), "The 'Acting White' Myth," **2005**, pp. 115–117.

Lanier, James R., "The Empowerment Movement and the Black Male," **2004**, pp. 143–148.

Ross, Ronald O., "Gaps, Traps and Lies: African-American Students and Test Scores," **2004**, pp. 157–161.

Taylor, Robert D., "Wealth Creation: The Next Leadership Challenge," **2005**, pp. 119–122.

West, Cornel, "Democracy Matters," **2005**, pp. 129–132.

Overview

Morial, Marc H., "Black America's Family Matters," **2003**, pp.9-12.

Price, Hugh B., "Still Worth Fighting For: America After 9/11," **2002**, pp. 9-11

Politics

Coleman, Henry A., "Interagency and Intergovernmental Coordination: New Demands for Domestic Policy Initiatives," **1992**, pp. 249–263.

Hamilton, Charles V., "On Parity and Political Empowerment," **1989**, pp. 111–120.

———, "Promoting Priorities: African-American Political Influence in the 1990s," **1993**, pp. 59–69.

Henderson, Lenneal J., "Budgets, Taxes, and Politics: Options for the African-American Community," **1991**, pp. 77–93.

Holden, Matthew, Jr., "The Rewards of Daring and the Ambiguity of Power: Perspectives on the Wilder Election of 1989," **1990**, pp. 109–120.

Kilson, Martin L., "African Americans and American Politics 2002: The Maturation Phase," **2002**, pp. 147–180

———, "Thinking About the Black Elite's Role: Yesterday and Today," **2005**, pp. 85-106.

McHenry, Donald F., "A Changing World Order: Implications for Black America," **1991**, pp. 155–163.

Persons, Georgia A., "Blacks in State and Local Government: Progress and Constraints," **1987**, pp. 167–192.

Pinderhughes, Dianne M., "Power and Progress: African-American Politics in the New Era of Diversity," **1992**, pp. 265–280.

Pinderhughes, Dianne, "The Renewal of the Voting Rights Act," **2005**, pp. 49–61.

———, "Civil Rights and the Future of the American Presidency," **1988**, pp. 39–60.

Price, Hugh B., "Black America's Challenge: The Re-construction of Black Civil Society," **2001**, pp. 13-18.

Tidwell, Billy J., "Serving the National Interest: A Marshall Plan for America," **1992**, pp. 11–30.

West, Cornel, "Democracy Matters," **2005**, pp. 129–132.

Williams, Eddie N., "The Evolution of Black Political Power", **2000**, pp. 91–102.

Poverty

Edelman, Marian Wright, "The State of Our Children," **2006**, pp. 133–141.

Prescriptions for Change

National Urban League, "Prescriptions for Change," **2005**, pp. 133-135.

Religion

Lincoln, C. Eric, "Knowing the Black Church: What It Is and Why," **1989**, pp. 137–149.

Richardson, W. Franklyn, "Mission to Mandate: Self-Development through the Black Church," **1994**, pp. 113–126.

Smith, Dr. Drew, "The Evolving Political Priorities of African-American Churches: An Empirical View," **2000**, pp. 171–197.

Taylor, Mark V.C., "Young Adults and Religion," **2001**, pp. 161–174.

Reports from the National Urban League

Lanier, James, "The National Urban League's Commission on the Black Male: Renewal, Revival and Resurrection Feasibility and Strategic Planning Study," **2005**, pp. 107–109.

Jones, Stephanie J., "Sunday Morning Apartheid: A Diversity Study of the Sunday Morning Talk Shows" **2006**, pp. 189–228.

Sexual Identity

Battle, Juan, Cathy J. Cohen, Angelique Harris, and Beth E. Richie, "We Are Family: Embracing Our Lesbian, Gay, Bisexual, and Transgender (LGBT) Family Members," **2003**, pp. 93-106.

Sociology

Teele, James E., "E. Franklin Frazier: The Man and His Intellectual Legacy," **2003**, pp. 29-40.

Special Section: Katrina and Beyond

Brazile, Donna L., "New Orleans: Next Steps on the Road to Recovery," **2006**, pp. 233–237.

Morial, Marc H., "New Orleans Revisited," **2006**, pp. 229–232.

National Urban League, "The National Urban League Katrina Bill of Rights," **2006**, pp. 239–243.

Surveys

The National Urban League Survey, **2004**, pp. 35-51.

Stafford, Walter S., "The National Urban League Survey: Black America's Under-35 Generation," **2001**, pp. 19-63.

Stafford, Walter S., "The New York Urban League Survey: Black New York—On Edge, But Optimistic," **2001**, pp. 203-219.

Technology

Dreyfuss, Joel, "Black Americans and the Internet: The Technological Imperative," **2001**, pp. 131-141.

Wilson Ernest J., III, "Technological Convergence, Media Ownership and Content Diversity," **2000**, pp. 147–170.

Urban Affairs

Allen, Antonine, and Leland Ware, "The Socio-Economic Divide: Hypersegregation, Fragmentation and Disparities Within the African-American Community," **2002**, pp. 69–92

Bates, Timothy, "The Paradox of Urban Poverty," **1996**, pp. 144–163.

Bell, Carl C., with Esther J. Jenkins,"Preventing Black Homicide," **1990**,pp. 143–155.

Bryant Solomon, Barbara, "Social Welfare Reform," **1987**, pp. 113–127.

Brown, Lee P., "Crime in the Black Community," **1988**, pp. 95–113.

Bullard, Robert D. "Urban Infrastructure: Social, Environmental, and Health Risks to African Americans," **1992**, pp.183–196.

Chambers, Julius L., "The Law and Black Americans: Retreat from Civil Rights," **1987**, pp. 15–30.

———, "Black Americans and the Courts: Has the Clock Been Turned Back Permanently?" **1990**, pp. 9–24.

Edelin, Ramona H., "Toward an African-American Agenda: An Inward Look," **1990**, pp. 173–183.

Fair, T. Willard, "Coordinated Community Empowerment: Experiences of the Urban League of Greater Miami," **1993**, pp. 217–233.

Gray, Sandra T., "Public-Private Partnerships: Prospects for America...Promise for African Americans," **1992**, pp. 231–247.

Harris, David, " 'Driving While Black' and Other African-American Crimes: The Continuing Relevance of Race to American Criminal Justice," **2000**, pp. 259–285.

Henderson, Lenneal J., "African Americans in the Urban Milieu: Conditions, Trends, and Development Needs," **1994**, pp. 11–29.

Hill, Robert B., "Urban Redevelopment: Developing Effective Targeting Strategies," **1992**, pp. 197–211.

Jones, Dionne J., with Greg Harrison of the National Urban League Research Department, "Fast Facts: Comparative Views of African-American Status and Progress," **1994**, pp. 213–236.

Jones, Shirley J., "Silent Suffering: The Plight of Rural Black America," **1994**, pp.171–188.

Massey, Walter E. "Science, Technology, and Human Resources: Preparing for the 21st Century," **1992**, pp. 157–169.

Mendez, Jr. Garry A., "Crime Is Not a Part of Our Black Heritage: A Theoretical Essay," **1988**, pp. 211–216.

Miller, Warren F., Jr., "Developing Untapped Talent: A National Call for African-American Technologists," **1991**, pp. 111–127.

Murray, Sylvester, "Clear and Present Danger: The Decay of America's Physical Infrastructure," **1992**, pp. 171–182.

Pemberton, Gayle, "It's the Thing That Counts, Or Reflections on the Legacy of W.E.B. Du Bois," **1991**, pp. 129–143.

Pinderhughes, Dianne M., "The Case of African-Americans in the Persian Gulf: The Intersection of American Foreign and Military Policy with Domestic Employment Policy in the United States," **1991**, pp. 165–186.

Robinson, Gene S. "Television Advertising and Its Impact on Black America," **1990**, pp. 157–171.

Sawyers, Dr. Andrew and Dr. Lenneal Henderson, "Race, Space and Justice: Cities and Growth in the 21st Century," **2000**, pp. 243–258.

Schneider, Alvin J., "Blacks in the Military: The Victory and the Challenge," **1988**, pp. 115–128.

Smedley, Brian, "Race, Poverty, and Healthcare Disparities," **2006**, pp. 155–164.

Stafford, Walter, Angela Dews, Melissa Mendez, and Diana Salas, "Race, Gender and Welfare Reform: The Need for Targeted Support," **2003**, pp. 41–92.

Stewart, James B., "Developing Black and Latino Survival Strategies: The Future of Urban Areas," **1996**, pp. 164–187.

Stone, Christopher E., "Crime and Justice in Black America," **1996**, pp. 78–94.

Tidwell, Billy J., with Monica B. Kuumba, Dionne J. Jones, and Betty C. Watson, "Fast Facts: African Americans in the 1990s," **1993**, pp. 243–265.

Wallace-Benjamin, Joan, "Organizing African-American Self-Development: The Role of Community-Based Organizations," **1994**, pp. 189–205.

Walters, Ronald, "Serving the People: African-American Leadership and the Challenge of Empowerment," **1994**, pp. 153–170.

Ware, Leland, and Antoine Allen, "The Socio-Economic Divide: Hypersegregation, Fragmentation and Disparities Within the African-American Community," **2002**, pp. 69–92

Wiley, Maya, "Hurricane Katrina Exposed the Face of Poverty," **2006**, pp. 143–153.

Welfare

Bergeron, Suzanne, and William E. Spriggs, "Welfare Reform and Black America," **2002**, pp. 29–50.

Covington, Kenya L., "The Transformation of the Welfare Caseload," **2004**, pp. 149–152.

Spriggs, William E., and Suzanne Bergeron, "Welfare Reform and Black America," **2002**, pp. 29–50.

Stafford, Walter, Angela Dews, Melissa Mendez, and Diana Salas, "Race, Gender and Welfare Reform: The Need for Targeted Support," **2003**, pp. 41-92.

Women's Issues

Stafford, Walter, Angela Dews, Melissa Mendez, and Diana Salas, "Race, Gender and Welfare Reform: The Need for Targeted Support," **2003**, pp. 41–92.

West, Carolyn M., "Feminism is a Black Thing"?: Feminist Contribution to Black Family Life, **2003**, pp. 13–27.

APPENDIX IV

About the Authors

DONNA L. BRAZILE is the Founder and Managing Director of Brazile and Associates, LLC. Brazile, Chair of the Democratic National Committee's Voting Rights Institute (VRI) and an Adjunct Professor at Georgetown University, is a senior political strategist and former campaign manager for Gore-Lieberman 2000—the first African American to lead a major presidential campaign. Brazile is a weekly contributor and political commentator on CNN's Inside Politics and American Morning. In addition, she is a columnist for *Roll Call Newspaper* and a contributing writer for *Ms. Magazine*. Brazile, a native of New Orleans, Louisiana, earned her undergraduate degree from Louisiana State University in Baton Rouge.

GEORGE E. CURRY is editor-in-chief of the National Newspaper Publishers Association News Service and BlackPressUSA.com. His weekly column is syndicated by NNPA to more than 200 newspapers. He has appeared on virtually every major TV program, including the Today Show, Nightline, 20/20, CBS Evening News, NBC Nightly News, ABC World News Tonight, CNN, Fox, C-SPAN, BET, MSNBC and ESPN. Curry's work at the NNPA News Service has ranged from being inside the Supreme Court to hear oral arguments in the University of Michigan affirmative action cases to traveling to Doha, Qatar to report on America's war with Iraq. Before joining the NNPA, Curry was editor-in-chief of *Emerge* magazine and served as New York bureau chief and as a Washington correspondent for the *Chicago Tribune*. He also worked as a reporter for *Sports Illustrated* and the *St. Louis Post-Dispatch*. He is the author of three books, *Jake Gaither: America's Most Famous Black Coach* (Dodd, Mead & Co., 1977), *The Affirmative Action Debate* (Persus, 1996) and *The Best of Emerge Magazine* (Ballantine, 2003). The National Association of Black Journalists (NABJ) named Curry its 2003 "Journalist of the Year." He is past president of the American Society of Magazine Editors, the first African American to hold the association's top office.

MARIAN WRIGHT EDELMAN, Founder and President of the Children's Defense Fund (CDF), has been an advocate for disadvantaged Americans for her entire professional life. Under her leadership, CDF has become the nation's strongest voice for children and families. The mission of the Children's Defense Fund is to Leave No Child Behind and to ensure every child a Healthy Start, a Head Start, a Fair Start, a Safe Start in life and successful passage to adulthood with the help of caring families and communities. Mrs. Edelman has received countless honorary degrees and awards for her tireless efforts to children and families. She is a graduate of Spelman College and Yale Law School.

LANCE FREEMAN, Ph.D., is an Assistant Professor in the Urban Planning program at Columbia University in New York City where he teaches courses on housing policy and research methods. Dr. Freeman has published several articles in refereed journals on issues related to neighborhood change, urban poverty, housing policy, urban sprawl and residential segregation. He is also the author of the forthcoming book, *There Goes the Hood: Views of Gentrification from the Ground Up* by Temple University Press. Dr. Freeman holds a master's degree and a Ph.D. in City and Regional Planning from the University of North Carolina at Chapel Hill.

DARRICK HAMILTON, Ph.D., is an Assistant Professor at Milano— New School of Management and Urban Policy, and an affiliated faculty member in the Department of Economics at The New School for Social Research. Dr. Hamilton's research agenda involves examining the welfare of less privileged groups and ethnic/racial group competition for pre-ferred economic and health outcomes. Dr. Hamilton earned his Ph.D. from the Department of Economics at the University of North Carolina, Chapel Hill.

NATHANIEL R. JONES became Senior Counsel with Blank Rome LLP following his retirement in March 2002 as Judge on the United States Court of Appeals for the Sixth Circuit. Appointed by President Carter, Judge Jones took his oath of office on October 15, 1979. His career has included: Executive Director of the Fair Employment Practices Commission of the City of Youngstown; Assistant United States Attorney for the Northern District of Ohio in Cleveland; Assistant General Counsel to President Johnson's National Advisory Commission on Civil Disorders and from 1969-1979 served as general counsel of the NAACP. Judge Jones earned both his A.B. and LL.B. from Youngstown State University; and was admitted to the Ohio Bar in 1957.

STEPHANIE J. JONES is the Executive Director of the National Urban League's Policy Institute located in Washington, D.C. Ms. Jones joined the League in 2005, and prior to that she served as Judiciary Committee Counsel to Senator John Edwards. Other professional experiences include Chief of Staff for Representative Stephanie Tubbs Jones, Associate Attorney at Graydon, Head & Ritchey. She also taught Civil Rights Law at Northern Kentucky University. Ms. Jones received her B.A. from Smith College and her law degree from the University of Cincinnati.

MARC H. MORIAL is the president and Chief Executive Officer of the National Urban League. He is a former two-term Mayor of New Orleans, Louisiana. Before becoming mayor, Morial served as a Louisiana State Senator for two years. He holds a bachelor's degree from the University of Pennsylvania, a law degree from the Georgetown University Law Center and honorary doctorate degrees from Xavier University and the University of South Carolina Upstate.

BRIAN D. SMEDLEY, Ph.D., is Research Director and co-founder of a new communications, research, and policy organization, The Opportunity Agenda. Smedley has received accolades for his work in the area of health from organizations such as the Rainbow/PUSH coalition and the Congressional Black Caucus and work in psychology from the American Psychological Association (APA). Dr. Smedley received his Ph.D. from the UCLA Department of Psychology.

MARK D. TURNER, Ph.D., founder, president and Principal Associate at Optimal Solutions Group (Optimal), has many years of experience in designing research studies and conducting policy research and empirical studies, as well as management experience and skills in the supervision of large-scale multi-site studies. Dr. Turner received his bachelor's degree in economics from Michigan State University and a Ph.D. in economics from the University of Maryland.

MAYA WILEY, J.D., is the founder and director of the Center for Social Inclusion in New York City. The Center for Social Inclusion (CSI) is an intermediary organization that supports community-based and other organizations to understand structural racism and to identify and promote effective policy reform strategies. CSI conducts applied research, analysis, strategic support for multi-racial alliance building, and works to build policy education and policy reform models. Ms. Wiley received her law degree from Columbia University School of Law and B.A. in psychology from Dartmouth College. Previously, she has served as Assistant Counsel at the NAACP Legal Defense & Educational Fund, Inc.; Assistant United States Attorney for the Southern District of New York, Civil Division, and a consultant for the Open Society Institute.

In Memoriam

RENALDO BENSON

Renaldo Benson was a soul and R&B singer and songwriter. He was best known as a member of the Motown group, the Four Tops. He joined the Four Tops in 1953 and continued to perform with the group for more than five decades.

The group signed with Red Top Records and Riverside Record before joining Columbia Records, where they released "Ain't That Love" in 1960. Benson was also the choreographer for the group in the early years.

In 1963, the group signed with Motown, first under the Motown Workshop Jazz label. From there, they produced a number of soul music hits, such as "I Can't Help Myself (Sugar Pie, Honey Bunch)" and "Reach Out I'll Be There." Benson was also a songwriter. He collaborated with lyricist Al Cleveland to produce the song "What's Going On" sung by another music great, Marvin Gaye. The song has been acknowledged as one of the greatest rock or R&B songs of all time and rated as one of The Rock and Roll Hall of Fame's 500 Songs that Shaped Rock and Roll.

Benson was admitted as a member of the Four Tops to the Rock and Roll Hall of Fame in 1990. The group was awarded a star on the Hollywood Walk of Fame in 1997, followed by the Vocal Group Hall of Fame in 1999.

Benson's last performance as a Four Top was in April 2005, a live appearance on the Late Night with David Letterman show. He died on July 1, 2005.

SHIRLEY CHISHOLM

Shirley Chisholm was a great American politician, educator and author. She was viewed as a woman before her time, breaking some of the barriers of sexism and racism, especially in politics. As a Congresswoman, she represented New York's 12th District for seven terms, from 1969 to 1983. In 1968, she became the first African American woman to be elected to Congress and in 1972, became the first African-American and first woman to make a serious run to become the president of the United States.

Shirley Chisholm was born in Brooklyn, N.Y. as Shirley St. Hill. She spent part of her childhood in Barbados with her grandmother. She then attended Brooklyn College and graduated with a Bachelor's of Arts degree in 1949. That same year, she married Conrad Chisholm. While working as a teacher, Chisholm earned a Master's degree in elementary education from the Teachers College at Columbia University. From 1959 to 1964 she was director of the Hamilton-Madison Child Care Center and from 1959 to 1964 was an educational consultant for the Division of Day Care.

Chisholm ran and was elected to the New York State Legislature in 1964. She soon campaigned as the Democratic candidate for New York's 12th District Congressional seat and was elected to the House of Representatives in 1968. She became the first African-American woman elected to Congress by defeating Republican candidate James Farmer. Chisholm joined the Congressional Black Caucus in 1969 as one of its founding members.

In the later years, Chisholm authored two books, *Unbought and Unbossed* (1970) and *The Good Fight* (1973). She was inducted into the National Women's Hall of Fame in 1993.

Chisholm resided in Florida until her death on January 1, 2005.

JOHNNIE COCHRAN JR.

Johnnie Cochran Jr., was known as one of the nation's best criminal defense lawyers and rose to fame when he uttered the phrase, "If the glove doesn't fit, you must acquit." He helped win an acquittal for O.J. Simpson in a double-murder trial. Cochran was born in Shreveport,

La., the oldest of four children. While still young, his family moved to Los Angeles.

Cochran graduated from the University of California-Los Angeles (UCLA) in 1959 with a Bachelor's degree in Business Administration. Three years later, he received his Juris Doctor (J.D.) degree from the Jesuit Loyola Law School (Loyola Marymount University). After passing the bar in 1963, he took a job as deputy city attorney in the criminal division. He entered a private practice and soon opened his own law firm, Cochran, Atkins & Evans.

In the late 1970s, he made a name for himself in the black community by litigating numerous high-profile police brutality and criminal cases. Cochran joined the Los Angeles County district attorney's office in 1978 but later returned to private practice in 1983.

Cochran founded the Cochran Firm, a group of lawyers specializing in personal injury cases. His high-profile successes helped him to open law offices in California, Florida, Louisiana, New York, Texas, and in Washington, D.C.

Johnnie Cochran died on March 29, 2005.

SHIRLEY HORN

Shirley Horn was an American jazz pianist and vocalist who got her start opening for Miles Davis. She became revered as a master interpreter of American standards. She recorded several albums on different labels in the 1960s, creating little fanfare. Horn began performing locally in her native Washington, D.C. while rearing her family.

Horn began to tour more in the later years after her children were grown. Her best-known recordings were with Verve Records. Horn was often compared to great jazz vocalists like Sarah Vaughan, Ella Fitzgerald and Carmen McRae as such she was considered one of the last great jazz vocalists of her era.

Over the years, Horn was nominated for nine Grammy Awards and won in 1999 for Jazz Vocal Album, "I Remember Miles," a tribute to her friend and mentor.

Shirley Horn died October 20, 2005 in Washington, D.C.

JOHN H. JOHNSON

John H. Johnson was one of the most influential African-Americans of our time. He was the founder of the Johnson Publishing Company, an international media and cosmetics giant that includes *Ebony* and *Jet* magazines, Fashion Fair Cosmetics and EBONY Fashion Fair. John Johnson was the first black person to appear on the Forbes 400 Rich List with a fortune estimated at about $600 million.

He was born in Arkansas City, Ark. and moved with his family in the 1930s to Chicago. He attended both the University of Chicago and Northwestern University. He was drawn to his entrepreneurial endeavors and soon began to publish his first magazine, *The Negro Digest* in 1942. Later would come the highly-successful *Ebony* magazine, a photo-oriented publication patterned after *Life* magazine.

Johnson served on numerous boards. Howard University renamed its School of Communications after Johnson and awarded him an honorary doctor of humane letters degree. John H. Johnson died August 8, 2005 at the age of 87.

VIVIAN MALONE JONES

Vivian Malone Jones was one of two black students to enroll at the University of Alabama in 1963. She and another student, James Hood, were enrolled by U.S. marshals and the federalized Alabama National Guard after Gov. George C. Wallace made his famous "Stand in the Schoolhouse Door" on June 11, 1963 in Tuscaloosa, Ala. She became the first African American to graduate from the University of Alabama. She joined the civil rights division of the United States Department of Justice. Jones was director of the civil rights and urban affairs for the U.S. Environmental Protection Agency until her retirement in 1996. In his later years, Wallace disavowed his white supremacy stance and apologized to Jones and other African Americans. The George Wallace Family Foundation, named after the former governor, selected her as the first recipient of its Lurleen B. Wallace Award of Courage. In 2000, she also received an honorary doctorate degree from the University of Alabama.

Vivian Malone Jones died on October 13, 2005 at the age of 63.

ROSA PARKS

Rosa Parks' refusal to give up her bus seat to a white man in 1955 sparked a citywide bus boycott in Montgomery, Ala. and launched the career of a then-obscure minister, Martin Luther King, Jr.

More important than elevating Dr. King, Parks' act of courage inspired an all-out assault on segregated institutions in the South that included boycotts, street protests, legal challenges and massive civil disobedience. An inspired modern civil rights movement, led by King and others, brought down barriers that relegated blacks to second-class citizens.

Technically, Parks was arrested for violating a city ordinance upholding segregation. However, the charge was eventually overturned and the U.S. Supreme Court outlawed segregated buses as unconstitutional.

Parks didn't set out to challenge the segregated bus system. In fact, she boarded the Cleveland Avenue bus and took a seat on the fifth row, the first row of the "Colored Section." It was when the bus became crowded that the driver ordered Parks to the back and she refused.

Knowing of Parks' sterling reputation, local civil rights leader E.D. Nixon said at the time, "My God, look what segregation has put in my hands!" It wouldn't take long for the world to find out.

Parks and her husband moved to Detroit, where she began working in the office of Congressman John Conyers.

Parks published *Rosa Parks: My Story*, an autobiography for younger readers in 1992. In 1995, she published her memoirs, titled *Quiet Strength*, which focused on how faith played a significant role in her life.

Rose Parks died on October 24, 2005. She was 92 years old.

BROCK PETERS

Brock Peters achieved his dream of becoming an accomplished actor. At the young age of ten, he set his sights on a show business career. He was a product of NYC's famed Music and Arts High School. Peters slowly worked his way up from poverty by doing various odd jobs. He landed a stage role in "Porgy and Bess" in 1949, and quit CCNY to go on tour with the acclaimed musical. His film role came in Carmen Jones in 1954, however he really began to make a name for himself—having dropped his real name, George Fisher, in 1953 in such films as To Kill a Mockingbird (1962) and The L-Shaped Room (1962). He received a Tony nomination for his starring role in Broadway's "Lost in the Stars."

Brock Peters died on August 23, 2005. He was 78 years old.

RICHARD PRYOR

Richard Pryor, an actor-comedian known for his groundbreaking comedy albums and countless stand-up comedy appearances, greatly influenced most of today's comedians. Pryor was clearly the biggest name in comedy in the 1970s, earning several Grammy awards.

His first professional performance was at the age of seven where he played drums at a nightclub. Pryor moved to Berkeley, Calif. in 1969. There, he signed with the comedy independent record label Laff Records in 1970 and recorded Crap (After Hours). In 1972, Pryor appeared in his first film, a documentary called Wattstax, where he spoke about and put a comical spin on race relations in Watts and the U.S. By 1983, Pryor became a worldwide celebrity and he signed a five-year contract with Columbia pictures for $40 million.

Pryor also wrote for famous television shows such as Sanford and Son, The Flip Wilson Show, and others. He also appeared in several popular films including Lady Sing The Blues, Uptown Saturday Night, Car Wash, Harlem Nights and Superman III. During his career, Pryor hosted the Academy Awards twice and was also nominated for an Emmy for a guest role on Chicago Hope.

Richard Pryor died December 10, 2005. He was 65 years old.

BOBBY SHORT

Bobby Short, was a three-time Grammy award winner and was considered the world's greatest cabaret entertainer, known for his New York style.

His musical styles were similar to the sounds of Duke Ellington and Cole Porter, which helped him gain well-known fans such as Jacqueline Kennedy Onassis, Barbara Walters and Dominick Dunne. He performed at the White House for Presidents Nixon, Carter, and Clinton.